...Y OF
...MPIRE
...PLAN
...EPARTMENT
...ETURN TO
MARKETING DEPARTMENT

STRATEGIC
MARKETING
COMMUNICATIONS

PROPERTY OF
INLAND EMPIRE
HEALTH PLAN
MARKETING DEPARTMENT
IF FOUND...RETURN TO
MARKETING DEPARTMENT

STRATEGIC MARKETING COMMUNICATIONS

NEW WAYS TO BUILD AND INTEGRATE COMMUNICATIONS

Paul Smith, Chris Berry and Alan Pulford

**KOGAN
PAGE**

We dedicate this book to:

Bev, Aran, Cian and Lily

Martha, Zoltan and Antonia

Jean, Claire and Richard

The masculine pronoun has been used throughout this book. This stems from a desire to avoid ugly and cumbersome language, and no discrimination, prejudice or bias is intended.

First published 1997
Reprinted with corrections 1997
Reprinted 1998
Revised 1999
Reprinted 2000

Apart from any fair dealing for the purposes of research or private study, or criticism or review, as permitted under the Copyright, Designs and Patents Act 1988, this publication may only be reproduced, stored or transmitted, in any form or by any means, with the prior permission in writing of the publishers, or in the case of reprographic reproduction in accordance with the terms and licences issued by the CLA. Enquiries concerning reproduction outside those terms should be sent to the publishers at the undermentioned addresses:

Kogan Page Limited
120 Pentonville Road
London
N1 9JN
UK

Kogan Page Limited
163 Central Avenue, Suite 2
Dover
NH 03820
USA

© Paul Smith, Chris Berry and Alan Pulford, 1997, 1999

The right of Paul Smith, Chris Berry and Alan Pulford to be identified as authors of this work has been asserted by them in accordance with the Copyright, Designs and Patents Act 1988.

British Library Cataloguing in Publication Data

A CIP record for this book is available from the British Library.

ISBN 0 7494 2918 6

Typeset by JS Typesetting, Wellingborough, Northants
Printed and bound in Great Britain by Clays Ltd, St Ives plc

Contents

Foreword

Strategic Marketing Communications tackles an area of growing importance to both marketing managers and marketing students – that of developing effective strategies that are the heart of the marketing communications of the organisation. Strategies must be integrated into an overall programme that effectively, efficiently and economically meets the business and marketing objectives of the organisation. Yet in spite of the importance of this strategic level subject, it is my belief that too often practitioners are concerned with the tactics of marketing communications and not with strategy, and it is certainly the case that too few books of quality have been written to meet this specific need.

I therefore recommend this book, *Strategic Marketing Communications – New Ways to Build and Integrate Communications*, as being of real benefit to both practitioners and students of marketing. *Strategic Marketing Communications* is more than an ordinary textbook – it is an interactive learning tool packed with practical examples, case studies, checklists and model documents. In particular, a powerful planning system called SOSTAC (Situation, Objectives, Strategy, Tactics, Action and Control) is introduced and explained.

Although *Strategic Marketing Communications* has been specifically designed to cover the Chartered Institute of Marketing Diploma subject, Marketing Communications Strategy, I particularly recommend it also to experienced managers in both agency and client organisations. This book will stimulate discussion between agency managers and client managers. It will also help to strengthen the strategic role of agencies, particularly in a climate where, it is argued, agencies have lost out to management consultancy organisations.

At Saatchi and Saatchi Advertising, we pride ourselves on our strategic contribution to the development of our clients' organisations and we have invested heavily to ensure that marketing communications planning is at the heart of the agency's business.

Strategic Marketing Communications has been written by a team of academics all with substantial business experience. The same team are responsible for developing a world class, comprehensive and definitive series of 10 CD ROMs on Marketing. The CDs are a source of reference for this book. So, here we have electronic text based resources working in harmony.

Finally, I am pleased to write this foreword because we at Saatchi and Saatchi Advertising are supporting the Institute of Practitioners in Advertising initiative to bring industry and academia together to raise understanding and performance standards.

I am sure you will enjoy and benefit from this challenging and stimulating book.

Marilyn Baxter, Vice-Chairman, Saatchi and Saatchi Advertising.
Chairman of the IPA Advertising Effectiveness Committee.

Acknowledgements

The authors have benefited enormously from the interactions over many years with colleagues in the worlds of both business and academia. In particular our ideas, concepts and dreams have been shaped by the marvellously rewarding job of teaching undergraduate, postgraduate and professional marketing managers at London Guildhall University and the Manchester Metropolitan University.

We gratefully acknowledge the manifold contributions of these colleagues and students to our thinking. The Chartered Institute of Marketing has also been influential in shaping our work and we hope that the book fulfils the needs of both professionals already working in marketing and the thousands of students who take the Diploma in Marketing examinations each year.

Clearly we cannot mention all those to whom we collectively owe a debt, but the following list illustrates the breadth of the help we have had from our many colleagues. Special thanks to:

Jeremy Baker, London Guildhall University
Enzo Balzanelli, Gillette Europe
Ross Barr, BMP DDB
Marilyn Baxter, Saatchi and Saatchi *Advertising*
David Beckett, The Marketing Council
Peter Betts, the Manchester Metropolitan University
Steve Cuthbert, Chartered Institute of Marketing
Martin Davis, Marketing Communications consultant
Peter Doyle, University of Warwick
Chris Easingwood, Manchester Business School
John Farrell, DMB&B
Madeline Hamil, Coca-Cola
Angela Hatton, Tactics
Brian Haworth, CIA Conzept International
Janet Hull, Institute of Practitioners in Advertising
Peter Jones, IBM
John Leftwich, Microsoft
Theodore Levitt, Harvard Business School

Martin Lewis, Broughton Jacques
Peter Liney, British Airways
Mike McGuire, Procter and Gamble
Owen Palmer, Consultant
John Stubbs, The Marketing Council
Rex Sweetman, Muscutt Sweetman
Norman Waite, Chartered Institute of Marketing

Introduction

During the four years we have spent researching and writing this book, we have discovered that most organisations and their marketing professionals understand and use the communications tools to a reasonable extent. They also understand and use marketing strategies and sometimes advertising, PR and direct mail strategies, but they rarely have communications strategies that pull all these communications tools in the same direction. Many of the biggest and best companies world-wide have no communications strategy, but, as they told us, they would very much like to know how to implement one. This book attempts to show you and them how.

It tackles an area of growing importance for all marketing professionals – that of developing effective marketing communications strategies for all types of organisations. Strategies that are integrated into an overall programme that effectively and efficiently meet both corporate and marketing objectives. New ideas, new models and new ways of thinking are blended together and reflected in the subtitle – New Ways to Build and Integrate Communications. *Strategic Marketing Communications* is more than an ordinary textbook: it is an interactive learning tool packed with practical examples, short cases, model documents and checklists.

By working through it we hope it will start you on the road towards better communications strategies. The thoughts and ideas contained here should help you to start building and using communications strategies that give you a competitive edge.

There is always plenty of room for improvement. It will enable you to develop your own approaches which will work best for you. Please let us know how you progress in this voyage of discovery towards developing winning communications strategies. We welcome your thoughts, criticisms, ideas, improvements, stories and examples (for the next edition).

Please write to Paul Smith c/o Kogan Page or visit us at the Multimedia Marketing Consortium's Web site: www.lgu.ac.uk/lgu/mmm where you can send comments directly to us.

Thank you

Paul Smith, Chris Berry and Alan Pulford

1

O N E

The nature of marketing communication

LEARNING OBJECTIVES

- Understand that marketing communications seeks to change ideas.
- Be able to distinguish between intended and unintended communication.
- Recognise centrifugal and centripetal marketing organisations.
- Be aware of current levels of expenditure on communications mix.
- Know how the communications tools available from internal and external programmes can be used to create a consistent image of the business.

TOPICS COVERED BY THIS CHAPTER

3

THE NATURE OF MARKETING COMMUNICATION

Communication is a constant activity. It is a universal and essential feature of human expression and organisation. Its scope is as broad as society itself, for every social act involves communication. Communication is concerned with *sending and receiving knowledge, ideas, facts, figures, goals, emotions and values*. It is much more than an occasional technique employed to convey a message. It is a ceaseless activity of all human beings, and therefore also of all human organisations. Communication is also a central element of the way in which people relate to and cooperate with each other, the interpersonal event which is the building block of society. Individuals not only send and receive information in order to cooperate, but parallel with this individuals are constantly communicating their self-images to all around them. Whether we like it or not, whatever a person does as a social act will be observed by others, and is therefore a communication about themselves. Chapter 2 analyses and explains the process of communication from a marketing perspective with detailed models. This chapter explains the very broad role which marketers need to take in managing communications, examines the key organisational role for marketers, and discusses how that role now needs to change quite fundamentally as we move into the 21st century.

Communication is more than a marketing tool. It is also an important basis of culture. It has fostered language and music, literature and philosophy, science and poetry. So in one sense, communication can be viewed as neutral and benign, a form of human interaction which helps society and the organisations within it to work well, and which can only benefit those who take part in it. This would be a reasonable approach to a definition if every communication included everything that could possibly be said on a subject, but of course this would be impossible. Communication is a selective art, as important for what it does not convey as for what it does convey.

Communication is also a human skill, so it is concerned with the state of mind of the communicator, and with the state of mind of the person intended to receive the communication. Communications objectives are often specified as outcomes of attitude change.

Conditioned optimistic lifestyle?

Compare two sets of attributes for instant coffee: Brand A is tasty, unsexy, solitary and rather introvert; Brand B is tasty, sexy and extrovert. If Brand A users are to be converted to Brand B, creative strategy for the whole communications mix needs to change some of the ideas about Brand B in the minds of Brand A users. Both brands are tasty, but unsexy needs converting to sexy and introvert must be change to extrovert. This is not a simple task, but if this can be achieved for at least a proportion of Brand A users through an appropriate creative strategy, is this responding to customer need or is it a form of conditioning? Most marketers would argue that they are creating better value and a more optimistic lifestyle for those that convert to Brand B.

Does this mean that marketing communication is propaganda? To qualify as propaganda, business communication must be seeking to influence the emotional attitudes of others without allowing them to make an effective or rational choice (Brown, 1963). This is never the situation in business, where in every market there are competitors, and for every product or service there is an alternative or substitute. Indeed, the existence of competition is now arguably a necessary precondition for business strategy (Porter, 1979). Communication by a business is a creative form of differentiation, always competitive, always seeking to persuade customers, shareholders and employees that its own market offerings are the best choice available. That is the sales pitch of the marketplace, not the imperative of propaganda.

INTENTIONAL AND UNINTENTIONAL COMMUNICATION

Where communication is person to person, for the communication to be successful there generally needs to be an intention by both parties that communication should take place, but there are many ways in which a person also communicates to other people unintentionally. The way a person dresses may be important for a specific occasion, such as a wedding or a sales conference, which will require a carefully constructed style of dress to communicate a particular self-image. This kind of image is an *intentional communication*, aimed at communicating specific lifestyle values to other identified people on a specific occasion. At the same time, the style and dress will be observed by others and will send unintended messages to other people about style, tidiness, convention and social role. This is *unintentional communication*. It will always be present when intentional communication is taking place, and it will affect the way in which the intended message is believed. People usually base their style of dress on the style of a preferred reference group (Smith, 1993). This not only enables them to conform to the style values of their chosen group, but also, wherever they are observed, they present a clear and unambiguous image to the world, a constant communication of at least some of their lifestyle values. Personal communication thus consists of both intentional messages targeted at certain identified people, and unintentional messages which are there for anyone to read (see Figure 1.1).

In business organisations, communication with customers, shareholders and employees is now regarded as a major resource, requiring careful management and adequate investment. Some of that communication is internal, involving the flow of information within the organisation, both to provide information for decision-making and to maintain a focus among staff on what the organisation is seeking to achieve. Without effective and managed internal communication, the activities of a business will become uncoordinated and focused more on individual goals than on operational objectives (Griffin and Moorhead, 1986). Much business communication is external, and without effective external communication between a business and its customers, the benefits needed and wanted by the market will not be understood, leading to loss of market share, loss of profitability and loss of jobs (Smith, 1993).

Poor or ineffective communication with key stakeholders, such as shareholders and banks, can cause a collapse in share price. Situation analysis should therefore include an audit of all the firm's external visibility, from signage to van livery, as well as assessing the effectiveness of its current communications programmes. (See Chapter 7.)

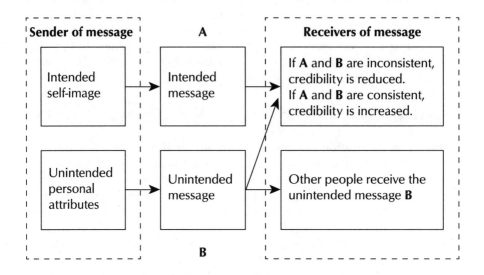

Figure 1.1 Impact of intended and unintended communication on person-to-person communications

If the intended communication is consistent with the unintended communication, the source credibility of the sender of the message will be enhanced and the message is more likely to be accepted and believed. If the unintended communication is inconsistent with or contradicts the intended communication, the source credibility of the sender will be reduced and the message is less likely to be believed.

CENTRIFUGAL AND CENTRIPETAL COMMUNICATIONS

Organisations communicate in much the same way as individual people. They seek to transfer and share ideas, and they convey intended and unintended messages. Unlike people, however, organisations do not possess a unified psychology (Argyris, 1960), and do not therefore automatically develop a self-image. Organisations have to create a corporate image, the organisational equivalent of an individual's self-image, through management of corporate culture and consequent marketing and communications mixes. If adequate management processes and structures are not in place, the corporate image will be uncoordinated and confused (see Table 1.1). This will have both internal and external market effects. Internally, when there is confusion within a

Table 1.1 Reasons for confused communication

- In an organisation many people in different departments tend to become involved in communication. This can often result in a variety of different styles and policies of communication within the same organisation, and lead to fragmentation of the organisation's public image. Two different departments, for example, may print their own variations of the organisation's letterhead.

- Organisations communicate with other organisations at a variety of levels and functions. There can thus be several communications about the same problem taking place simultaneously between different pairs of people in both organisations. An accounts clerk may be pursuing a payment from a customer by talking to their accountant at the same time as a sales representative is seeking further business from a buyer in the same customer.

- Coordination of communication is often made difficult by directors refusing to surrender even partial control of the departments reporting to them.

- In many organisations the concept of communication is limited to the formal sending of messages (such as letters, advertising, press releases), and there is little understanding of the constant communication by every visible part of the organisation. A dirty delivery van, for example, does not communicate high quality and care, and with products such as fresh foods will communicate the opposite.

- Many businesses lack a marketing communications strategy covering at least all intended and (hopefully) unintended communication (see Chapter 4).

business about what kind of identity is needed, it soon shows. Lack of cohesion quickly leads to weaker decision-making by staff and the lowering of motivation for a workforce which does not know what is expected of it. This results in contradictory design signatures and messages, badly briefed sales reps, and the neglect of basic business housekeeping such as keeping the delivery vans washed and clean.

Business organisations may have well-developed marketing systems and plans, with carefully crafted marketing mixes and communication programmes, but if they do not have a cohesive corporate identity, the image of them perceived by customers, shareholders and employees will be fragmented. This was highlighted almost 40 years ago by Theodore Levitt (1962) in his essay on centripetal marketing:

> Too often a company will imply one thing about its product in its mass-media ads and contradict it at point of sale, deny it with its direct-selling tactics, and muddle it with its product service policy... In short, the

communications job which advertising and good product design so laboriously and expensively undertook is scuttled by the customer's actual experience with the many other communications the company sends out. The overall message that will finally have got through to the customer will be self-contradictory and confusing instead of self-reinforcing and reassuring.

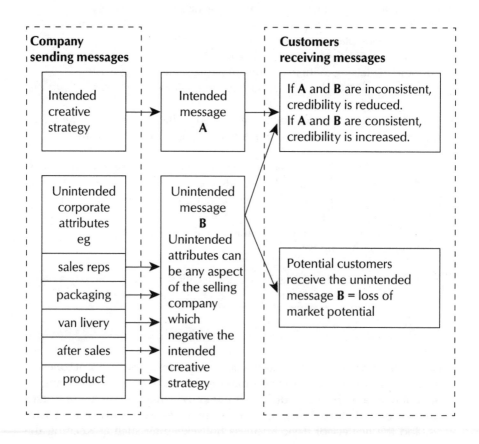

Figure 1.2 Impact of intended and unintended communication on business communications

If the corporate attributes intended to be communicated by the creative strategy are consistent with other corporate attributes, the source credibility of the company will be enhanced and communications are more likely to be accepted and believed by customers. If those other corporate attributes tend to negative the attributes intended by the creative strategy, unintended communications will be inconsistent with and contradict intended communications and the source credibility of the company will be damaged, with the result that all communications by the business are less likely to be believed.

In such a business, some or all of the unintentional messages sent to the market will contradict the messages intended to achieve its market objectives. Levitt termed this as a characteristic of *centrifugal marketing*, as most activities in the business tend to shift progressively away from what the business is trying to deliver. This contradiction will destroy the credibility of its advertising, sales promotion, public relations and design programmes (see Figure 1.2). The more effective kind of organisation, in which all activities are focused towards achieving specific marketing objectives with specific customers, Levitt termed *centripetal marketing*. The approach of the centripetal business towards communication will be to coordinate unintended and intended communication in order to create a consistent image. For example, its service engineers will be trained to handle customers with extra care, politeness and respect, and customers will be telephoned to check that they received a high standard of after-sales service. The centrifugal business will simply lack the management willingness, systems and resources to create consistency, as its managers will be motivated to achieve only basic levels of customer service and will therefore be at a major disadvantage when positioning against a centripetal business.

For many businesses, and particularly for those in consumer goods markets, communication is the major weapon employed to achieve positioning. Even if a business has no formal positioning strategy, it will nevertheless have a *de facto* position against competition. However, as Mintzberg and Quinn (1996) have pointed out, the market position achieved by a business is always a combination of some strategic objectives achieved and others not achieved as a result of managers responding to changing circumstances and improvising strategy different from that originally planned. The centripetal marketing business will focus its communications on a cohesive set of messages to the customer, seeking to maximise consistency between intended and unintended communication. It will therefore be able to adjust its objectives towards the most effective positions in its markets because its managers will be able to improvise with the advantage of a cohesive (and customer-orientated) corporate image. Managers in the centrifugal business will simply create a more and more confused image as they try to improvise, because its unintended communication will become more and more inconsistent with its intended communication.

Leaky communications?

For example, UK water companies have generally much higher water wastage through leaks in the main supply pipes than water suppliers in other European countries. This contributes significantly to the annual summer water shortages and consumers tend to point the finger of blame at the water companies for paying too much out in dividends to shareholders and investing too little in improving the quality of the main piping. The water companies respond by advertising, but this has little effect in changing consumer attitudes because of the high inconsistency between the water companies' intended and unintended communication. This reduces the credibility of all communications from these companies, who then have to spend even more on advertising, and carry more administration costs from customers querying their water bills.

LACK OF STRATEGY MEANS WASTED BUDGET

This process of information and message transfer is an important investment for any business. Doyle (1994) suggests that businesses typically spend around 15 per cent of turnover on marketing communication such as advertising and the salesforce. Internal communication could increase this percentage significantly. Unlike other key investments, however, such as finance, human resources, production and logistics, businesses seldom have an overall communications strategy, plan and budget which covers all communication, both intended and unintended.

- Very few businesses have an overall communication strategy to coordinate their communication activities. Most business identities are therefore to some extent fragmented and are not perceived as cohesive images in the minds of customers, shareholders or employees. Even businesses which have very large advertising budgets do not have formal communication strategies as a framework for budgets and programmes.
- Businesses generally have marketing plans with detailed tactical plans and budgets for some areas of marketing communication, such as an advertising plan. Almost never are these tactical plans coordinated into a coherent communication plan for the whole business.
- Without any overall strategy and plan, typically at least 15 per cent of turnover is being spent by businesses on communication in an unco-ordinated and *ad hoc* way. This is equivalent to almost a sixth of the factory space, time and materials being set aside for production workers to manufacture anything they fancy.
- This also means that there will be considerable duplication and sub-optimisation of communication cost. A railway company can suboptimise its cost by spending money on advertising to reassure its customers that its services run mostly on time, when it should be spending some of that money to hire additional drivers or buy additional rolling stock so that its services *will* run on time.

THE SCOPE OF MARKETING COMMUNICATIONS

The scope of *marketing communications* is much wider than is generally assumed in practice. Marketers have a direct interest in the effectiveness of internal as well as external communications by a business, and the scope of marketing communication therefore encompasses *both the internal information and decision-making system, and the messages and images put across by the business to its present and potential customers and other stakeholders.*

The conventional communication tasks of marketers are generally confined to the *communications mix*. This is the combining of communications tools to achieve a specified amount of weight and cover in a target market within a defined budget.

Target market cover:

Target market cover is the percentage of the target market which comes into contact with a communications tool (eg advertising, point-of-sale promotion) at least once in a defined campaign period. If, for example, *News at Ten* reaches 10 million viewers, 70 per cent of whom are ABC1 male, then an ad in the centre break will reach 7 million ABC1 men. If ABC1 men are the primary target group for the campaign, and there are 9 million ABC1 men in the UK, then the advertisement will reach seven out of nine of the total target market. This will be a target market cover of 77 per cent (Smith, 1993).

Weight:

Weight is the relative share of campaign budget spent on a particular communications tool, and it will depend on the nature of the market and the kind of strategy being employed. For example, in industrial marketing personal selling is typically given much more weight than advertising, because deals are made person to person with a relatively small number of customers. In consumer products, on the other hand, sales promotions and advertising will be given more weight than personal selling, and where they are used within a pull strategy, the focus of these communications tools will be on the customer at the end of the channel. (See Chapter 4, The communications process and the marketing mix, for details on how to give appropriate weight to each communications tool so that the budget can be shared across the tools in the communications mix.)

The *marketing communications mix* consists of the following *communications tools*:

- salesforce (personal selling);
- advertising;
- sales promotions;
- direct marketing (sometimes called *database marketing*);
- public relations;
- sponsorship;
- exhibitions;
- corporate identity;
- packaging;
- point-of-sale promotions and merchandising;
- word of mouth;
- Internet and new media.

When combining these into a communications mix, the marketer needs to take account of their particular appropriateness for the target market, the rate at which each tool will generate sales or awareness, and the rate of sales response when the tools are combined into the mix. The importance of each communications tool will vary according to the type of customer and the general pattern of communication in a market. This is explained in more detail in Chapter 2. Estimates for the total UK spend on the main communications tools are shown in Figure 1.3, but it is important to bear in mind that there is a wide range of communications tools which are not generally included in the marketing communications mix as they are controlled by other functional and line managers (see Table 1.2 on page 13).

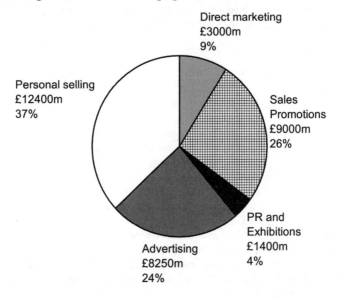

Figure 1.3 Estimates of total communications mix spend in the UK for 1995 (Source: Advertising Association and industry estimates. Sales promotions' estimates are based on a wide definition which includes discounting into distribution channels)

INTERNAL PROGRAMMES AND COMMUNICATIONS TOOLS

Internal communication within a business is a major area of interest for the marketer for several reasons:

- Marketing management seldom has line authority within a firm, and marketers therefore have to achieve results through persuasion rather than command.
- Many marketing activities are key sources of information for a business, such as the records of the customer database (customers' names, addresses, telephone/fax/e-mail numbers, buying and production managers, purchases from the business, credit ratings, payment performance and other information provided from the salesforce representatives).

Table 1.2 Internal programmes with which the marketer must be involved

Internal programmes	Intended and unintended communications tools
Corporate identity and image	Corporate identity design manual and policy, eg logo, design signature, signage, van livery, uniforms, letterheads, compliment slips, personal cards, gifts, annual report, design specifications for packaging and promotional literature.
Internal marketing communications	This is a system for telling staff what is happening in the business in order to reinforce motivation, eg new campaigns about to break, newsletters, training awards, news from international subsidiaries. Staff are also important sources of word-of-mouth communication, 24 hours a day.
Salesforce training and development	Brochures, sales manuals, technical manuals, sales conferences.
Dealer/distributor network	Conferences, training, manuals, brochures, dealer agreements.
Retailer merchandising plans	Display and shelf-facings in own outlets, point-of-sale materials, annual market analysis.
First-contact customer service training and design	Training telephonists and reception staff, brochures, name badges, security clearance.
After-sales service	Training, manuals, brochures, point-of-sale literature.
Production quality assurance	Product/service design to reach the required quality level for the market(s), training, quality assurance procedures and manuals, motivation of staff to achieve target quality.
Managing global/international brands	Contacts with world staff, setting common standards, after-sales service, training, sales conferences.

- Marketing management will normally provide market data for strategic planning from its own analysis and research (market sizes, potentials, medium- and long-term trends, competition analysis, product portfolio analysis and assessment of brand equity).
- Internal communication can play a major role in motivation of staff performance, which in most businesses will have a significant impact on quality of product and service delivered to the customer. In service-based businesses, such as a travel agency or a bank, quality of staff performance is often the only image which the customer sees, so motivation and training is an essential element of the marketing mix.
- Many programmes and projects regarded as internal to the business, and therefore developed as purely internal communications, have a significant impact on elements of the marketing mix and on communications tools in particular (for example, salesforce training, sales contracts and after-sales service specifications).

For these reasons, marketers need to become involved in all the internal communications programmes which can result in both intended and unintended messages being sent to the market. These are normally extensive in a business and include the internal programmes listed in Table 1.2.

In addition, marketers should be involved in the design of the customer database and all specifications for market research to ensure senior management of the business is receiving valid and correctly interpreted data to feed into its strategy development. Involvement and a degree of control is often achieved by marketers through taking information initiatives, for example providing relevant data in short routine reports with both analysis and proposals for action. Marketers also tend to focus their planning activities through task groups or venture teams, as this provides more credibility for any recommendations going to senior management.

EXTERNAL PROGRAMMES AND COMMUNICATIONS TOOLS

The main external programme which generates communications tools is the communications mix, which is generally under the marketing manager's control. There is a tendency to think of communications tools as one-way channels which send messages from a business to its customers, but because of the necessity for feedback in communication (see Chapter 2) all communications tools listen to messages coming from the market as well as sending messages to customers. *Market research* is therefore a key external programme for marketers as it provides much of the qualitative feedback from the market. There are other external programmes which use communications tools, some of which are under marketing control (eg advertising) and some of which are not (eg community relations programmes). All ingredients of the *marketing mix*, which are also under marketing control, have potential for producing both intended and unintended communication. In Table 1.3 these are shown for a marketing mix of *seven Ps*, including *people, processes* and *physical evidence,* which are important ingredients of the marketing mix in service-based businesses and also now increasingly for product-based businesses. In effect, all businesses now build their market offerings around the notion of service to the customer.

Table 1.3 External programmes with which the marketer must be involved

External programmes	Intended and unintended communications tools
Marketing mix: Promotion	Communications mix should also plan the integration of all messages produced by ingredients of the marketing mix.
Marketing mix: Place	Distribution is in itself a major method of communication with the market, through gaining effective shelf-facings and merchandising for the product.
Marketing mix: Price	Messages about quality and status.
Marketing mix: Product	Quality must be consistent with advertising, sales and packaging messages. This plays a significant role in stimulating repeat purchase.
Marketing mix: People	More marketing budget is invested in personal selling than in any other communications tool. The salesforce both sells and listens (the voice, eyes and ears of the business) and its effectiveness depends on the quality of individual sales reps, their training and levels of preparation. Other staff also convey important messages about the business, eg after-sales service technicians, delivery drivers, service receptionists. When customers are assessing a service-based business where there is no apparent and physical product, they look first at the quality of staff in the business.

(continued over)

External programmes	Intended and unintended communications tools
Marketing mix: Processes	In service-based businesses, production often takes place at the same time as customers use the service, so the method and technology of production conveys messages to the customers and others. A cash machine which says 'out of order' or chews up a bank card is a negative and unintended communication.
Marketing mix: Physical evidence	The overall visual presentation of the business is a major communications tool. Van livery and cleanliness of transport is a mobile message with high but unmeasurable market cover. Shop signs and window displays should be treated as reminder advertising. Product packaging is the 3-D advert on the shelf.
Market research	Most market research is not about discovering new markets, but about what the established customers are thinking. Many large businesses also use routine market research to monitor the image which customers have of them. Unfortunately, instead of this prompting these businesses to develop cohesive communication strategies, it appears to drive them to more advertising spend.
Public relations	PR is only occasionally under marketing control and is difficult to cost within a marketing budget. Some PR cover, such as sponsorship of sports and cultural events, can be measured and costed.

THE NEW AGE OF THE CYBER CONSUMER

Until the mid-1980s, the process of mass marketing communication was a partial one. Marketers had the capacity to reach whole populations, and specific target market groups within them, and this access was guaranteed provided they bought the appropriate television slots. Marketers also now had a range of powerful communications tools (television advertising, personal selling and sales promotion) with which to promote their brands. However, most of this communication was one-way, and only personal selling provided real interaction with the customer. For the other major communications tools, marketers had to rely on a combination of sales analysis and market research for feedback in order to know what effect their messages were having in the market. This built a time delay into the marketing communication process, as it could be several weeks before the effects of a particular communication could be calculated. Some limited experiments in television home shopping were carried out by retailers (such as Sainsbury in the UK) during the 1980s, but were not developed into full projects. Both satellite and cable television now have home shopping channels, but they are not interactive. In addition, most communications tools available had limited capacity for being customised towards individual customers. Database marketing had gone some way towards this through the merging of databases with direct mail, but the extent of customisation allowed by this in the mid-1980s was generally limited to name and address details.

Changes in the communications landscape in the early 1990s provided some of the answers to these problems, driven by a combination of new technology and better use of existing techniques and technologies. These changes have been principally as follows.

- Personal computers have reduced in size, increased in capacity and reduced in price through the 1980s as a result of improved chips and miniaturisation. Ownership of PCs has risen dramatically both in Europe and in the US. In the UK, for example, over 30 per cent of adults own a PC, and almost 60 per cent of households have one. Increasingly, therefore, homes have a potential IT terminal for interactive communication.
- New television media such as satellite and cable provide a multiplicity of channels to carry communications, and also in the case of cable have capacity for interactivity with individual households.
- Information technology has developed faster and more efficient systems for databases which can now store very large populations of personal data. This, combined with more efficient technology for printing and distributing personalised direct mail, provides a capacity for customised communication on a large scale.
- New combinations of IT and machines into integrated manufacturing systems controlled by CAD-CAM (computer aided design – computer assisted manufacturing) systems now provide a capability of manufacturing to individual customer requirements on a scale of, and at a similar cost to,

mass manufacturing. Not only can communications now be customised, but so can products and services.

- New forms of electronic communication such as e-mail and the Internet now provide a capacity to interact with customers in a variety of new ways. The Internet can provide shopping malls, product details, pictures as well as words, and Web sites designed around particular brands and companies. The Internet shopper can ask questions, and so can the marketer. This provides the final closing of the mass marketing communications loop. Feedback can now be real time on a mass scale.

- Communication in cyberspace, as on the Internet, is a great leveller of competition, as the quality of a Web site depends on creativity rather than on market power. Marketers will need to develop ways of differentiating communications effectively in cyberspace. (See Chapter 10 for much more detail.)

The customer now no longer exists in an armchair, in front of a television, remote from the marketer and probably several weeks away from reacting to a communication. Neither need the customer exist in the shop, where shelf-facings have to be paid for by heavy discounts to the retailer. The customer can now exist in cyberspace, and increasingly will do so. Connections to the Internet are increasing dramatically in both the US and Europe. In the UK, in 1997 the 3 million Internet users were expected to grow to 8 million by the year 2000. Many of these use it to gain product information prior to purchase. This is from a zero base in 1993, which indicates an exponential growth in access to and use of the Internet. This is the cyber consumer, who can be anywhere on the planet, and has no geographical limits. This means that marketers will have to deal increasingly with cyber markets, which are global, and where target segments will be capable of being finely identified, possibly to the level of focus of niche markets, as global segments. Already there are some Web sites on the Internet which have millions of cyber consumers visiting them each year. Do these Web sites contain the cyber brands of tomorrow?

The value of studying marketing history lies in the analysis of long-term trends and acquiring the insight and understanding of past masters. For example, *The Art of War* by Sun Tzu (around 300 BC) has been the basis of American, Swedish, Japanese and Chinese texts, and it is discussed in Chapters 4 and 5. Marketers survive by anticipating and predicting the future, and this is impossible without an understanding of the past. Marketers now stand at the beginning of a new century, in which the technologies of miniaturisation, robotics, computer design and control, information systems and logistics are converging and synergising into a totally new regime of production, distribution and communication. There is the capacity, waiting now to be used, to work on a global scale, recording and assessing the needs of countless millions of individual customers, and to deliver to them products and services customised to their own individual requirements. This is *dynamic relationship marketing*, and it is put in an Internet and database context in Chapter 10.

Marketers are now in a world of cyber brands and cyber marketing space. The future of marketing communications will increasingly be with the cyber consumer.

DISCUSSION TOPICS FOR CHAPTER 1

1) What are the differences between intended and unintended communication?
2) What could be the effect of unintended communications reaching people other than the intended receiver?
3) Identify examples of centrifugal and centripetal businesses.
4) How would you ensure that communications by a business are not confused and inconsistent?
5) What should you include in a communications budget for a UK water company?
6) List the tools in a marketing communications mix. Which three would be most important for a European car manufacturer?
7) Why is spend on personal selling more than on other marketing communications tools?
8) Outline a training programme for after-sales service staff of a domestic washing machine manufacturer.
9) Why are people, processes and physical evidence important in service marketing?
10) What roles does market research perform in marketing communications?
11) What are a cyber consumer, a cyber market, and a cyber brand?
12) How will marketers communicate in 3000 AD?

REFERENCES

Argyris, C (1960) *Understanding Organisational Behaviour*, Tavistock, London

Borden, N H (1964) The concept of the marketing mix, *Journal of Advertising Research*, June, pp 2–7

Bovee, C L *et al* (1995) *Advertising Excellence*, McGraw-Hill, Maidenhead

Brown, J A C (1963) *Techniques of Persuasion*, Penguin, Harmondsworth

Doyle, P (1994) *Marketing Management and Strategy*, Prentice Hall, Hemel Hempstead

Griffin, R W and Moorhead, G (1986) *Organisational Behavior*, Houghton Mifflin, Boston, MA

Levitt, T (1962) Centripetal marketing, in *Innovation in Marketing*, McGraw-Hill, Maidenhead

Mintzberg, H and Quinn, B (1996) *Strategy Process*, Prentice Hall, Hemel Hempstead

Porter, M E (1979) How competitive forces shape strategy, *Harvard Business Review*, March–April

Rodzinski, W (1991) *The Walled Kingdom*, Fontana, London

Smith, P R (1998) *Marketing Communications – An integrated approach*, 2nd edn, Kogan Page, London

Wright, J S *et al* (1977) *Advertising*, Tata McGraw-Hill, NY, USA

T W O

The theory of the communications process

LEARNING OBJECTIVES

- Understand what communications is.
- Consider the importance of sender credibility.
- Appreciate the nature and importance of feedback in communication and common errors that distort it.
- Understand the importance of overlapping fields of perception.
- Know the role of transmitters and the problems of noise in the channel.
- Appreciate how marketing communications must reflect the overall objectives of the organisation.

TOPICS COVERED BY THIS CHAPTER

WHAT IS COMMUNICATION?

Communication is the act of sending information from the mind of one person to the mind of another person. This is easy to define. There is a *sender* and a *receiver*, and a *message* passing from one to the other. In practice, however, communication is a very complex activity, and presents a number of concepts and relationships which are important to the marketer:

- Communication is an interpersonal activity. It is dependent on the social context in which it takes place, and the person sending the information will do so in a variety of ways, all at the same time. It is easy to recognise salesforce activity as interpersonal, but even advertising uses personal surrogates and times messages to coincide with different likely social contexts at different times of the day.
- The sender will need to identify in advance the person to whom they wish to send the message, and will therefore need to know how the receiver (the audience) will interpret it. Market research is carried out to establish this.
- The sender will also need to see evidence that the message has been not only received but also understood. The marketer collects certain feedback data which can show the effect of the message in the market, and incorporates this data in their marketing information and intelligence system.
- The sender will need to persuade the receiver that the message is worth listening to, and the message itself will need to be in a form of language which the receiver can understand. Messages need to be designed by professionals who understand how to make them effective.
- There will need to be a clear and unobstructed route or channel through which the message can be sent, and through which the receiver can indicate that the message has been received and understood. The message will need to be recognised through the distractions (noise) in the channel, and the feedback will need to be interpreted correctly.

In order to clarify these concepts and relationships, a number of models of the communication process will be helpful to the marketer.

Models of the communications process

Having a clear model of the business system and the marketing process he is engaged in can help the marketer identify quickly what he needs to do next, what others need to do next, in what order this should be done, and what may be wrong with what he or others have been doing. To that extent a model is similar to a checklist. And like a checklist it can be learned and absorbed into the routine of everyday practice. Unlike a checklist, however, a marketing model also helps to explain how and why he is doing it. It represents the characteristics of the real world, and compresses the complexities of that real world into a simpler, usually graphic form, so that the relationships between different parts of a process can be understood and related to some specific marketing activity. The more a marketing model is used, the more it becomes a part of a marketer's experience, and therefore of a marketer's implicit assessment of a problem. When a marketer senses that prices can be increased with very little effect on sales, he is using an *implicit model* of inelasticity of price to demand. Sometimes, however, it is necessary to find and use a new model, or to take the components of an existing model and put them together in a different way to meet a new situation. When this is necessary, the marketer is using an *explicit model*, and this can help him both to think through the problem and also to convey the ideas to other people in the business.

Work or romance on Eurostar?

It is common for service marketers to use specialised models such as Shostack's molecular model (see Shostack, 1977) to identify formally the intangible (non-physical) elements of their service and how these can be promoted together with the tangible (physical) elements. Shostack proposed a molecular model of service marketing, and this is now widely used by service marketing planners. At the centre is the intangible (non-physical) 'atom' of the key service benefit (eg 'Don't waste valuable time on other airlines when you can still carry on working on this one!') and arranged around it are other 'atoms' representing the tangible (physical) elements of the service (eg the seats, the legroom, the in-flight food) and the intangible (non-physical) elements of the service (eg safety, security, membership of an executive travel club, standard of cabin staff). The model helps the service marketer to create synergistic relationships between the subsidiary atoms and the central key benefit.

This results in airlines – which are dependent on business travellers – often featuring aircraft seats as relaxing workstations rather than emphasising the time taken for the journey which is seen as an interruption to business activity. Cross-Channel ferry operators, on the other hand, who are much more dependent on excursion and holiday travellers, often emphasise the old-fashioned romance of the sea, so that travellers can feel that the grind of crossing the Channel is the start of a romantic holiday. It is not surprising that, uniquely, Eurostar tries to do both.

The basic personal communications model

The most basic communications models identify three components (see Figure 2.1):

1) a *sender* of a message;
2) a *receiver* of a message;
3) a *message* passing from a *sender* to a *receiver*.

Figure 2.1 A basic communications model

(Source: Schramm, 1955)

These three components form the basic model of personal communication, showing the *transferring of an idea from the mind of the sender to the mind of the receiver*. The basic model suggests that the receiver must be aware that a message is being sent to him, and from whom. This in turn implies that the credibility of the sender will affect how much attention is paid to the message. If credibility is high, the intended *receiver*s will give it attention and believe it. Establishing sender credibility in the target market is a key part of the marketer's role in getting effective messages across, and this is especially important with new brands and new products.

It may be good to talk, but who cares?

BT is a major consumer advertiser. In the mid-1990s, BT was spending between £150 m and £200 m a year on advertising, with a focus on its 'good to talk' campaign, which launched in 1994. This campaign was aimed at encouraging customers to use the phone more, and featured both TV and press advertising. Simultaneously, BT was direct mailing its extensive customer base to promote special tariffs and products again designed to encourage use of the telephone. Then, in late 1996, BT's regular feedback from market research noticed a small rise in negative reaction to its advertising. This meant that as a sender of marketing communications, BT was no longer believed by a proportion of its market. This proportion was relatively small, at less than 10 per cent, but if it continued to grow, it would damage BT's credibility and reduce the effectiveness of its advertising. BT's advertising agency, Abbott Mead Vickers DDBO, was also aware of research carried out by MORI in 1996, which showed that over 80 per cent of those questioned thought, when considering the image of an organisation, that it was fairly or very important to know what social and community activities that organisation was involved in. So just before Christmas 1996, BT launched a TV and press campaign specifically intended to tell its customers about some of its socially responsible services (eg providing telephones for people with disabilities) and the successful social and community projects funded by BT.

Established brands will normally have credibility already built into them, often over many years of advertising and development. New brands will take time to establish their credibility, and the launch campaign will need to focus on this. Six months after the launch of Mr Kipling cakes, a substantial part of the market claimed to remember their grandmothers buying them. In some special situations, sender credibility derives from matching social identification of the sender with that of the receiver, as with the need to match the dress and personal grooming of retail sales assistants to that of their predominant customers. In industrial business-to-business marketing, the social matching of the salesforce is even more important, and tends to follow a company pattern. Until fashion hit 'Big Blue', the IBM sales representative was always recognisable by his 'white shirt, dark suit and sincere tie'.

In marketing communications, the identification of the sender is crucial to the effectiveness of the communication. If the sender is identified as credible, then the message will be believed. The sender is identified by the customers in the market in two ways:

1) the organisation which is sending the message;
2) the 'person' identified in the communication as sending the message (eg the managing director signing the direct mailshot, or the personality endorsing the product in an advertisement).

The credibility of the sender will depend on: *their perceived expertise* (eg in TV ads technical explanations are often given by characters dressed in laboratory overalls, looking like research chemists); *how far they can be trusted* (a well-known scientist will be seen as both knowledgeable and honest); and *whether or not they are liked* by the target audience (actors from popular TV series are likely to score high on this) (Kelman and Hovland, 1953). Initially, a high credibility sender will have a much greater effect on the audience's opinions than a low credibility sender. However, over a period of time, this effect disappears, unless the audience is reminded again of the identity of the sender (Hovland, Janis and Kelley, 1953).

The game of damage limitation

If you are a major international business active in many consumer markets and your oil tanker has just covered a nature reserve in crude oil, what do you do to recover your hard-earned public image as an environmentally sensitive company? The answer to this is fairly simple. First, check with market research to see what the public really thinks about the disaster. Then feed stories to the press about how much cost and effort your managers are putting into cleaning up the mess for 2–3 weeks to counter the protests of the environmental lobby. After that, launch a corporate advertising campaign designed to be seen by as much of the public as possible, fronted by the corporate logo, showing all the wonderful ways in which you as a business have protected the environment all over the globe. Maintain this campaign for three weeks and then stop. After a further 3–4 weeks, the negative effect of your company's reduced sender credibility will disappear, and the audience will remember only the messages about protection of the environment. In addition, a large amount of the negative perception of the initial disaster will have disappeared. This classic PR game plan is used for damage limitation by most large international businesses. Environmental lobby organisations, such as Greenpeace, maintain their own advertising and PR feed to the press partly in order to keep the name of the errant business in front of the public as a counter to this game plan.

Feedback

This basic model immediately raises three questions:

1) How do I as a sender know that my message has been received?
2) How do I as a sender know that my message has been understood in the way I intended?
3) If my message has not been received or understood, how can I improve it?

These are answered by introducing into the model a component which will enable us to assess whether the message has been received and how it is being understood. This additional component is called *feedback* (see Figure 2.2).

In personal one-to-one communication, the sender watches the responses of the receiver. These are normally eye-contact, facial expressions of interest and verbal responses from the receiver. 'Really?' 'My goodness!' 'I absolutely agree...' These are indications that the receiver has registered something of what has been said. Even someone sending a message to a large group, such as a lecturer or an after-dinner speaker, looks for signs of interest and response in the audience (students start making notes, dinner guests stop talking). In personal communication it is often relatively simple to monitor feedback, and to take action on the basis of it. If the students look as if they are falling asleep, a good lecturer will normally make a joke, or refer to the exam at the end of the course. Either of these will generally stimulate fresh interest in what the

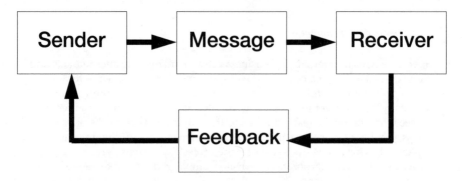

Figure 2.2 Feedback tells the sender the message has been received

lecturer has to say. Good after-dinner speakers will pepper their delivery with anecdotes designed to stimulate laughter and applause, two physical acts which help to keep the audience awake.

Compared with personal communication, businesses operate on a much larger scale, monitoring in a variety of ways feedback from messages sent to the target market, as well as much other information which can be used in developing the medium and long-term plans of the business. Some of this information is quantified (eg sales figures) and some is non-quantified (eg possible changes in government taxation policy). This data is fed into the company business information system as a whole, and some is fed only into the marketing intelligence and information system (MIIS) (Smith, 1993) used by the marketer to make effective decisions.

There are four main sources of feedback from the market which are fed into the MIIS: sales, market research, customer activity in addition to sales (eg completing and sending product enquiry cards from a trade magazine) and agency research. Most of this data is under the control of the marketer (eg market research on attitudes towards a brand and its competitors will be commissioned directly by the brand manager) but some is developed by agencies employed by the marketer (eg advertising, PR, design and product development agencies will all carry out research into their own specialised problems) and fed back into the MIIS only after it has been interpreted by the agency (see Figure 2.3).

Some of this monitoring is personal and one to one, as with a sales representative leading the prospect towards a purchase order, waiting and watching for buying signals. Problems encountered by the sales representative in making a deal will be reported to sales management daily or weekly and then fed into the MIIS. This feedback information will be non-quantified, with the sales representative giving their personal assessment of what is happening in the customer's mind, and because it is subjective, it needs careful analysis. There is also important information flowing into the MIIS from non-purchase activity by the customer which indicates strong interest in the product or brand, such as promotional competition entries. These, along with customer complaints,

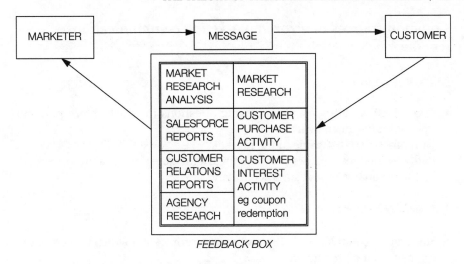

Figure 2.3 Marketing communications feedback

will be monitored by a customer relations department, and are important data in assessing how the market is responding to marketing communications.

Most of the monitoring by marketers, however, is non-personal and quant-ified feedback and often consists of statistical data which needs to be analysed and interpreted. Sales might increase during an advertising campaign, but analysis of the sales data will be needed before a connection can be made between the two events, and that means eliminating other factors which might have caused the increase, such as seasonality. Some feedback is easier and faster to analyse, as with coupons redeemed in a below-the-line promotion. Normally, campaigns require the use of a number of marketing communic-ations tools, such as salesforce, point-of-purchase and advertising. The feed-back to these will need to be measured both cumulatively (to know how the target market has received and understood the whole campaign) and separately (to discover if certain communications tools will work better than others with this particular target market). A market research agency may often be commissioned to measure awareness, attention, perception and trial against each of the communications tools used in the campaign. This can be expensive, but if a marketer is investing in a multi-million pound communications campaign, it will be important to assess as accurately as possible the responses of the market to the messages that are sent. With a major campaign, the advertising agency will carry out its own research to ensure that the message is designed in the most effective way, and delivered through the most appropriate channel. At a minimum, feedback data will come from the salesforce sending back information on how the market is responding.

Common sources of error in marketing communications feedback

Market research

- Poor questionnaire design (eg asking questions to which the respondent may not have an answer).
- Unrepresentative sample of the market.
- Badly trained researchers (who do not ask the questions in a uniform way).
- Failure to analyse the results accurately.

Salesforce reports

- Sales representatives will often not report information which reflects badly on their own performance.
- They will often report only information they are asked for (and sometimes they are not asked at all).
- As the sales report information is processed by sales management, information which reflects negatively on the salesforce performance will be edited out.
- Sales representatives sometimes don't spot significant events in the marketplace.

Customer interest activity

- Customers will report complaints more often than satisfaction.
- Rate of coupon redemption will be affected by special factors built into the design of each coupon promotion (eg period of validity, amount of market covered in distributing the coupons).
- The novelty factor boosts sales to new customers, but sales tail off as the number of repeat purchases declines.

Agency research

- Agencies depend on selling their services, and their research will tend to reflect a need for the services they provide (eg advertising agency research will show a need for advertising).
- Some agency research will present spurious data analysis to show their services are needed (eg while PR is valuable in building sender credibility and its visibility can be measured, its direct effect on sales cannot be measured easily or at all).

HOW MESSAGES ARE UNDERSTOOD

When a message is sent, not all of it may be understood by the receiver. Not only that, but sometimes a receiver may completely misinterpret the message, and appear to receive an idea quite different from the one which the sender intended to communicate.

Millions die from ineffective communications:

A mistake in translation may have triggered the atom bombing of Hiroshima. There is evidence that the word 'mokusatsu' used by the Japanese government in response to the US surrender ultimatum was translated as 'ignore' instead of its correct meaning 'withhold comment until a decision has been made' (Cutlip, Center and Broom, 1985).

Even when people speak the same language, messages can be misinterpreted by the receiver. For example, a message which repeatedly asserts that a washing powder will whiten clothes will be understood but may be interpreted negatively by someone who needs to wash coloured fabrics such as football shirts.

To correct this problem, three more components need to be added to the communications model:

1) An understanding of the experience from which both sender and receiver perceive the message. These are called *fields of perception* and market research is normally used to identify these.
2) The sender needs to construct the message with care so that it can be understood in the way intended. This is called *encoding the message*. This can involve not only language, verbal and visual, but also combinations of these which when read together have specific meaning to consumers in the target market (the field of semiotics).
3) Just as the sender encodes a message, so the receiver needs to look at the message and work out what it means. This is called *decoding the message*.

With the addition of encoding, which often includes implicit as well as explicit messages, the model is now becoming more complex but much closer to a representation of what is happening in the marketing communications process. Few advertisements ever say 'but' although that is what is intended; they are usually dressed up in images which send out an encoded message.

The *field of perception* is all the accumulated experience of the individual over their lifetime. It includes language, culture, knowledge, values, social-isation and self-image. It is the individual's view of the world, how it is and how it ought to be, and that individual's place within it. For effective marketing communication to take place, the fields of perception must overlap, so that sender and receiver have a common basis for talking to and understanding each other (see Figure 2.4, page 31). They do not need to have identical views of the world, but they do need sufficient common understanding for communication to be understood. Both message and feedback take place in the overlap between the two fields.

Lunch without frontiers – an overlap of two fields

Sheila Turner is a sales representative for a UK automotive components manufacturer. She lives and works in Warwick in the English Midlands, reads Stephen King novels, dresses business style, plays the piano a little, eats Chinese when she goes out, holidays in Provence, goes to aerobic classes on Fridays, and her only secret vice is a love of processed low-fat cheese. For two years she has been negotiating for her company to become a recognised supplier of drive belts to a French motor car manufacturer. Sheila learned French at school and has improved it on holiday in Provence. Jean-Pierre Fabou is the buyer with whom she has been building the deal. He is learning English but is reluctant to speak it, so most one-to-one discussions with Sheila are in French. Sheila has made a number of visits to the French factory, and Jean-Pierre has always taken her to the same local restaurant for lunch, where they dine at a table on the edge of the street, drink a few glasses of wine, and watch a suburban Paris afternoon drift slowly by.

On price, Sheila can beat other European competition because of the lower UK labour costs, but French motor manufacturers generally have not used UK components suppliers since the 1970s, when component quality and reliability became apparently unreliable. So Sheila has concentrated on building an image of good production and effective technical specification for her company. When Jean-Pierre has visited her company's factory in Warwick, she has hosted him closely and guided him through its quality assurance system. She has also personally translated most of the technical specifications and her factory's quality assurance documentation into French.

On his first visit to Warwick, Sheila took Jean-Pierre for an English pub lunch, to give him a bit of local flavour, but it was not a success. He insisted on wine, which was almost undrinkable, and the food arrived cold at the table. This would clearly not earn points from a French buyer, and she felt defeated in her efforts to build a good personal relationship with him. On his second visit, she decided to fight on her own culinary ground, and booked a table at a Chinese restaurant in the old medieval quarter of the town, where lime trees planted in the last century shaded the north wall of Warwick Castle. They drank green tea and she discovered in conversation that Jean-Pierre ate out at Vietnamese restaurants in Paris, but had always assumed she would want to eat French cuisine when she was visiting France.

Sheila had consistently developed an overlap of mutual perception between herself and Jean-Pierre in the key areas of the transaction: the quality and reliability of her company's products. She had also developed the encoding within that overlap in a number of ways, both in facilitating Jean-Pierre's knowledge about her company's manufacturing competencies and its quality assurance system, and in building socialisation through taking the food battle to her own territory. She had continually enhanced her own source credibility (and she had by chance neutralised any negative effects from the disastrous pub lunch), and had constructed a common basis for discussion and under-standing. It was only a matter of time, now, before she closed the deal with Jean-Pierre.

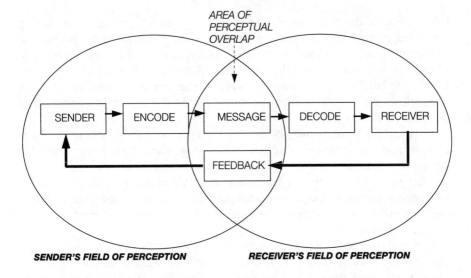

Figure 2.4 Overlapping fields of perception enable communication to take place

Identifying the area of overlap is crucial to effective encoding of a message by the sender, and for decoding of that message by the receiver. In personal communications this is often a matter of style and language. Communication between a Russian and an Italian, for example, will be difficult unless either understands the other's language, or unless they both understand a third language, such as English. One reason for the predominance of English as a world business language is that it often provides a commonly accepted overlap in fields of perception so that encoding and decoding can take place without an interpreter. Sometimes this is, of course, not an option, as happened in Sheila Turner's sales deal.

However, the fields of perception are much wider than mere common language. If sender and receiver are both business managers, they will understand the transaction they are both trying to achieve, such as an export deal. Even if both speak English poorly, each will understand what the other is trying to achieve. So the *context* in which the communication is taking place will also influence both encoding and decoding. This context may involve many things which are cultural, and which may be important to one party or the other. Jean-Pierre took Sheila to a good restaurant, and no doubt chose the wine with care. This is one of the joys of doing business in France, and Sheila had to think carefully how to respond to that. Likewise, some cultures, such as Japanese, place very great importance on politeness, which affects the ways in which messages might be understood.

In non-personal communications, the fields of perception and the ways in which encoding and decoding are carried out are also important. In marketing, they are arguably much more important, because many people depend on the communication being effective. A misinterpreted message from a sales manager to a distribution manager could result in wrong goods being delivered, perhaps to a key customer, reducing the possibility of a repeat order. This could affect the workforce, the shareholders and possibly other customers. Even worse, a poorly encoded advertising campaign could cause a new product to fail. For this reason, an advertising agency will normally carry out meticulous market research before, during and after the development of an advertising campaign.

Yet, even if the perceptions of the target market are thoroughly researched, and the message creatively and perceptively encoded, the message may still not reach a sufficient number of receivers in the target market. The message needs to be carried to the target market in a way that will reach most of the consumers at whom it is aimed. This means selecting the most appropriate carrier to take the message to the consumers. This carrier is called the communication channel.

In personal communication, the channel is relatively simple. A sales manager giving a presentation at a sales conference will communicate to the audience through the space between them, often in a variety of ways such as speaking, using an overhead projector or computer projection, giving out handouts or showing a video. The air between the manager and the audience is the channel. Light from an overhead projection slide will travel through it and so will sound. As the manager speaks, his voicebox vibrates the air and sound waves travel through it to the ears of the audience. Without this, encoding and decoding cannot take place, however much the fields of perception overlap. So selecting an appropriate channel, and using it effectively, require some technical understanding of how that channel works. In a large conference theatre, for example, the sales manager will use a microphone with a sound amplification system, because their voicebox on its own will not produce sufficient vibration of the air to reach the ears of all the audience. Video will be projected onto a large screen, because the sales representatives in the back row will not be able to see what is on a small television screen at the front of the conference theatre.

Listening to the message

Technology may also be important to the way in which a receiver listens to a message. In the European Parliament, for example, the MEPs put on earphones, so that they can hear a simultaneous translation of a speech in their own language. These technical tools used by *senders* and *receivers* take the message and make it heard. They are called *channel transmitters*.

They are operating at the same time as the message moves from sender to receiver, and they cannot be separated from it. So the communications channel is a sub-model of the whole marketing communication process (see Figure 2.5).

In marketing communications, these transmitting technologies require special and expert technical planning.

CHANNEL OF COMMUNICATION

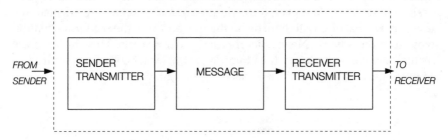

Figure 2.5 The communication channel

No FT – no airline seat

An airline is launching a new transatlantic executive class. The *Financial Times* is an obvious media choice, as it will be read by most of the end-users (the executives), who will then influence the buyers (their PA or the company travel office). But which is the best day to advertise? Certainly not on Monday morning, when most reader attention is concentrated on catching up with weekend developments. And on which page? UK News, American News, Asia Pacific News? And then, how can the advert draw and keep attention for the precious 30 seconds it needs to deliver its message? These are technical questions, and the airline's advertising agency should have the research to answer them.

Receiving transmitters need just as much technical attention as sender transmitters. A television commercial has typically 30 seconds in which to communicate. Family television sets are smaller than most other items of furniture in a room. The family may all be focused on a football match, but there will be other activity as soon as the break starts. There will be intense discussion of the game so far; someone may pass around cans of beer or cups of tea; chairs may be rearranged for a better view. Who is watching the advert? How many eyes and for how long? How much of the message will be understood and accepted amidst the other activity? These are technical questions, and the advertising agency will use specialist media researchers to provide the answers.

Noise in the channel

Understanding how the technology of the channel transmitters works is only a part of what is needed to identify a useful communication channel. The receivers may be there at the end of the channel, transmitters fully switched on to listen, but other sights and sounds may obscure the message. Every business manager has at some time been in a meeting near a main road in summer with the windows open. Even with a microphone and sound amplification, the speakers' messages can be drowned in the thrumming of a passing diesel lorry. And even if the right page and position are selected in a newspaper, what else will there be on that page to take the reader's attention away from the advert? News, pictures and other adverts. This clutter in the channel, which draws away the attention of the target consumer or drowns the message, is called *channel noise* (see Figure 2.6).

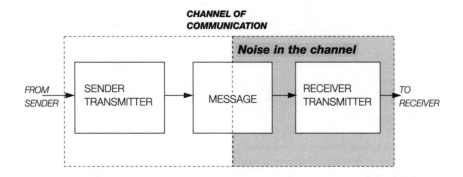

Figure 2.6 Noise in the communication channel

It is the reason why newspapers charge more for 'boxing' classified adverts. In a page of 30–100 small classified messages, the box stands out from the surrounding channel noise, and it will draw the reader's attention before the other adverts on the same page.

All channels used by marketers have considerable amounts of noise, and a key task of the marketer is to make sure his message stands out clearly from it. This is often a much more complex problem than simply making the message louder or more attention-grabbing.

Boxing clever

Most newspapers carry hundreds of small adverts, often classified according to what they are advertising, eg motor cars. There are hundreds of these adverts on each page of the 'classified' sections, and there may be many adverts for exactly the same product, such as a specific model and year of motor car. If an advert in this 'classified' section of a newspaper is 'boxed' (bordered with a thick dark line), it will stand out clearly from the other adverts on the same page and attract the reader's attention before those other adverts. However, if every advert in the classified section of a newspaper were to be boxed, they would all attract attention equally, and no individual advert would stand out from the page. Newspapers charge a premium for a boxed advert, so only a small proportion of classified adverts have this special attention-getting quality.

Marketing messages need to stand out from their surrounding noise in two ways:

1) They need to stand out from all the surrounding non-marketing noise so that they can be seen as marketing messages. This is because customers search for marketing messages and pay a special kind of attention to them. Marketing communications are not simply a process of specific attention and information; over the past 100 years they have become an institutionalised system of commercial information and persuasion (Williams, 1980). In a consuming society, marketing communications are a basic part of the process by which consumers search for products and services. Consumers depend on the social status of specific products and services to explain to themselves and others what and who they are. Marketing communications such as advertising provide this non-functional status value, and when products or services are branded, this produces an even higher level of consumer loyalty and attention to those products or services. Marketing communications thus perform a function similar to a newspaper, providing news and information which will assist buyers to make effective purchases.

Some modern philosophers go further than this (Berger, 1972), and suggest that the nature of advertising in particular explains why consumers search for and pay special attention to marketing communications. Advertising not only conveys information about the function and performance of products and services, but also gives social and personal meanings to them. The need for the status sought by consumers through purchase of these social and personal meanings is constant and always waiting to be satisfied. However, once a purchase is made, the product or service acquired will last only a certain amount of time until it is consumed. After consumption, the need for status will remain, and that will be satisfied only through further purchase. So the status acquired is always merely temporary, and the consumer will only be as good as their next purchase. There is thus a strong social and personal compulsion for consumers to seek and look at marketing communications.

Marketers do not therefore try to disguise their messages to the market, but rather seek to emphasise their marketing nature. This means that marketing messages must be designed to stand out from the noise of all the other messages seeking to gain attention. Adverts need to stand out from news in newspapers; commercials need to stand out from programmes on television; poster hoardings need to stand out from street signs and public notices.

2) Marketing messages need to stand out from surrounding marketing noise so that they can attract, inform and persuade those target customers at whom they are aimed. This means that a marketing communication must both differentiate itself from other marketing messages, and stimulate attention from those particular customers at whom it is aimed. With some forms of communication, such as direct mail, this is achieved through the nature of the channel and how the communication is designed to move

through it. The direct mail promotion is personally addressed to a target prospect using address information from a marketing database. With point-of-sale promotions, where the communication has to stand out from other packaging treatments, this is achieved largely by design, colour, graphics, contrasts and a prominent *promise* such as a competition or a price-off offer. To make display advertising stand out on hoardings or in newspapers is more difficult and often involves an element of shock or surprise designed into the advertisement, as with the Benetton 'shock' photographs' campaign.

Underlying all these forms of attention-getting is the set of values and status which marketers have persuaded the consumers in the market to associate with their product or service. In consumer products this is generally represented by the brand, and the design signature used to represent that brand. In industrial business-to-business marketing, quality, reliability and delivery are generally much more important to buyers than status, and these values are conveyed through a design signature, often the corporate identity, representing the selling business. (Note that successful businesses which are acquired by other businesses often keep their original name, functioning as a division of the acquiring business.) As more and more advertising is produced for the brand, or the corporate identity is repeatedly used in product or service advertising, the values associated with them are reinforced in the minds of buyers in the market.

This is a learning process, in which both the private consumer and the professional buyer learn about the values associated with a brand or a corporate identity, and then have those values and their association with the brand or corporate identity reinforced through subsequent marketing campaigns. The more the buyer sees the brand or the corporate identity associated with a specific range of products, services or messages, the more the brand and corporate values will be recognised by the market. To make a marketing communication stand out from other marketing communications, brand and corporate identity are used on all forms of communication to the market. If the presentation of these is not consistent, the learning process will be distorted or blocked. It is therefore important for effective long-term marketing communications that wherever the brand or the corporate identity appear, they have exactly the same design features and carry the same values and attributes. The same golden thread of cohesion should run through every component of a marketing communications mix.

INTEGRATING THE MODEL WITHIN OVERALL BUSINESS STRATEGY

Marketing communications is a part of the overall marketing process, and is therefore dependent on the policies and strategies set for the whole business organisation by its controlling board of directors. As you will see in Chapter 4 on strategy, strategy cascades down the organisation from the chief executive through the functional managers to the line managers, who adopt and modify the chief executive's strategy to achieve results in their own areas of operation. This means that the policies and strategies of the whole business need to be integrated with the strategies of all levels of management involved in marketing communications.

In successful businesses, the strategy process starts with the customers, current and potential, and the extent to which their needs and wants can be satisfied by the business or by its competitors. This is what you would expect in a marketing orientated business. It is therefore important that the top planning level of the organisation, in particular the chief executive, receives the most accurate and current data on what is happening in the market. Much of the key data required for this top-level strategy development is produced by marketing managers in the organisation (eg company sales, market share penetration, competitors' sales, competitors' advertising spend, new products coming into the market). As can be seen in Figure 2.7, this data is captured in the MIIS (Marketing Intelligence and Information System) and then fed into the information system of the whole business. It will not only be analysed by the marketing managers, but also by the business planners who develop overall strategy for the whole organisation. The results of that analysis will be fed back to the marketing managers in the form of justified strategic objectives for the business. These objectives then become the basis on which the marketer defines all planning objectives, including marketing communications objectives.

The whole communications model which can be applied to the marketing communications process is thus both about the planning and encoding of

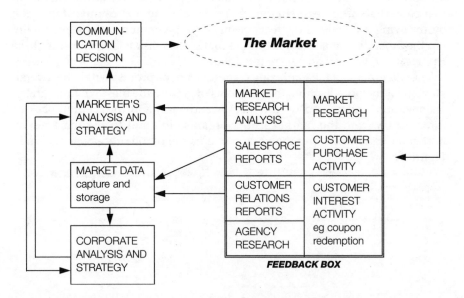

Figure 2.7 Integration of market feedback information and strategy development

marketing communications, but also about the strategic direction of the whole business. When all information and analysis is assembled, the communication decision is made. There may be a wide variety of justifications for this decision, including:

- *a short-term need* to use marketing communications tools to correct under-achievement of a marketing plan (eg if sales are not hitting target);
- *a need to defend* against anticipated action by competitors (eg to spoil the launch of a competing product);
- *a planned routine* of reminding the market about a brand (eg to maintain brand awareness and foster brand loyalty).

Whatever the reasons for deciding to use marketing communications, they must reflect the overall objectives of the organisation as well as the immediate needs of the marketer to communicate with a market. Every communication of the firm will have an effect in the mind not only of customers, but also of other stakeholders in the organisation such as shareholders and employees. This is more important with marketing communications than with any other communications of the organisation, because marketers use the most powerful communications tools in any organisation, and those which are likely to have the strongest and widest effect. There are two reasons for this. Firstly, even if a communication is carefully targeted at a specific segment in the market, the rest of the population cannot be blindfolded and will be subject to possible influence by it. Secondly, much marketing communication takes effect through word-of-mouth communication in which the receiver of a message passes their interpretation of that message on to other people who may or may not be in that particular target segment (Smith, 1993). Like the ripples caused in a lake by throwing a pebble, the effects of marketing communications eventually lap the most distant shore. Part of the marketer's task is to make sure these ripples move faster than nature intended.

This integration of the marketing communications process within the overall strategy of the organisation, the problems of getting the message through the channel and understood by the market audience, and the feeding back of information from the market to the organisation and to the marketer in particular, can now be put together in one model of the process, as shown in Figure 2.8.

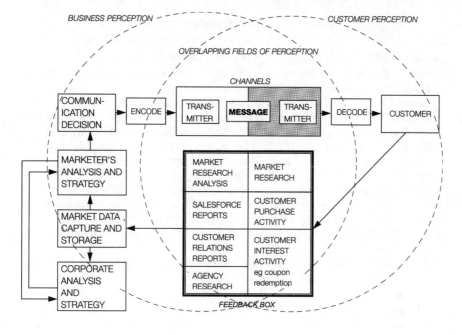

Figure 2.8 The marketing communication process – a feedback model

DISCUSSION TOPICS FOR CHAPTER 2

1) How are the different roles of sender and receiver in a communication process?
2) Select an advert from a newspaper. Identify sender, intended receiver and message.
3) What is sender credibility and how does it affect the communication process?
4) What are the main human feedbacks monitored by marketers?
5) Suggest ways in which feedback from salesforce reports can be made more reliable.
6) Select a full-colour advert from a magazine. Identify the message and describe how it has been encoded.
7) Discuss the importance of fields of perception in international marketing negotiations.
8) Identify the receiver transmitters you use in a typical day. What technical problems do you have with them?
9) Discuss noise in television advertising.
10) Why do people pay attention to adverts?

REFERENCES

Berger, J (1972) *Ways of Seeing*, BBC/Penguin, London

Cutlip, S, Center, A and Broom, G (1985) *Effective Public Relations*, 6th edn, Prentice Hall, Englewood Cliffs, NJ (cited in Smith, 1993)

Financial Times (1997) BT seeks to reassure 'caring' consumers, 13 January

Hovland, C I, Janis, I L and Kelley, H H (1953) A summary of experimental studies of opinion change, in *Communication and Persuasion*, Princeton University Press, NJ

Kelman, H C and Hovland, C I (1953) Reinstatement of the communicator in delayed measurement of opinion change, *Journal of Abnormal Psychology*, **48**

Schramm, W (1955) How communication works, in *The Process and Effects of Mass Communication*, ed W Schramm, University of Illinois Press, Urbana, IL

Shostack, G L (1977) Breaking free from product marketing, *Journal of Marketing*, April

Shostack, G L, How to design a service, *European Journal of Marketing*, **16** (1)

Smith, P R (1998) *Marketing Communications – An integrated approach*, 2nd edn, Kogan Page, London

Williams, R (1980) Advertising: the magic system, in *Problems in Materialism and Culture*, Verso, London

T H R E E

The communications process and the marketing mix

LEARNING OBJECTIVES

- Understand how communication tools convey direct and indirect benefits.
- Distinguish different types of customer and the different stages in the buying readiness process.
- Contrast different hierarchy of effects models.
- Appreciate the response curves of the main communications tools.
- Understand the communications mix characteristics for industrial and consumer markets.
- Communication in push and pull marketing strategies.
- Understand the principles of integrated marketing communications.

TOPICS COVERED BY THIS CHAPTER

THE SPECIAL FEATURES OF MARKETING COMMUNICATIONS

Some of the ways in which elements of the personal communications model are adapted by marketers, such as special forms of feedback, have been explained in Chapter 2. There are, in addition, a number of special features of marketing communications which make them different from other forms of communication.

Marketing communications is a systematic relationship between a business and its market in which the marketer assembles a wide variety of ideas, designs, messages, media, shapes, forms and colours, both to communicate ideas to, and to stimulate a particular perception of products and services by, individual people who have been aggregated into a target market. The result of this process of assembling is referred to by marketers as the *communications mix*, and this is what is seen, heard and hopefully understood by the customers in the market. To assemble this mix, the marketer uses a number of *marketing communications tools*: personal selling, advertising, sales promotions, public relations, direct marketing and marketing design and much more.

DIRECT AND INDIRECT BENEFITS

Each marketing communications tool will convey either direct or indirect benefits, and will be used to communicate to the customer either close to where the buying decision is made, or at a distance away from where the buying decision is made (see Table 3.1).

Table 3.1 The relationship of marketing communications tools to distance from buying point

	Direct tools	**Indirect tools**
Distant from the buying point	**Advertising**	**PR** (public relations) Sponsorship Corporate identity
Close to or at the buying point	**Personal selling**	Point-of-sale promotions Other **sales promotions** (eg price-off coupons)
Close to and/or distant from the buying point	**Direct marketing** and promotions (eg exhibitions) Direct mail offers (eg database marketing)	**Design** (eg packaging, brand signatures and corporate identity) **Word-of-mouth**

Direct tools convey direct benefits; indirect tools convey indirect benefits. A *direct benefit* is the main want normally fulfilled by the product or service. It is the main reason why the customer buys, and for this reason, direct benefits are usually communicated by the most powerful communications tools: advertising and personal selling. An *indirect benefit* is some ancillary want which can also be fulfilled by purchase, but it is never the main reason why the customer buys. These indirect benefits are conveyed by the less powerful communications tools: sales promotions, public relations and marketing design.

Beanz meanz benefitz

Heinz's main communication of its baked beans is through display and television advertising in which the product is always seen providing a convenient fast meal for the family and the children in particular. This is the key direct benefit and is the main want fulfilled by the product. These communications ensure that baked beans are kept on the family shopping list, and are therefore aimed at maintaining the overall size of the market for baked beans and Heinz's position as brand leader. Periodically, Heinz will support this message with price-off coupons distributed through household magazines, or by special price-off promotions on the tin itself. They might also arrange some public relations support by way of household magazine articles on the nutritional value of baked beans, backed up with recipes for a variety of easily prepared dishes. Some food manufacturers publish recipe booklets, for which the customer sends so many labels from the product. These are indirect benefits, and while they will have some effect on how the customer decides whether or not to buy Heinz Baked Beans, they will only be important after the main decision has been made – to keep baked beans on the family shopping list. To ensure that the customer sees both forms of communication as one overall cohesive message, both direct and indirect benefits are given the same marketing design treatments (colours, graphics, shapes) and use the same brand and corporate identity (Heinz).

CLOSENESS TO THE BUYING DECISION

Some communications tools, such as personal selling and point-of-sale promotions, are used at or close to where the customer makes their decision to buy (see Table 3.1, page 42).

In personal selling, the communication is an interactive one between a salesperson and a prospect, in which the salesperson seeks to impose a predetermined pattern of personal communication on the prospective buyer. This pattern will vary slightly from one organisation to another, depending on the attitude of the sales manager, but will always include the seven Ps of selling (Smith, 1993):

- Prospecting (looking for potential customers);
- Preparation (objective setting, customer research, etc);
- Presentation (demonstration, discussion);
- Possible problems (handling objections);
- 'Please give me an order' (closing the sale or getting the order);
- Pen-to-paper (record the details accurately);
- Post-sales service (building a continuing relationship).

Some salesforces will build in other 'Ps' according to their own ways of dealing with the market eg the salesforce of a branded food manufacturer selling to small and independent retailers will normally include 'Payment' so that the credit position of the retailer is checked early in the transaction before other credit is offered.

Since the Second World War, as the marketing concept has been progressively adopted in business, the role of personal selling to the consumer-buyer has declined, and is now used mainly in industrial or business-to-business marketing. For most consumer goods, and for many consumer services, the buying process no longer contains any active face-to-face selling. Brands and market-led product designs, supported by advertising and sales promotions, have taken its place. Even when stores are staffed by sales assistants, their role is to guide the customer through a range of known branded alternatives rather than to sell to them. Much consumer marketing is thus dependent on non-personal selling techniques called *merchandising* (Buttle), in which the store layout, the design of the product packaging and the position of products on the shelves are the main factors in achieving sales. With the development of self-service retailing, merchandising has evolved through agreements between manufacturers and retailers which allow the manufacturers' brands specific spaces on the shelves (known as *shelf-facings*). These shelf-facings are often maintained by specialist sales representatives known as *merchandisers*, who are employed by the manufacturer to ensure that its brands are displayed as agreed with the retailer.

Point-of-sale communications are of two kinds:

1) *Incentives on the shelf or pack or attached to goods on display*. These encourage the customer to try a new product or experiment with a change of brand, and include price-off offers (price reductions indicated on-pack), more-for-same (additional quantity for the normal price) and banded offers (two products banded together with a free gift). Until recently, these point-of-sale promotions were assumed to be effective in breaking brand loyalty, but recent research by Ehrenberg has shown that these promotions stimulate only short-term trial of new products or different brands, after which the customer returns to the brand to which they were previously loyal. To be effective in seducing customers away from their normal brand, these promotions need to be integrated with a range of other communications tools such as advertising, so that the experimental choice of the customer is supported and reinforced over a period of several weeks.

2) *Point-of-purchase advertising*. This consists of advertising messages created and displayed at the point where the customer pays for the goods, usually at or close to a till or check-out. They include *box-talkers* (eg the strap-line on the side of boxes holding canned beers, designed to hold the product on the shelf and to be seen by the customer), *shelf-talkers* (brand messages attached to the shelf) and special display stands with promotional messages on them. Point-of-purchase advertising provides an easy solution for the retailer for displaying small items bulked in boxes which would otherwise be difficult to display on conventional shelving, and is used extensively in the confectionery sector for displaying small branded sugar confectionery rolls (eg Trebor Extra Strong Mints) close to the till in a CTN (confectioner, tobacconist and newsagent) or at the check-out in a supermarket.

Some marketing communications tools, such as advertising and public relations, operate at a distance in time and place from the point where the buying decision is made, and are less likely to have an immediate effect on sales, since the messages reach the customer when they are not in a buying situation. These communications tools generally carry messages which are intended to support and develop awareness of the brand rather than causing immediate buying activity. Even newspaper advertising by supermarket multiples on Thursdays and Fridays, giving information on price-off offers available that weekend, are more in the nature of 'reminder' advertising, to reinforce the store loyalty of weekend shoppers and bring them into the supermarket for their weekly shopping, rather than to promote the particular products featured in the advertising.

STATE OF MIND OF THE CUSTOMER

Just as it is important that the communication takes place within the overlap of the fields of perception, the area of common understanding between the marketer and the customer, it is also necessary for the marketer to recognise that there are different ways in which customers will assess the communication and then decide how to respond to it.

While all customers are unique, there are four typical types of customer each of whom will have a different way of assessing a marketing communication and responding to it. These are the learning customer, the self-justifying customer, the routine customer and the professional customer.

The learning customer

Some customers become highly involved in a buying decision, looking at a wide range of alternatives, developing detailed information on them, and comparing prices and methods of payment. This is usually the case with purchases which for the customer are infrequent, high cost and when there are many alternative products in the market all with significantly different features. Gathering information and evaluating it will be important for this customer, who will become highly involved in detail and who will see significant risk in making their choice.

PC Personal Computer or Purchase Chaos?

No modern family is complete without its personal computer. It will work out the shopping budget, help with schoolwork, keep father entertained in the evenings, print letterheads and Christmas cards, play multimedia games and learning programs, provide a handy dictionary and encyclopaedia, and link the family into the world wide web. It is the modern equivalent of the Edwardian piano, a family-focused piece of technology. Families learn that they need a PC from friends who already have one, from teachers who teach their children to use them and from the constant flow of PC-related news in papers and television. Like the Edwardian piano, they are major items of investment for the family and can cost more than a second-hand family car. The range of features which can be included with a PC is almost endless – colour printer, fax modem, Internet modem, 17" low energy monitor, multimedia CD player, acoustic speakers, business software, home entertainment software, educational software, on-site service warranties, off-site service warranties. What does the family really need out of all these choices? And what if they don't buy some of the add-ons and then find that they need them? The family will spend some time gathering information about the different PCs available, and will look around the shops at the different prices and deals. The parents will be advised by a friend who already has a PC. The children will be advised by their schoolmates. The parents will probably buy a computer magazine to see what is available and what the different options mean. At that point, even if there is a computer 'expert' in the family, confusion will reign. They find that they have to learn a new and strange language. What is a RAM and why should they opt for an 8 Mb RAM rather than a 4 Mb RAM? Is it really necessary to have 1Gb of hard disc, and what is a hard disc anyway? Should the CD drive be quad-speed and what is a sound card, let alone what brand and type of sound card to have? Maybe they need a computer to work out which computer they should buy. The parents will carry out most of the analysis of the information, though it is quite likely that children over the age of 11 will have a clear idea of what they want in a home PC, and that will probably be multimedia game playing capacity which comes expensive. The parents will be considerably dependent on anyone or anything that will reduce the risk in this complex buying process. A retail sales assistant may appear reliable and knowledgeable, and they may respond to that. They may recognise a well-known brand such as IBM and decide to go for that. This still does not reduce the technical complexity as IBM make a wide range of PCs, but it at least reduces the number of manufacturers they need to consider. Liking and preference for a particular brand will be an emotional response, as will the process of making a final decision on price and optional extras. After they have made the purchase, the parents will talk to their friends and to other parents about what a good deal they made, and the children will once again be able to hold their heads high among their peer group, and swap CD games with their friends.

The family has employed a problem-solving approach to buying a PC. The sequence of stages in their problem-solving was: gather information, analyse and try to understand it, develop a preference, find an affordable price, work out a risk-reduction strategy, and then purchase a PC (see Figure 3.1). For the family dealing with a strange technology, a key part of this process was not only gathering information, but also comprehending it. Even after purchase, they will continue to assess the features, finding out more and more that the PC can do, and talking to friends and other parents about it. The process has involved considerable learning by the family.

Figure 3.1 Learning customers: stages in the buying-readiness process

These customers are learning about their buying problem as they progressively solve it. They spend a great deal of time, effort and thought on the purchase, and are therefore called *high-involvement* customers. Effective marketing communications should therefore provide technical detail, for which newspapers and magazines will be the best media. Sales staff, particularly in retailing, should be trained to spot this learning customer and to assist them in making a firm choice. These customers are also likely to rely on the advice of friends and will eventually advise other friends, so messages should be designed to achieve multi-step communication (Smith, 1993).

The self-justifying customer

Some customers make up their minds fairly quickly, especially when there is little differentiation between products and brands available. Festinger (1957) developed his hypothesis of cognitive dissonance to explain that this type of customer buys quickly and then evaluates the purchase. If the product turns out to have features or qualities which are not what the customer expected or which the customer did not want, they will adjust their original expectations to fit the features and qualities of what they have bought. The dissonance between what they expected and what they have got is reduced by this adjustment.

Buying a family car

The UK car market, like most national car markets, is actually made up of three distinct groups of customers – car leasing companies, companies buying for their own fleets and the private buyer. Purchasing for the first two groups is made by professional buyers who generally get 40 per cent off list price. Not so the private buyer, who is paying near list price for a family car. The search process is generally prolonged, with information from friends, acquaintances, long copy press adverts full of splendid technical detail and of course the manufacturers' brochures. Then there are the romantic TV adverts promising that a family saloon is really a sports car in disguise, all based on the concept that a man can be unfaithful to his wife as long as it is only with a motor car.

Every one of the family's needs will be calculated and taken into account, and every one will be consulted in the process. The husband's romantic dream will be constrained by the wife's sense of the practical. The children will say they like this one but they don't like that one, and will inevitably opt for anything with a digital dashboard and lots of buttons to press. The search is high involvement but an impossible one, as there is really little difference between one 1.6L family saloon and another within the same price range. The apparent learning process does not really involve learning, and the decision to buy a particular model is arrived at through a process of impulse rather than logical assessment of alternatives. If the family is replacing a reliable car, it will probably opt for the same brand. The excitement of real choice evaporates.

Once the new car arrives home, the whole family goes to work exploring it. The husband will sit in it for hours, poring over the manual. The children will bounce in and out, trying levers, pushing buttons, discovering a wonderful new toy. The husband soon discovers that it is not like the old car at all. It has special levers that move the steering wheel this way and that, and so many buttons to press he can't remember what they all do, let alone the illuminated ashtray. Although he doesn't smoke, he leaves it open driving at night, to get the full effect. It feels faster than it did on the test drive. He stands and looks in awe at the headlamp washers. He leaves it outside the pub, and with apparent reluctance is compelled to spell its wonders to his companions who had warned him so carefully against buying that brand. He reads the long copy adverts in the Sunday papers all over again, and returns to the pub with yet more startling revelations about the car to end all cars. Resolving the dissonance between his romantic dream and the staid reality of yet another family car, the only logical analysis he carries out is after he has bought it. This is the self-justifying customer.

This customer buys quickly because they assume that they know the products available, then develop ways of confirming that perception of themselves, and finally acquire the knowledge to support that perception (see Figure 3.2). Marketing communications again need to supply technical detail for this type of customer, but with messages designed to encourage the customer to evaluate the product in specific ways that help them to justify the purchase.

Buying problem $\Longrightarrow$ Action $\Longrightarrow$ Feelings $\Longrightarrow$ Knowings

Figure 3.2 Self-justifying customers: stages in the buying-readiness process

These customers can play an important role in word-of-mouth communication as they will need to express their self-justification, and messages should be designed to turn these customers into key steps in multi-step communication. Brand advertising will support self-justification and will help to build brand loyalty for repeat purchase.

The routine customer

Most purchases which people make are routine – buying a light bulb, selecting a pack of breakfast cereal, taking clothes to the dry-cleaners. These are not generally risky decisions as the products or services are very similar and are therefore said to have *low differentiation*. Even with brands which are routinely selected, say as part of the weekly grocery shopping, the customer choice is out of habit rather than because of brand loyalty. Routine customers have low involvement in their buying decisions, partly because it is a routine choice which does not involve searching for information, and partly because there is little differentiation between products and brands in the market other than the design of the packaging. Marketing communications therefore need to focus on supporting this routine, reminding the customer that the brand is still there and providing simple reasons why that brand should remain part of the customer's routine. Packaging design is important in the communications mix as it helps the customer to recognise the brand on the shelf and save time comparing different brands. Television advertising using short, frequently repeated messages will reinforce routine.

This routine customer can be induced to switch brand using sales promotions such as price-off coupons, point-of-sale promotions, on-pack offers and competitions. Once they have switched, they will have a tendency to return to their previous brand, but this can be restricted by repeat advertising to maintain their choice of the new brand. This is not a simple process, as the routine customer has low involvement, does not feel intensely about the choice, and will swing between the old and the new brand. The sequence of buying-readiness stages for this customer is knowing the brand they usually buy, taking it off the shelf and later feeling comfortable with the purchase (see Figure 3.3). Merchandising is therefore important, and part of the marketing communications planning should involve negotiating with the distribution channel for high-impact shelf-facings for the brand to maximise the communication to the customer from the supermarket shelf. For the same reason, the design of the packaging should be reviewed regularly to ensure that it maintains a distinctly different image from that of competing brands, so that the customer can recognise it easily and at a distance.

Buying problem ⇨ Knowings ⇨ Action ⇨ Feelings

Figure 3.3 Routine customers: stages in the buying-readiness process

Now hands that do dishes can save the planet:

For almost 20 years Fairy Liquid has been supported by a series of mother and daughter TV commercials focused on the hands of the mother. Apart from the impossible creative problem of making washing-up look interesting, the advertising is a useful example of reminder advertising for the routine customer. Washing-up liquids have very little differentiation from each other, apart from colour of packaging and the occasional reassuring promise that the fragrance of fresh lemons will attach to your crockery. So the main task of the advertising is to be as memorable as it can, and provide attributes which will reinforce the habit of the shopper in taking it off the shelf and putting it in the supermarket trolley. The commercials have successfully used the jingle 'Now hands that do dishes can be soft as your face', which helps to distinguish the TV commercial from other commercials, so that it can reinforce and remind the shopper that the usual choice will be quite safe.

Some daughters, of course, have grown up into fierce environmentalists and switched over to brands such as Ecover, which differentiates itself in a variety of ways. The container is biodegradable, as well as the liquid, and there is even a translucent strip down the side to show the user how much is left. It is unlikely that Ecover is bought as routine, and it is more likely to be purchased initially by a high involvement customer who will be only a small proportion of the market. No amount of creative jingles about saving the planet will entice the routine customer away from the main manufacturer and own-label brands. It is simply not within the routine, as the repeat advertising assures the shopper.

The professional customer

Most organisations have professionally trained buyers who manage their procurement budgets, negotiate supply contracts and manage the flow of components, goods and services into their factories and offices. These are the professional buyers, the main point of contact for sales representatives involved in business-to-business (or industrial) marketing. Many sales representatives who have learned what it is to be shredded by a hardened buyer will agree with Elbert Hubbard's description of professional buyers as 'intelligent, cold, passive... a human petrification with a heart of feldspar, and without charm... minus bowels, passions or a sense of humour. Happily they never reproduce, and all of them finally go to Hell' (Hill and Hillier, 1977: 80). They use their specialised experience to purchase goods and services for the organisation on the terms and at the quality levels which the organisation needs. From the outside, this appears to be a high-risk occupation, but buyers are methodical and follow set procedures to manage risk. They will set up supply contracts with a particular supplier for a period, often 12 months, and draw on that as and when they need supplies, so that they do not have to enter fresh negotiations every time they buy anything. Such a supply contract would be reviewed by the buyer every year, when other suppliers would be invited to bid for the contract, and the supplier would be decided through negotiation.

So sometimes the professional buyer is buying in a similar way to the learning customer, and sometimes they are operating like a routine customer. When they are reviewing and negotiating an annual supply contract, they are *highly involved*, as the outcome can be critical to the manufacturing and market performance of their company, and they will develop a detailed analysis of alternative suppliers and products. The things they buy vary from technically highly differentiated products, such as integrated manufacturing systems, to components with very low apparent differentiation, such as nuts and bolts, but the buyer's job is to seek out, identify and use differentiation as a tactic in negotiating price and delivery. So industrial marketers, like professional buyers, treat all supplies being sold from business to business as highly differentiated, even if objectively they are not.

Professional buyers therefore follow two different sequences of stages in the buying-readiness process (see Figure 3.4). When they are finding new or reviewing existing suppliers, they first search for information and then negotiate with sales representatives before awarding a supply contract. When they are buying from existing suppliers under an existing contract they first place the order, then evaluate the supplier after they have received information about how the order has been met by the supplier.

The first stage of a new contract negotiation will typically be an exchange of information between a buyer and a sales representative. The buyer will be given technical specifications by other people in the organisation such as production managers, and will ask a number of suppliers to make presentations of the terms on which they can supply. This is characteristic of high involvement customers, and it is a way of reducing uncertainty for the buyer. Presentations may be made to production management as well as the buyer, so the sales representative needs to make effective relationships with both. These personal relationships are important in industrial marketing, as is the quality of presentation made by the sales representative (Hill and Hillier, 1977), which can change the feelings of the buyer and their technical adviser about the supplier. Following this feelings stage, the contract will be awarded. When the buyer is operating as a routine customer, they do not waste time renegotiating the supply contract, but simply check that supply is available and order it. This routine enables them to reduce risk. Any changes in specification will probably be handled between the production management who will use the components and the sales representative, and that will then be communicated to the buyer to be included in amended terms of contract. So as a routine customer, the organisational buyer will act first, get information

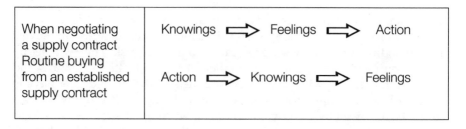

Figure 3.4 Professional customers: stages in the buying-readiness process

second and develop fresh perceptions of the supplier afterwards. Once a sales representative has gained a supply contract, they will work to maintain the relationship with regular visits to the factory to check that quality and delivery are what the production manager wanted, and this will involve the occasional lunch, possibly with the buyer as well. This is a key opportunity for the sales representative to maintain the image of their company in the minds of both the buyer and the production manager.

Profiling the customer

Some markets will contain several of these customer types eg a proportion of customers who are intensely environmentalist will search for information about household and grocery products before evaluating them, although the majority of customers will buy them as routine items. It is important therefore at the beginning of the marketing communication process to develop an analysis of the segments in the market which conform to one of the profiles of characteristics shown in Table 3.2.

HIERARCHY OF EFFECTS MODELS

The three stages in the customer's response described above – knowings, feelings and action – have been used in models of the marketing communication response process since the 1920s. Whatever the end result required by the marketer, the customer will go through these stages of response to the marketing communication, and each stage will be the logical outcome of the stage preceding it, like a hierarchy of related levels in an organisation. For this reason, this process of the customer passing through stages of gradually developing response to marketing communications is referred to as the *hierarchy of effects* concept (the term was first used by Lavidge and Steiner (1961)). A variety of models of this concept has been developed over the past 70 years, mainly derived from attempts to measure advertising effectiveness, and a summary of the more well-known models is shown in Table 3.3. Over the years, the models have moved progressively from classical learning models (eg Strong's AIDA, 1925) to attitude change models (eg McGuire's processing model, 1969).

Table 3.2 Matching customer profiles with marketing communications factors

	Customer types			
	Learning customer	**Self-justifying customer**	**Routine customer**	**Professional customer**
Involvement	High	High	Low	Annual: high Routine: low
Typical products and services	PC, family holiday, life insurance	Family car, fashion accessories, DIY tools	Washing-up liquid, petrol, air flight	Machine tools, nuts and bolts, security services
Product differentiation	High	Low	Low	High
Brand loyalty	High after purchase	High before purchase	Habit not loyalty	No loyalty
Information	Technical	Detailed and technical	Reminders of the brand	Technical as requested
Assessment of risk	High risk	Avoids or ignores risk	Low risk	Annual: high risk Routine: low risk
Evaluation	Rational	Emotional	Little evaluation or emotional	Annual: rational Routine: emotional
Attitude to price	Rational	Insensitive	Sensitive	Sensitive
Design focus	Technical	Features	Branding, packaging	Technical, safety, reliability
Message	Detailed and rational	Detailed and emotional	Brand support	Annual: rational Routine: rational and emotional
Main marketing communic-ation tools	Advertising, print media, direct mail, Internet	Advertising, print and TV, word-of-mouth, sales pro-motion, direct mail	Advertising, TV and radio, point-of-sale, sales promotions, merchandising, packaging	Personal selling, exhibitions, public relations, direct mail

Table 3.3 Hierarchy of effects models: the sequence of stages typical for a high involvement customer responding to mass communications about highly differentiated products

	COGNITIVE (Knowledge)		AFFECTIVE (Feelings)		CONATIVE (Motivation to action)
AIDA (Strong, 1925)	Attention	Interest		Desire	Action
DAGMAR (Colley, 1961)	Awareness Comprehension		Conviction		Action
3-D (Lavidge and Steiner, 1961)	Awareness Knowledge	Liking Preference	Conviction		Purchase
Adoption (Rogers, 1962)	Awareness	Interest		Evaluation	Trial Adoption
Processing (McGuire, 1969)	Presentation Attention Compre-hension	Yielding (attitude change)		Retention (of new attitude)	Behaviour
Marketing communications priorities	Communicate information (rational appeal)		Persuade eg through fear-reassurance (emotional)		Keep repeating the message (motivate to action)

The changes in customer response assumed to occur in each stage are defined differently by each author according to the results of their research and analysis. Strong (AIDA – 1925), for example, assumed the knowings (cognitive) stage to be concerned mostly with gaining the attention of the customer to the message. Later authors, such as Colley (DAGMAR – 1961) and Lavidge and Steiner (3-D – 1961) concluded that attention was only the start of the cognitive stage, and that a more substantial mental process of awareness, understanding and cognition-modification was taking place. The problem for all authors has been simply how much knowledge is necessary before the customer starts to change attitude and behaviour towards a product or brand. Once that can be ascertained, an appropriate communications mix can be developed and scheduled.

DIFFERENT TIMES TO RESPOND TO EACH COMMUNICATIONS TOOL

Some marketing communications tools will cause a measurable response in a market in a short period of time (eg personal selling). Other tools have a drip-feed effect, difficult to isolate and measure, over a much longer period (eg public relations).

The time taken for the different marketing communications tools to have an effect in the market will vary. Those tools which operate close to where a customer makes a buying decision, such as an effective retail sales assistant or a price-off promotion in a shop, will have an immediate effect on sales, as the customer is generally in a situation where they wish to buy and can be guided through their choice. Other tools, such as advertising and public relations, which operate at a distance in time and place from the point where the buying decision is made, are less likely to have an immediate effect as they reach the customer when they are not in a buying situation and are often messages which are intended to support and develop awareness of the brand rather than cause immediate buying activity. These relationships of cause and effect can be calculated mathematically as response functions for each communications tool, and the typical response curves of marketing effort for the main communications tools is charted against sales in Figure 3.5.

The effect of a communications tool will not always follow the response curves illustrated, and it is therefore important in assembling a marketing communications mix for the marketer to make some initial estimate of how fast the market will respond to each tool. An experienced brand manager who has used a variety of communications tools for the same brand will have a clear idea of the speed of response, and will therefore have a reasonably clear idea of how to balance the mix. If the marketer has no experience of the response in a market, then the following general rules for each tool can provide a starting point for balancing the effects over time of the communications mix.

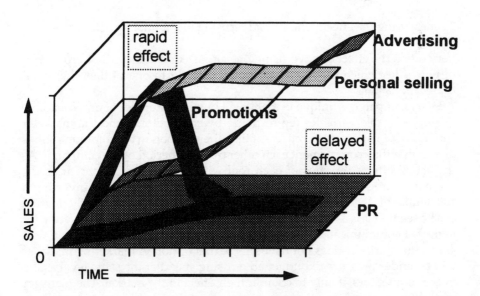

Figure 3.5 Response curves of the main marketing communications tools

- *Advertising:* may have an early effect on the perception of a brand, but it usually takes some time to have an effect on sales. This is because advertising is often taking the market through a learning process, and because advertising tends to be used more in the early stages of the buyer response process (eg attention, information and interest). Advertising often responds on an S-curve, with a measurable effect on sales some way into the campaign.
- *Personal selling:* will have an early effect on sales, depending on the size of the salesforce, as the whole purpose of personal selling is to close deals, generate sales and get the product or service into distribution.
- *Sales promotions:* will also have an immediate effect, as they tend to stimulate impulse purchasing (ie buying decisions which have not been preplanned by the customer).
- *Public relations:* is generally a constant communications activity by a business. It will build its effect on sales slowly, as its main function is to make the other communications tools more credible to the customer (eg by reinforcing source credibility).

As the marketing communications plan is being implemented, the marketer should monitor the effect of each communications tool on sales. There will be a variety of data which can be used for this, such as level of deals achieved by the salesforce and sales promotion coupon redemptions. Part of the effect of advertising can be measured by market research into recall of advertising, but the marketer needs to distinguish between:

1) measuring the effectiveness of advertising in getting the attention of, and communicating ideas to, the customer (which may or may not result in sales); and
2) measuring the effectiveness of advertising in stimulating actual sales.

Very often, the effect of advertising on sales is equivalent to that proportion of new sales which cannot be attributed directly to one of the other communications tools.

Every campaign is unique in that it will involve a number of unmeasurable or unpredictable variables (eg response by competitors), and the marketer should seek to integrate the effects of the different tools in the communications mix so that they complement each other over the period of the campaign. As the actual effects on sales of each tool will only become apparent as the campaign progresses, the marketer should be cautious about investing a substantial budget in communications tools until their effects in the market can be seen. This is a strong argument in favour of regional test marketing for high-cost communications campaigns before national roll-out. In some situations the marketer does not have this partial option. A marketing manager will be under pressure to budget advertising spend at the same level as the major competitors, if only to counter their effect in the market. The manager may also wish to avoid alerting competitors to the launch of a new product, as they could then mount a spoiler campaign to destroy the national roll-out of the new product or brand. A brand manager making a deal with a national supermarket buyer will need to show the forthcoming campaign in detail as part of the negotiations for additional shelf-facings or primary selling space for the brand.

DIFFERENT COMMUNICATIONS MIXES FOR DIFFERENT MARKETS

The ways in which marketing communications mixes are assembled will vary according to the type of market targeted (see Figure 3.6). In business to business or industrial marketing, the salesforce normally has the major role, supported by exhibitions and database direct communications. Advertising is only a small proportion of the industrial marketer's communications budget.

With consumer brands, the reverse is true – advertising will generally take the largest share of the communications budget, supported by sales promotions. Some consumer *services*, such as fast food, use substantial sales promotions in addition to advertising, and focus message content on the personal touches of service. Image and people are two key variables in the way customers assess service businesses, so design and staff training are key elements of the marketing communications mix.

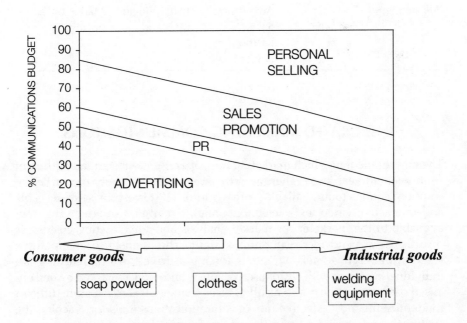

Figure 3.6 Relative expenditures on communications tools

DIFFERENT COMMUNICATIONS MIXES FOR DIFFERENT DISTRIBUTION CHANNEL STRATEGIES

When a new product is launched, one of the most important tasks of the marketer is to get the product or service into distribution. That means promoting to the intermediaries in the distribution channel (the agents, retailers and wholesalers). This is called a *push strategy*, as it is forcing the product down the channel with personal selling, discounts and special deals. Retailers will want to be reassured that an eventual pull strategy will follow.

Once the product is being stocked by these intermediaries, the task of the marketer changes, and the communications mix is redirected towards the end customer, to attract them into the shops to purchase the product. This is called a *pull strategy*, and it will require a shift in the communications mix towards mass advertising, sales promotions and point-of-sales promotions (see Table 3.4).

Whichever strategy is being used, it is important to integrate the marketing communications mix with the other elements of the strategic marketing mix.

Table 3.4 Main elements of push and pull strategies

Pricing	Target market	Marketing communications		Product
Push strategy	Wholesalers Retailers	Personal selling	Differentiate by packaging	Discounting to channel
Pull strategy	End user End buyer	Advertising Sales Promotions Point of sale	Differentiate by brand	Market-based pricing

INTEGRATED MARKETING COMMUNICATIONS

The environment in which marketing now operates is substantially different from even 20 years ago. There is now an enormous variety of marketing communications tools available – press, radio, TV (terrestrial, satellite, cable and interactive video text), telephone, mail, e-mail and Internet. The data available to the marketer for market analysis and for targeting customers directly is vast and increasing almost daily. The intensity of competitive reaction in all consumer markets is forcing a drive towards reaching the individual customer with customised products and services backed by personalised communications. As a result of these changes, it is much more difficult to identify the most effective mix of communications tools for reaching the customer, and indeed quite different communications mixes may now be competing against each other for the attention of the same customers.

There is therefore a major problem for marketers. They have the technical ability to communicate personally to large numbers of customers, but many of the messages received by those customers are not coordinated within the business. For example, advertising, public relations, salesforce and corporate identity are often under the control of different main board directors. The classical communications model (see Chapter 2, Figure 2.8) no longer adequately represents the marketing communications of a business as there are today many messages from different parts of the business reaching the customer.

There is now, in moving into the 21st century, a need for marketing communications to be coordinated and budgeted around the needs and perceptions of the customer. As technology develops, in both manufacturing and marketing, that customer becomes more and more accessible as an individual rather than as just one person in an aggregated mass market. Store loyalty cards, for example, already enable a retailer to profile the typical buying pattern of individual customers. This new direction for marketing is called *integrated marketing communications* (IMC).

The idea of integrating marketing communications has been discussed by marketers for some time. In 1962, Levitt suggested the concept of centripetal marketing, in which:

> The business firm has to be systematically self-conscious about every commercial message it sends out – whether it concerns its ads, its product design, its packages, its letterhead, how its salesmen dress… its point-of-sale materials, its trucks, or the conditions under which its products are displayed and sold. It is essential that the messages of each of these be carefully coordinated to achieve one overwhelming, self-reinforcing, simple and persuasive story… The effective modern corporation needs a constant top-down look at its total communications consequences, so that the total communications programme is always designed for maximum customer penetration.
>
> (Levitt, 1962)

Shultz, Tannenbaum and Lauterborn devised an integrated marketing communications model in 1993 which proposed that, unlike the classical communications model, marketing communications should start with what the customer is doing – purchasing activity. If that is the point at which the effect of advertising on sales can be measured, then that is the point at which advertising objectives should be set. If not, move back one step in the model to measure a partial transaction – action short of purchase which signals an interest (eg completing and sending in an on-pack competition entry). This approach of starting analysis with the customer rather than with the marketer sending the communication fits appropriately well with the marketing concept and the authors suggest initial analysis using a database of demographic, psychographic and purchase history details. It also reflects recent concepts in linguistics such as relevance theory, which suggest that models of interpersonal communication should start with the receiver and work back to the sender.

If this coordinated marketing communications is to be built around the customer, clearly the starting point of an IMC model needs to be not only a statistical definition of the customer, but also the customer's way of perceiving the product/service offering and their different types of buying process. This perception will manifest itself in activity by the customer – not only purchase, but many other kinds of activity (eg coupon redemption, competition entries, direct mail questionnaires). At the same time the marketer needs to evolve a strategy for the market and for the brand based on what can be observed and measured in customer activity. The meeting point of these two processes is in brand activity – how the customer relates to the brand and how the marketer develops the brand. The two processes need to be integrated in planning communications, as they are in fact integrated in market activity (see Figure 3.7).

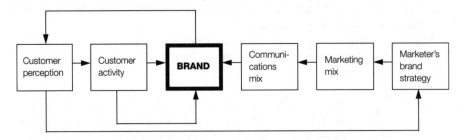

Figure 3.7 The process of integrated marketing communications using the brand as the integrator in the channel

IMC therefore focuses development of the marketing communications mix on the relationship between customer activity in relation to the brand and marketer activity in relation to the brand. It assumes that brands are the basis for the way customers perceive products and services.

Principles of IMC (Integrated Marketing Communication)

IMC is based on a number of principles which derive from the marketing concept and it is addressed fully in Chapter 9. For now, here are some key principles to consider in the context of the marketing communications process.

- *IMC starts with customer perception and activity.* All products and services have brand attributes (to a greater or lesser extent) and therefore involve values perceived by customers over and above the specific function of those products and services. In buying behaviour, it is inevitable that customers form relationships with brands. This may amount to brand loyalty or it may be a lesser relationship. The brand is therefore the mediator between the business and its customers.
- *IMC integrates the strategy of the whole business with the needs and activities of the customer.* Simply producing a product or service which is needed and

wanted by the customer is not enough because there are so many other ways in which a business relates to its customers. Many delivery vans now have a rear bumper sticker saying, 'If you think the driver of this van has driven politely, please ring this number…' Businesses now spend substantial sums on social and community projects, to integrate their activities more with the social reality in which their present and potential customers live.

- *IMC coordinates all the communications of the business within an IMC mix*. Many businesses still have different communications with their markets reporting to different directors. Public relations, salesforce, advertising and product packaging can easily be out of coherence with each other, sending different messages to the market. Chief executives should ask themselves more often the question posed by Levitt in 1962: where is the overwhelming, self-reinforcing, simple and persuasive story? Do the delivery vans reinforce the brand messages? There should be one line of management responsibility for all messages sent to the market by the business, from factory signs to share certificates.

- *IMC creates dialogue with the customer.* Communication is a two-way process. The sterile feedback of sales data is not enough. Tesco now use their loyalty card database to invite selected customers into their stores in the evenings for tastings of products which feature in those customers' 'loyalty profiles'.

- *IMC seeks to customise communications towards individual need.* It is now technically feasible to build databases which identify customers in terms of their individual social and economic traits, their buying activity and their activity in relation to a particular brand. Some businesses already do this. It is equally feasible to customise communications, products and services to individual need. This is now the basic communications methodology adopted by the financial services sector.

Integrating the process of the customer and the process of the marketer

Any marketing process starts with the perception of need by the customer and further perceptions of possible ways in which that need can be met. This typically leads the customer into activity such as searching for information. In our communications saturated society, the customer's previous experience of searching will include knowledge of the existence of products or services which have brand attributes and values with which that customer feels comfortable. This knowledge will to some extent constrain their search process, which will be defined partly in terms of seeking a brand as well as, or even rather than, simply a product. A brand will, for example, carry with it attributes of reliability, and the total communications of the business will add to or detract from the attributes of its brands, as can be seen in the model in Figure 3.8.

In the full IMC model shown in Figure 3.9, it can be seen that there will be activity by the customer demonstrating interest in the brand before formal buying activity takes place, and even before the customer is aware of an unfulfilled need. The brand becomes the focus of customer activity before

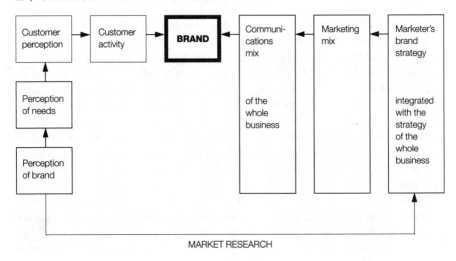

Figure 3.8 IMC model showing flows of main activity

and during the search for information, and that search and subsequent purchase become involved within the general area of brand interest activity. All functions within a business, both at head office level and at local level, can contribute to this brand interest activity (eg the local factory manager may become involved in local small business development, or the fast-food restaurant manager may sponsor and help organise a pensioners' coffee

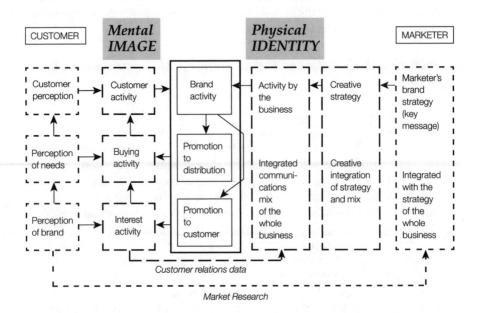

Figure 3.9 IMC model showing relationship between flows of marketing activity and brand interest activity

morning). Public relations and corporate identity can play a significant role, which is sometimes more than passive (eg sponsored events such as the London Marathon and community projects such as working with schools to clear derelict land).

The integrated marketing communications mix assembled by the marketer should take into account both market research on the perception of the brand to enable the brand to be constantly retuned to market perception, and data derived from customer interest activity. *An important and often absent element of the communications mix should be the fostering of this interest activity, so that there is a latent demand for the brand which can transform into overt demand when a customer develops needs which that brand can satisfy.*

The IMC model implies much more than this marketing transaction relationship between a business and its potential customers. If a business is to build a bank of potential customers-in-waiting, it will clearly need to respond to a wide range of social and ethical values held by its potential customers. These will also need to be assembled within the business's marketing communications mix and should be developed as part of the IMC strategy. This points to one of the unmeasurable but certain benefits of effective public relations in providing a bedrock of social and ethical values on which brands can be developed and maintained. This implies more than lip-service to such values, but requires their adoption by the business as a part of its corporate value system. Many businesses fail to maximise the benefit of their public relations activities by leaving them outside the marketing communications process. Yet it is only the marketers in a business who are trained to comprehend the symbiosis in brands anchored to a market-based corporate value platform, rather than being set adrift along with so many other free-floating brand platforms.

DISCUSSION TOPICS FOR CHAPTER 3

1) What indirect benefits can be provided by point-of-sale promotions?
2) Discuss merchandising as a form of marketing communication.
3) What are the differences between the learning customer and the routine customer?
4) Identify a recent purchase you have made in which you acted as a self-justifying customer.
5) What are the differences between the buying techniques of a professional customer and a routine customer?
6) How important is price in a buying decision?
7) Distinguish and discuss cognitive, affective and conative stages in a buying-readiness process.
8) Why does advertising often operate on an S-curve to sales?
9) Why is personal selling so important in marketing industrial goods?
10) Discuss the role of brands in IMC.

REFERENCES

Buttle, F, Merchandising, *European Journal of Marketing*, **18** 6–7

Colley, R H (1961) *Defining Advertising Goals for Measured Advertising Results*, Association of National Advertisers, New York

Ehrenberg, A S C (1994) The after-effects of price-related consumer promotions, *Journal of Advertising Research*, July

Festinger, L (1957) *A Theory of Cognitive Dissonance*, Harper & Row, New York

Hill, R W and Hillier, T J (1977) *Organisational Buying Behaviour*, Macmillan, London

Lavidge, R J and Steiner, G A (1961) A model for predictive measurements of advertising effectiveness, *Journal of Marketing*, October

Levitt, T (1962) Centripetal marketing, in *Innovation in Marketing*, McGraw-Hill/Pan, Maidenhead

McGuire, W J (1974) An information processing approach to advertising effectiveness, in *The Behavioral and Management Sciences in Marketing*, ed H Davies and A J Silk, Ronald Press, New York

Rogers, E M (1983) *Diffusion of Innovations*, 3rd edn, Free Press, New York

Shultz, D E, Tannenbaum, S I and Lauterborn, R F (1993) *Integrated Marketing Communications: Putting it together and making it work*, NTC Business Books, IL

Smith, P R (1998) *Marketing Communications – An integrated approach*, 2nd edn, Kogan Page, London

Strong, E K (1925) *Psychology of Selling*, McGraw-Hill, Maidenhead

F O U R

The nature of strategy

LEARNING OBJECTIVES

- Understand the nature and purpose of strategy.
- Consider the components of strategy.
- Use the list of tips when writing strategies.

TOPICS COVERED BY THIS CHAPTER

WHAT IS STRATEGY?

The problem with strategy

When it comes to defining strategy, there is no general consensus. Authors, experts and practitioners all have differing opinions. Some see it as retrospective, others as prescriptive and others as iterative. These opinions will be considered later. When it comes to defining marketing communications strategies, there is an even bigger problem. No one knows much about communication strategies because no one (or very few) appears to use them. Advertising strategies are common. Marketing strategies are common. But marketing communications strategies are uncommon. These marketing communications strategies integrate and drive all the communications tools in a single purposeful direction. The agencies cannot agree what a communications strategy is. Many clients have not got the faintest idea. Marketing professionals often refer to advertising strategies when asked about marketing communications strategies. Even textbooks (see Appendix 5.1) don't agree on a common definition, let alone a common approach to developing good strategies. So what chance is there of crystal-clear successful strategies emerging if both the basic understanding and the development process are blurred? (See variety of communications strategies and different levels of strategy in Appendix 5.2.)

This chapter attempts to solve the mystery surrounding the general nature of any type of strategy by looking at a range of definitions, examining the benefits of strategy and finally offering some guidance on the components of strategy. The next chapter looks at marketing communications strategy specifically. This chapter considers the overall nature of all kinds of strategies.

Forward or backward strategy?

Two common schools of thought cover the development of strategy. One school advocated by Igor Ansoff makes strategy out to be a carefully planned, heavily analysed, prescriptive activity far removed from the details of tactical creativity. The other school championed by Henry Mintzberg suggests that strategy is an emergent pattern in organisational actions to which managers give legitimacy by ascribing the label of strategy to what has already happened, ie tactics are rolled out and eventually someone tries to make sense of the basket of tactical activities by trying to sum them up as a strategy – an umbrella that covers everything that has happened so far (Murray and O'Driscoll, 1996). It is the authors' opinion that this type of retrospective strategy development is rampant, particularly in marketing communications. This means that tactics are developed firstly and strategies are then written around them to pull them all together.

At any level, whether corporate, marketing, total communications or just advertising, strategy should flow from the simple yet logical structure of the SOSTAC planning system – which applies to any kind of plan and any kind of strategy.

S   stands for *Situation*, which means where are we now?
O   stands for *Objectives*, which means where do we want to be?
S   stands for *Strategy*, which summarises how we are going to get there.
T   stands for *Tactics*, which are the details of strategy.
A   stands for *Action* or implementation – putting the plans to work.
C   stands for *Control*, which means measurement, monitoring, reviewing, updating and modifying.

This means that strategy should come before tactics. Strategy should drive the tactics in an overall direction otherwise the tactics can drift anywhere. Strategy summarises how the objectives will be achieved.

Before a strategy is chosen, options (strategic options) should be generated and weighed up. There is always more than one option, at least one good and one bad. In fact there are usually several, some better than others, and the easiest option is not always the best. However, before developing strategic options, let us consider a few more definitions of strategy.

DEFINITIONS OF STRATEGY

Dictionary definitions

There are many dictionary definitions, and even a pocket dictionary provides useful insights.

Strategy: the science of planning and directing military operations; a plan or action based on this; skill in managing or planning, esp. by using stratagems. (*Collins Pocket Dictionary*, 1986)

Stratagems: a trick or plan for deceiving an enemy in war; any trick or scheme. (*Collins Pocket Dictionary*, 1986)

Strategic: sound in strategy; advantageous; needed for carrying on war; directed against the military and industrial installations of the enemy. (*Collins Pocket Dictionary*, 1986)

Marketers' definitions

Here is how strategy has been defined by marketing professionals:

- 'a big picture';
- 'a longer-term view';
- 'a way of achieving objectives';
- 'a summary of the tactics';
- 'a guideline for tactics';
- 'a platform for integrating the marketing mix';
- 'a platform for integrated communications';

- 'a platform for combining positioning, segmentation and the mix';
- 'a way of making things fit better'.

Expert definitions

Experts have come up with many definitions of strategy. Below are just a few, starting with Mintzberg's ideas on strategy and moving on to more specific ideas about marketing strategies (not marketing communications strategies specifically) and finally considering a new definition of strategy.

Mintzberg's 5Ps of strategy

Henry Mintzberg (1996) suggests that strategy is used implicitly in different ways. He lists five definitions of strategy: plan, ploy, pattern, position and perspective:

- *Plan:* '... a unified, comprehensive, integrated plan designed to ensure objectives are achieved.'
- *Ploy:* '... a manoeuvre to attack or threaten to attack a competitor... threatening to enter a market, cut prices or launch lower priced "fighting brands".'
- *Pattern:* the summary of a series of actions ('consistency in behaviour whether or not intended').
- *Position:* how the organisation, or brand, wants to be seen in the marketplace and whether it wants to be a leader or a follower, in a niche or not.
- *Perspective:* permeates internally – within the organisation so that all employees see the strategy and feel part of it... the corporate culture.

Kotler's game plan

Philip Kotler (1996) says that the key, underlying strategic planning, is that of strategy. For each of its businesses, the company must develop a game plan for achieving its long-run objectives. Furthermore there is no one strategy that is optimal for all competitors in that business. Each company must determine what makes the most sense in the light of its industry position and its objectives, opportunities and resources.

Jain's direction

Subash Jain (1993) suggests that strategy specifies direction. Its intent is to influence the behaviour of competitors and the evolution of the market to the advantage of the strategist. It seeks to change the competitive environment. Thus a strategy statement includes a description of the new competitive equilibrium to be created, the cause and effect relationships that will bring it about, and the logic to support the course of action.

Doyle's target markets and competitive advantage

Peter Doyle (1996) believes a strategy means a choice of target market segments, which customers you are trying to serve to reach your objective, and secondly, strategy is about choosing a differential advantage. A business's core strategy defines how it will seek to gain a sustainable competitive advantage.

A new definition of strategy

Strategy summarises how objectives will be achieved.

The SOSTAC planning system (Situation analysis, Objectives, Strategy, Tactics, Action and Control) is explained fully in Chapter 8. We will concentrate here on the first part, 'SOS':

Situation – Where are we now?
Objectives – Where do we want to be?
Strategy – How do we get there?

How do we get there? How will the objectives be achieved? This is strategy – a summary of how objectives will be achieved. Strategy is a decision which will affect all the subsequent tactical details. Tactics, on the other hand, are the details of strategy. Tactics are driven by the strategy.

This is a very simple definition but it applies to any type of strategy: for example, a corporate strategy outlines how a corporate objective will be achieved; a marketing communications strategy outlines how the marketing communications objectives will be achieved. Strategy paints the big picture and gives direction for all subsequent tactical activities. Strategy involves a series of decisions of how you are going to get there, and keeps a record of these decisions. This, in turn, helps all subsequent tactical decisions since it gives clear guidance. It stops tactics from drifting in different directions – all tactics should fit in with the overriding strategy.

TYPES OF STRATEGY

There are many types and levels of strategy including corporate strategy, operational strategy, marketing strategy, product strategy, distribution strategy, marketing communications strategy, advertising strategy, etc. Here is a brief explanation of some of them:

- *Corporate strategy:* long-term moves made to achieve corporate plans and objectives. Corporate strategy involves senior management decisions, eg choosing what business to be in.
- *Operational strategy:* can cover manufacturing systems, eg McDonald's strategy was to systematise the franchising system so that it could deliver a consistent level quality, service, cleanliness and value around the world.
- *Marketing strategy:* involves the whole marketing mix and choice of target markets, exploiting competitive advantage, eg reposition the product as upmarket, state of the art, priced accordingly and distributed through exclusive retail stores, and supported by a major above-the-line campaign.

- *Product strategy:* determines and guides decisions about product development, eg to expand the range instead of restrict the range, focus on product enhancements only, utilise miniaturisation, etc.
- *Pricing strategy:* determines prices and pricing structures, eg adopt a premium pricing strategy (skimming the market) instead of a cut-price strategy (penetrating the market).
- *Distribution strategy:* determines the routes for distribution, eg to distribute directly through mail order instead of retail outlets or to develop multi-level channels instead of single-level channels.
- *Marketing communications strategy:* determines the message or sequence of messages which should be shared with specific target audiences through the optimum communications mix (eg advertising or direct mail).
- *Advertising strategy:* determines the message or sequence of messages which should be shared with specific target audiences through the optimum media mix (eg television or press advertisements). Note that, ideally, the communications strategy should drive this.

STRATEGY CASCADES

A strategy becomes another person's objectives as you go down the line of managers, eg the chief executive's strategy becomes the marketing director's objectives, etc.

Chief executive's strategies

The chief executive chooses strategies to fulfil the objective of, say, becoming the number one company within 24 months by:

1) becoming number one brand through expansion into the pan-European market sector;
2) becoming the trade's preferred supplier through developing specific channel marketing plans;
3) ensuring the company is always first to market with new product by having fast deployment groups.

Marketing director's objectives

These are the above strategy numbers 1, 2 and 3 (ie the chief executive's strategies become the marketing director's objectives).

Marketing director's strategies

The marketing director's strategies will specify how objective numbers 1 , 2 and 3 will be achieved. For example, to expand into the pan-European market, one of the strategies might be to recruit and retrain a larger pan-European salesforce (as opposed to developing a network of distributors and agents).

Sales director's objectives

The marketing director's strategies become the sales director's objectives, eg recruit and train a larger pan-European salesforce. The sales director's strategy then summarises how this will be achieved, eg by hiring a recruitment and training consultancy (as opposed to hiring from within the organisation itself, or establishing a continuous professional development programme for all of the existing sales team). (Note it is assumed in this case that the sales director reports to the marketing director. This is not always the case, ie some organisations' sales and marketing directors have equal weighting and report to the board separately.)

THE BENEFITS OF STRATEGY

Why bother with strategy? Other than looking good in front of other managers, what are the real benefits of developing strategy? It takes time and energy amidst an already busy schedule. Who can afford this luxury?

In the case of marketing communications strategy, carefully planning new strategies can create clearer communications with increased impact, cash savings and less stress. The planning process also encourages review and helps to give a manager an overall perspective, or bird's-eye view, which sometimes gets lost amidst a sea of busy day-to-day tactical activities.

Strategies have many benefits:

- Each tactical activity is able to build on the others to create strength through continuity and consistency.
- Tactical planning is that much easier and quicker when clear strategic direction is agreed.
- Marketing communications strategy creates many more benefits through integration. These are considered in more detail in the next chapter.

For now consider marketing strategy as a precursor to marketing communications strategy. Remember marketing strategy drives the whole marketing mix whereas marketing communications strategy drives only the communications and the communications mix.

WHAT ARE THE COMPONENTS OF MARKETING STRATEGY?

Before considering marketing communications strategy, consider what you would look for in a marketing strategy. What are the key components? What would make it incomplete? There is no common agreement here yet. There are several views about what should be in a strategy and what should not. Below is a selection of thoughts on what should be in a marketing strategy. It can be seen that many of the experts' thoughts overlap.

- Right products in the right markets:

  Strategic marketing focuses on choosing the right products for the right growth markets at the right time.

  (Jain, 1993)

- Clear market definition, competitive strength and performance:

  A good marketing strategy can be characterised by (a) a clear market definition; (b) a good match between corporate strengths and the needs of the market; and (c) superior performance, relative to competition, in the key success factors of the business.

  (Jain, 1993)

- Scope, objectives, resources, competitive advantage, functions:

  Scope of Business (product portfolio); Levels of Integration; Objectives; Strategic Business Unit Identification (managers know clearly what they are responsible for); Resource Allocation; Developing Sustainable Competitive Advantage; Effective Functional Strategy (manufacturing and marketing policies); Synergy (from resources and capabilities of management particularly with different Strategic Business Units).

  (Doyle, 1994)

- Scope, dimension, timing, commitment, dilution:

  Market Scope (serve an entire market or break it into segments); Geographic Dimension (local, regional, national or international); Time of Entry (into a market: first or last); Commitment (to achieve market dominance or merely play a minor role); Dilution (de-marketing – when the overall benefit a company derives from a market, either currently or potentially, is less than it could achieve elsewhere).

  (Jain, 1993)

- Three Cs – customer, competition and corporation:

  Within a given environment, marketing strategy deals essentially with the interplay of three forces known as the strategic three Cs: the customer, the competition and the corporation. Marketing strategies focus on ways in which the corporation can differentiate itself effectively from its competitors, capitalising on its distinctive strengths to deliver better value to its customers.

  (Jain, 1993)

The components could therefore be summarised as:

- products;
- markets/customers;
- strengths/competitive advantage;
- scope/scale;
- objectives;
- resources;
- timing.

The components of marketing communications strategy are discussed separately in Chapter 5. Before that here are some tips to bear in mind when developing any kind of strategy.

TIPS FOR STRATEGY MAKERS

There are many approaches and ideas to developing strategies. Here are a few which mix the ancient thoughts of Sun Tzu with some of today's more contemporary thinkers.

Sun Tzu's tips for strategy makers

More than 2300 years ago, Sun Tzu wrote *The Art of War*, an amazing book on the principles of military strategy. Below are some interpretations of his ideas – seven wise tips for strategy makers. (See Wing (1989) for a recent translation from this classic written some time between 480 and 221 BC.)

1) Adopt SOSTAC

He believed that it is essential first to carry out a complete analysis of the situation. The strengths and weaknesses of one's position, the relationship between one's goals and the goals of society at large, the intensity of one's courage and determination, and the worthiness and integrity of one's objective must all be carefully evaluated. Even then, it seems, SOSTAC was emerging – situation analysis, objectives and strategy.

2) Do your homework

> Those who triumph,
> Compute at their headquarters
> A great number of factors
> Prior to a challenge.

> Those who are defeated,
> Compute at their headquarters
> A small number of factors
> Prior to a challenge.

Much computation brings triumph.
Little computation brings defeat.
How much more so with no computation at all.

By observing only this,
I can see triumph or defeat.

3) Develop some options

Therefore, those who are not entirely aware
Of strategies that are disadvantageous,
Cannot be entirely aware
Of strategies that are advantageous.

4) Know your resources
You must be certain that your resources have been carefully evaluated before engaging in this challenge.

5) Win senior management support
Before engaging in a challenge, a leader must be certain that the organisation is prepared to support the expense of a confrontation.

6) Do not hurt your market or environment
Brilliant leaders are always aware of the entire system, both inside and outside of their organisations. They know that to harm or destroy what is outside will hurt their own growth, while employing their rivals and incorporating their resources will enhance their strategy.

7) Put everything in place before making a move
Sun Tzu believed that a true victory can be won only with a strategy of tactical positioning, so that the moment of triumph is effortless and destructive conflict is avoided even before considering a confrontation – for whatever purpose.

Contemporary thinkers' tips for strategy makers

Row in the right direction

The first principle of strategy is not to beat the competition but to deliver value to customers. Delivering value means operating with a keen and flexible sense of direction. Rowing harder does not help if the boat is headed in the wrong direction. Applying more muscle is no solution if the course is mistaken. Getting there quicker is no benefit if the route taken means there are no profits when you arrive. Beating competitors by ruining industries is not strategy. Yet this is what many Japanese companies have done in industry after industry.

(Ohmae, 1990)

Audience and message selection

There is plenty of potential for wrong strategies. Consider a brilliant idea which gains attention but wrong audience or worse, wrong message aimed at the right audience.

(Griffin, 1993)

Trends and assumptions

It is wrong to assume a stimulus response model, ie increase communications and sales increase. The soft drink, 7-UP, did not sell well in the late 1980s flop. An executive provided an insight: 'Perhaps in our zeal and in our euphoria over Cherry 7-UP we underestimated the trade's growing impatience with new brands... and pressure for shelf space' (Engel, Warshaw and Kinnear, 1994).

Enduring strategies

A strategy means something longer term, a sense of direction, an objective; a tactic is a means to accomplish that and I think companies ought to be highly flexible about tactics but a little more careful about choosing strategies that are more enduring. Tactics are changeable, strategies should endure.

(Kanter, 1996)

Core values

Organisations that enjoy long-term continuing success have 'core values and a core purpose that remain fixed while the business strategies and practices endlessly adapt to a changing world' (Collins and Porras, 1996).

Learn from other disciplines

- From the military world: 'A victorious army wins its victories before seeking battle.'
- From the diplomatic world: 'The demonstration of options is almost always an asset.'
- From the business world: 'A team that won't be beat – can't be beat.'
- From the world of games and sports: 'You have to care about losing.'

(Source unknown)

CHOOSING A PARTICULAR STRATEGY

The choice of strategy is obviously crucial as it guides all the other tactical activities. It is sensible to consider more than just the first strategy that comes to mind.

Strategic options must be generated before deciding on a strategy. There is always more than one strategy which can achieve a set of objectives. Some, however, are better than others. Consider marketing strategies for a moment. Say a marketing director is charged with delivering growth in sales. There are at least five strategic options: (1) overseas expansion; (2) innovation; (3) acquisitions; (4) new distribution channels; and (5) buying market share (through price discounting and/or heavy sales promotions) (Henkoff, 1996: 32–38). Having generated the strategic options, they can then be considered, analysed and the best one selected according to pre-set criteria (see pro forma strategy selection in Chapter 7).

As mentioned, some strategies are better than others, depending on the organisation, its resources, competencies, goals, etc. For example, consider the following three competitors in the tyre market, each of which has a different marketing strategy: Goodyear has chosen a strategy of mass volume, low cost market leadership; Michelin has chosen a product development strategy and invested in new technology and R&D (research and development) – this led to the development of the radial tyre which redefined customer needs and made the cross-ply tyre obsolete; Armstrong Rubber has adopted a third strategy – exploiting specialist applications by focusing on special tyres for agricultural, aviation and civil engineering market segments.

And it is possible to have more than one strategy (as long as they complement each other and do not compete with each other). Consider this example from Microsoft:

If our goal is to achieve a certain level of market share within a product category we could decide that, let's say we needed to achieve 50% market share. We could determine that our strategy would be to get 25% of that market share by encouraging new people to buy spreadsheets. So we would grow the overall market and consequently achieve 25% of market share. To secure the other 25% of the market share our strategy could be to progressively attack one of our competitors' customer bases and encourage them to move from their product to our own. So, you can build up there two different strategies: one of market expansion and creation of demand and the other of a competitive stand point encouraging brands which are within a competitor's base.

(Leftwich, 1997)

There are always strategic options and sometimes multiple strategies. Having considered the problems with strategy, definitions, types and cascading strategies along with the common components and tips for strategy makers, we are now ready to consider the more specific aspects of developing marketing communications strategies in Chapter 5.

The importance of strategic precision:

'It's not the value of something that counts but the worth of it. As in the case of an inexpensive but strategically placed button.' (Anon.)

APPENDIX 4.1

Strategic alliances

Marketing marriages and strategic alliances can help more than just distribution and production. Alliances can help communications whether with shared promotions or cooperative advertising, alliances demand new skills from marketing managers. Here is what Kenichi Ohmae has to say about the importance of alliances in general.

> Corporate leaders are beginning to learn what the leaders of nations have already known: in a complex, uncertain world filled with dangerous opponents it is best not to go it alone. Great powers operating across broad theatres of engagement have made common cause with others whose interests ran parallel with their own. There is no shame in this. *Entente* – the striking of an alliance – is a responsible part of every good strategist's repertoire. But managers are slow to experiment with genuine strategic alliances. They have tried joint ventures and long term contractual relationships, certainly but rarely attempting the forging of entente. A real alliance compromises the fundamental independence of economic factors, and managers don't like that. For them, management has come to mean total control. Alliances mean sharing control. The one precludes the other.
>
> (Ohmae, 1990)

Make strategic alliances now

> With enough time, money and luck you can expand brands and build up distribution yourself – you can do everything yourself. But all three are in short supply. In particular, you do not have enough time to establish new markets one by one throughout the triad (Japan, US and EC). The 'cascade' model of expansion no longer works. Today you have to be in all important markets simultaneously if you are going to keep competitors from establishing their positions. Globalisation will not wait. You need alliances and you need them now. But not the traditional kind.
>
> (Ohmae, 1990)

DISCUSSION TOPICS FOR CHAPTER 4

1) 'Strategy is for overpaid board members who have nothing else to do.' Do you agree? Give reasons.
2) 'Strategy should come before objectives and not after objectives.' Is this possible? Explain your answer.
3) 'Strategy does not apply to SMEs (small to medium-sized enterprises).' Do you agree? Explain your answer.
4) 'Stop flapping about with your high minded strategy – just get on with the job now.' How would you react?

REFERENCES

Collins, J C and Porras, J I (1996) Building your company's vision, *Harvard Business Review*, September–October, pp 65–77

Doyle, P (1996) Excerpt from *Marketing* (CD ROMs), Multimedia Marketing Consortium, London

Engel, J, Warshaw, M and Kinnear, T (1994) *Promotional Strategy: Managing the marketing communications process*, 8th edn, Irwin, Homewood, IL

Griffin, T (1993) *International Marketing Communications*, Butterworth-Heinemann

Henkoff, R (1996) Growing your company: five ways to do it right, *Fortune*, 25 November, pp 32–38

Jain, S (1993) *Marketing Planning and Strategy*, 4th edn, College Division, South Western Publishing, Cincinatti, OH

Kanter, R M (1996) Excerpt from *Marketing* (CD ROMs), Multimedia Marketing Consortium, London

Kotler, P (1996) Excerpt from *Marketing* (CD ROMs), Multimedia Marketing Consortium, London

Leftwich, J (1997) *Marketing Planning* (CD ROM), Multimedia Marketing Consortium, London

Mintzberg, H and Quinn, B (1996) *Strategy Process*, Prentice Hall, Hemel Hempstead

Murray, A and O'Driscoll, A (1996) *Strategy and Process in Marketing*, Prentice Hall, Hemel Hempstead

Ohmae, K (1990) *Borderless World*, Fontana, London

Wing, R L (1989) *The Art of Strategy* (trans of Sun Tzu (c 480–221 BC), *The Art of War*), Aquarian Press

Marketing communications strategy

LEARNING OBJECTIVES

- Understand where marketing communications strategy fits in.
- List the key components of communications strategy.
- Understand the diversity of approaches.
- Start to build your own communications strategy.
- Understand how SOSTAC and strategy fit together.

TOPICS COVERED BY THIS CHAPTER

STRATEGY AND SOSTAC

As mentioned in Chapter 4, the Nature of Strategy, many organisations have a marketing strategy and an advertising strategy (see Appendix 5.3) but they do not have a marketing communications strategy that drives and integrates all of the communications tools in a single purposeful direction. So what chance is there of crystal-clear successful communication strategies emerging if both the basic understanding (see Appendix 5.1) and the development process are blurred? Having acquired an understanding of the overall nature of strategy (Chapter 4), this chapter now looks specifically at marketing communications strategies, their benefits and key components, and provides tips and checklists for the strategy makers as well as a selection of examples from a range of different types of organisation.

Before considering the benefits of strategy, remember where strategy fits into the planning process. Using the SOSTAC approach the situation must first be analysed in detail to determine 'where we are now' in terms of market positioning, competitive strengths (sustainable), unfulfilled benefits sought by customers (but not yet delivered by competitors), status as follower or leader, etc. Next come the objectives or 'where we want to be'. These cover both marketing objectives (eg sales, market share, distribution penetration, number of new products, etc) and communications objectives (levels of awareness of the brand and of specific benefits/features, preference, positionings, intentions to purchase, etc). These should be defined and quantified within a specific time frame so that they can be measured and monitored. Then comes the strategy – 'How do we get there?' This should be clearly agreed before engaging in any of the details of tactical activities like advertising, sales promotion and PR. Although the strategy can include the use of these tools, it should bring the individual tools together in a strategic manner rather than in an *ad hoc* tactical manner. This means that the tools should be knitted together by a common strategy which integrates them in a purposeful way.

Before getting into the nuts and bolts of strategy and its key components, it is worth remembering that the development of a marketing communications strategy delivers many benefits. It is important to remember this because developing and agreeing strategic decisions costs time, money and energy. Many marketers have an inner urge to get on with the job – to get creative, to develop wonderful advertising campaigns, innovative sales promotions, delightful new sales literature, sensational exhibition stands and more. Other marketers are under pressure to get out and talk to customers, bring in some sales, to generate revenues and justify their existence. So, seemingly self-indulgent navel-gazing such as strategic contemplation may not always appear worth while – in the immediate term. But, beyond the immediate term, a good strategy will reap many benefits. Read on...

Note that it is possible to develop a strategic approach for each individual communications tool (see Appendix 5.2 for an example of an exhibition strategy).

THE BENEFITS OF A MARKETING COMMUNICATIONS STRATEGY

Despite the hard work, spare time taken and previous levels of 'success without strategy' there are many benefits to be derived from developing a marketing communications strategy.

- It enables each tactical activity to build on the others creating strength of communications through continuity and consistency.
- It helps to create clearer, sharper selling messages appropriately directed to target customers at various stages in their buying process.
- Tactical planning of each communications tool is made that much easier and quicker when clear strategic direction is agreed.
- It facilitates integrated marketing communications which saves time, money and stress as well as providing IMC's other associated benefits of consistency and clarity.
- It can facilitate the development of joint promotions and strategic alliances (see Appendix 1 in Chapter 4).
- It can encourage the development of hybrid marketing systems. The addition and integration of new communication tools/channels (eg telemarketing) to existing communications tools/channels (eg advertising or the salesforce) can create such a hybrid marketing system. Harvard professors Moriarty and Moran (1990) believe that a company that designs and manages its hybrid system strategically will achieve 'a powerful advantage over rivals that add channels and methods in an opportunistic and incremental manner'. A well-managed hybrid system allows an organisation to achieve what Moriarty and Moran call a 'balance between its customers' buying behaviour and its own selling economics'. (See Appendix 5.3 for more on hybrid systems.)
- As well as driving the external communications, a good communications strategy (when communicated internally) creates a bond within a company so that everyone knows what everyone else is trying to achieve.

These are some of the benefits to be derived from the development of a good marketing communications strategy. We will now consider what goes into a marketing communications strategy – the components.

THE COMPONENTS OF A MARKETING COMMUNICATIONS STRATEGY

The components of marketing strategy discussed in Chapter 4 on the nature of strategy include products, markets/customers, strengths/competitive advantage, scope/scale, objectives, resources and timing. With a more specific strategy such as marketing communications, it is worth considering some additional components. First, let us consider what some other authors see as the key components of a marketing communications strategy (sometimes referred to as 'promotions strategy').

As with the overall nature of strategy, again there is little consensus here. American authors such as Govoni, Eng and Galper (1986) see communications strategy consisting of four key communications tools (advertising, sales promotion, selling and PR), while the UK's Tom Griffin (1983) sees a thorough understanding of the customer as the key component. America's Donald Schultz (1993) sees the key component of communications strategy as based around the differentiated benefits which customers want, while Engel, Warshaw and Kinnear (1994) see integration, control and the communication of need-satisfying attributes/customer benefits as key components. But there are very few, if any, examples of communications strategy given in any of these sources.

From a search through these sources Table 5.1 lists what we consider to be the key components of a marketing communications strategy.

Table 5.1 Key components of a marketing communications strategy

Positioning	Should restate and consolidate the positioning.
Benefits	Should reinforce benefits wanted by customers (and unfulfilled by competition).
Strengths	Draws on the sustainable competitive advantage.
Competition	Has a competitive dimension.
Customers	Segments and targets the market plus considers all the stages in the buying process from generating awareness and enquiries through to maintaining repeat sales. Can also cater for different types of customers from heavy to light users, loyal to non-loyal/promiscuous, etc.
Direction	Gives clear direction (in terms of positioning, strengths, etc).
Tools	Defines the range of communications tools, eg above or below the line.
Integration	Ensures the communications tools are integrated.
Sequence of tools	Does the advertising need to build brand awareness before converting to sales with direct mail? Does the PR break before the sales launch? etc
Timescale	Is longer term than tactics and operational activities.
Resources	Indicates the emphasis and size of spend on certain tools (whether the communications are going to be advertising led or salesforce driven, etc).
Objectives	Can make reference to the overall objectives of the strategy.
Marketing strategy	Should be consistent with and draw from the overall marketing strategy.

If the list in Table 5.1 seems too cumbersome then you may be able to remember the acronym 'STOP & SIT' which covers the fundamental components: STOP – Segmentation, Targeting, Objectives (fulfilling the…) and Positioning – then add SIT – Sequence (of tools), Integration (of the tools) and Tools (the communications tools to be used). Somewhere in a communications strategy the main tool(s) have to be mentioned and preferably their sequence (eg advertising mailing before…, etc). Integration, although assumed, is always worth spelling out. Much of the rest of the table (eg segmentation, targeting and positioning) is fundamental to any marketing strategy and therefore spills over into any marketing communications strategy.

STRATEGIC COMMUNICATIONS LANGUAGE

Using the language of marketing and being able to expand on selected pieces of marketing jargon helps the strategic thinking process. For example, 'push' and 'pull' strategies are commonly referred to as when making a sales *push* into the trade (retailers and wholesalers) or using advertising, PR and promotions to get customers to *pull* the product off the shelf. In reality both are used with differing amounts of emphasis.

Below is a selection of strategic language taken from conversations about marketing communications strategy. These sound bites may help to stimulate ideas for building communications strategies:

- … grow the market (through advertising)…
- … educate the market (grow the market) to a point where it is predisposed to consider…
- … investing in demand building…
- … sowing seeds of awareness through advertising…
- … harvesting interested customer base…
- … advertising that capitalises on the brand heritage…
- … investing heavily in sales promotion…
- … combining media coverage with trade participation…
- … utilise both personal and mass communications…
- … building a database platform…
- … build and manage relations…
- … mailings supported by a follow-up telesales followed by a sales visit…
- … call – mail – call sequence…
- … developing loyalty schemes…
- … enhancing the product offering…
- … position the business firmly as…
- … distinguishing the brand from other brands…
- … reinforce the unique capability of…
- … repositioning the brand…
- … developing relationships…
- … a client relationship strategy as opposed to the previous machine gun approach (advertising led)…
- … growing lifetime customers…
- … focusing on specific target opinion formers…
- … generating opinion leaders' support before launching the main stream…
- … focusing on specific 'missed benefits' (benefits that buyers are missing)…

- ... forming new alliances to gain access to new customer groups and opinion leaders...
- ... stretch the budget through a wholly integrated communications campaign...
- ... fast marketing catch card approach (sampler card, gift, coupon, three million door drop, TV advertising burst after radio...)

TIPS FOR MARKETING COMMUNICATIONS STRATEGY MAKERS

Strategies vary depending on the primary audience – customers, distributors, opinion formers, stakeholders. The latter (stakeholders) require a message that communicates the organisation's values rather than specific offerings, whereas the former (customers) may want specific product offerings and benefits.

Strategic options must be generated before deciding on a final strategy. It is highly unlikely that the first communications strategy that emerges is going to be the best one.

This is just one of the tips from the great strategist Sun Tzu whose work is referred to in Chapter 4. Despite being over 2,000 years old, his ideas and tips for other budding strategists are perfectly valid. Here is a summary of the seven tips outlined in Chapter 4:

1) Adopt SOSTAC.
2) Do your homework.
3) Develop some options.
4) Know your resources.
5) Win senior management support.
6) Do not hurt your environment.
7) Put everything in place before making a move.

This is useful advice and prepares the way for the development of good strategies. When the strategic options have been developed, they can be compared in order to determine which strategy is more likely to deliver the best result. The key components of strategy (see Table 5.1), the communications strategy checklist on page 90 and the pro forma worksheets starting on page 113 can all be used when selecting strategies from a range of strategic options. The checklist can also be used to assess the real examples of marketing communications strategy shown on the next few pages.

Finally, remember 'STOP & SIT'. Ask whether the communications strategy breaks up the market into Segments and Targets the right customers. Will the strategy fulfil the marketing and communications Objectives? Is the Positioning made crystal clear? What Sequence of Integrated communications Tools will be used?

The five 'musts' for communicators:

1) Always define precisely your audience.
2) Avoid the predictable.
3) Keep the message simple.
4) Use power tools (images that last).
5) Say what only you can say.

(Source: Doug Ivester, Coca Cola's Chief Executive)

EXAMPLES OF DIFFERENT APPROACHES TO COMMUNICATIONS STRATEGY

A complete communications strategy should cover 'STOP & SIT' and also ideally include competitive benefits, customer buying cycles and timescale as well as resources. Below are some examples from a range of different organisations. Most do not cover all of these components but at least they give direction to all of the subsequent communications tactics. As mentioned earlier, few organisations get this far. Few organisations bother to develop their marketing communications strategies. Those that do use a variety of different approaches as will be seen.

Acura communications strategy

...initial strategy was to attract former Honda buyers who were ready to move up to a more expensive model... Acura directed its advertising against European automakers... early ads sought to distinguish Acura's upscale car line from Honda's other models and its traditional image in the car market, later ads capitalised on Honda's championship racing heritage... TV, radio and print ads emphasised Acura's high performance and speed, along with press critiques and awards.

(Engel, Warshaw and Kinnear, 1994)

Gold Heart Day communications strategy

...develop an annual fund-raising event, Gold Heart Day, by generating massive media coverage, with considerable retail and trade participation opportunities, thereby increasing awareness of the plight of the children, and the Variety Club's efforts to help them.

(Smith, 1993)

MCI communications strategy

...promotional strategy that utilised both interpersonal and mass communication was the key... the theme was expanded as the campaign continued to emphasise MCI's commitment to quality service and knowing what today's business people really want... mailings were supported by follow-up calls from MCI sales people... MCI was willing to invest heavily in promotion to support this strategy.

(Engel, Warshaw and Kinnear, 1994)

IBM Insurance Marketing Solutions communications strategy

...position the business as a solution provider who fully understands client needs and is easily able to provide complete and successful solutions. All communications reinforce our unique capability which combines marketing and IT in an integrated manner. The key target group is European insurers with medium to large customer bases (usually over 1 million). All communications are below-the-line, editorially driven, and drawn from sound research into leading-edge solutions. The published papers are used across a series of public conferences, own conferences, training awareness days along with a constant media relations campaign.

(IBM)

Tupperware communications strategy

...a multimillion dollar direct response campaign... the company maintained its personal selling approach but modified its party format to accommodate the increasing limitations for working women... installed a toll free number to link customers to a local dealer... catalogues were originally available only for dealers, hosts and hostesses, they were made accessible to everyone and reached 30 million people...

(Engel, Warshaw and Kinnear, 1994)

etc limited

A client relationship strategy focusing on a few key sectors (industry, health, local government and financial services) instead of the previous machine gun (broad advertising) approach. Direct mailings and seminar events aimed at key opinion formers developed through targeted mailings create a tightly focused database for future presentations and high value mailings. [See Chapter 8 for complete mini case.]

(etc limited)

The National Lottery communications strategy

The chance of winning is at the heart of all of the communications for the brand. The communications strategy of a regular *chance* of winning large amounts of money was identified as having the greatest and most universal appeal to the British consumer. It was also important that the brand was positioned as being accessible, fun, honest, harmless and for everybody. The strategy was deployed across all communication channels including television, press, posters and radio advertising but also on in-store material, merchandise and even ticket receipts and retailer signage. A single-minded strategic thought at the core of all activity allows for synergistic and integrated communications. [See Chapter 8 for complete mini case.]

(National Lottery)

Daewoo communications strategy

Position Daewoo as the most customer focused car company in the UK. Car buyers are happy with cars but unhappy with dealers. Daewoo must own customer service. This differentiates Daewoo.

- *Stage 1:* Build corporate credibility through TV and motoring press.
- *Stage 2:* Develop Daewoo dialogue collecting information about likes and dislikes about car ownership.
- *Stage 3:* Launch brand.

This necessitates integration throughout the marketing communications and operational implementation. Advertising will build brand awareness and direct people into Daewoo's telemarketing database. The complete mix includes retail design, interactive point of sale, sales promotion, direct marketing, database construction and management, PR and advertising. [See Chapter 8 for complete mini case.]

(Daewoo)

Telewest communications strategy

Create/educate the market (get consumers to a point where they are predisposed to consider cable (from Telewest Communications); build the brand (by teaching customers to value most what Telewest does best); stimulate acquisition (through three big sales promotion ideas); build and manage relationships (through good service and constant database dialogue).

The Multimedia Marketing Consortium communications strategy

Below-the-line and through-the-line activities are used instead of above the line. There is no direct salesforce. The publicity drive incorporating press launches, editorials, conferences and exhibitions builds a platform for harvesting through subsequent direct mailings and networked inserts.

Two distinct worldwide sectors are targeted: (1) *corporate training*, which includes human resource, personnel and training departments as well as marketing managers/directors; (2) *academic education*, which includes a top-down path of deans and heads of department along with a bottom-up path of lecturers and librarians. The CD ROMs and peripheral products are positioned as state-of-the art, world-class learning materials. All communications reinforce this. The strategy comprises a series of stages:

- *Stage 1:* Generate opinion formers' support (and endorsements) through personal presentations to key players within institutional networks.
- *Stage 2:* Use a sustained media relations campaign integrated with conferences and exhibitions to generate awareness among key user groups.
- *Stage 3:* Roll out (a), (b) and (c) simultaneously:
  - *Stage 3(a):* Harvest the awareness levels with highly targeted mailings networked within institutional groups. If successful continue to form new alliances with new networks.
  - *Stage 3(b):* Test banded offers in key marketing magazines. If successful roll out across other targeted magazines.
  - *Stage 3(c):* Release distributors' sales teams onto key accounts nationally.
- *Stage 4:* Develop a database for future updates and developments. Exploit and integrate the web resource.

(Multimedia Marketing Consortium)

United Airlines communications strategy

UA uses a variety of communications tools. UA puts the thought of United Airlines into the mind of the target traveller at every opportunity. This involves thinking through how business travellers spend their day, whom they speak to when booking a flight and even how they travel to the airport. Given the multitude of different ways that customers might be reached UA needs to ensure that, however the traveller receives a message about UA, the end result is always that they are more likely to consider the airline next time they fly.

The decision starts and ends with the traveller, but the person who books the flight, the agent who takes the booking and the travel policy maker within the company can all exert influence over the choice of airline. For example, the travel trade needs much more detailed information about routes, schedules and prices than business travellers, since UA wants to ensure that an agent is fully briefed about United if asked.

Because the core target is actually quite small in number – just over 100 000 people – it is recognised that there are many other demands on their time and many other products and services seeking to capture their attention and loyalty. Unless UA practises integration in both planning and execution there is a real risk of being swamped. Research into the target travellers and the way they spend their days allows UA to manage this relationship using a number of different contact points. Taking an integrated approach allows the communications budget to stretch much further than if UA limited themselves to traditional media. [See Chapter 8 for complete mini case.]

(United Airlines)

CONCLUSIONS

Despite the range of approaches and variations in size, succinctness and complexity, these companies are at least attempting to make strategic decisions which will affect all subsequent tactical communications tools, how they integrate, how they build on each other, how they wrap themselves around a customer, etc. However, there is always a counter-argument against taking the longer-term strategic perspective (see Appendix 5.4 – when tactics are preferred to strategy). The communications strategy shown in Checklist 5.1 on page 90 can help marketers to develop better marketing communications strategies firstly, by ensuring the key components of strategy are at least considered, and secondly, by encouraging the development of strategic options before choosing a final strategy.

Checklist 5.1 Communications strategy

	Does the strategy consider:	Does it specify:	Yes/No
1)	Segmentation?	What market?	
2)	Targeting?	Markets, stakeholders and DMUs?	
3)	Objectives?	Will the strategy fulfil the marketing and communication objectives? Are the benefits clear?	
4)	Positioning?	Reinforce the desired positioning?	
5)	Exploiting sustainable competitive advantage?	Cost leader? Differentiate? Focus/niche? Does the strategy play to our strengths? Does it address competitive benefits (benefits which customers want but competition does not supply)?	
6)	Type of purchase and the buying process?	Multi-stage strategy (enquiry; sale; repeat sales or straight sale; repeat sale)?	
7)	Timescale?	What timescales and/or phases are involved?	
8)	Sequence and timing of tools?	Does the strategy guide the sequence of communications tools?	
9)	Range of communications tools?	Does the strategy incorporate and integrate a range of tools?	
10)	Scale?	Global, national or local?	
11)	Resources?	Can we afford it? Is it the best way to spend a budget?	
12)	Lifetime customers?	Does it encourage repeat business and customer loyalty?	
13)	Brand enhancement?	Does the strategy enhance the brand?	
14)	Strategic options?	Were other strategies considered? Does the chosen strategy fulfil the marketing objectives better than others?	
15)	Homework done?	Has each option been carefully evaluated?	
16)	Fit with the overall marketing strategy?	Check the marketing strategy.	

APPENDIX 5.1: HOW OTHERS SEE COMMUNICATIONS STRATEGY

Govoni, Eng and Galper (1986)

Promotion as a strategic variable consists of four elements (advertising, personal selling, sales promotion and public relations) which must be coordinated to form the overall promotional strategy.

Griffin (1993)

The right communications strategy is built on a thorough understanding of buyers, DMUs (decision-making units), the buyers' characteristics, preferences, media habits... constraints imposed on them by their culture and other PESTED (political, economic, social, technological, environmental, demographic) factors.

Engel, Warshaw and Kinnear (1994)

Promotional strategy refers to a controlled, integrated programme of communication methods designed to present an organisation and its products or services to prospective customers; to communicate need-satisfying attributes to facilitate sales; and thus to contribute to long-run profit performance.

Strategy creates *customer benefits and exchange* (both sides benefit when done properly but both sides hurt when done improperly).

Strategy must be *guided by the marketing concept* (ie focus on customers and their needs, and, integrate all activities – communications mix and marketing mix).

APPENDIX 5.2: STRATEGY CAN APPLY TO A SPECIFIC COMMUNICATIONS TOOL

Working down the planning hierarchy, it is possible to build a strategic dimension to each and every one of the communications tools. Take, for example, sales promotions and exhibitions:

All sales promotions should be part of a bigger and longer-term strategy. Longer-term strategies are about building and reinforcing brand image, strengthening user loyalty, and even inviting new users to join the club, as opposed to short-term tactical sales boosts. Whether planned on a one-off tactical basis or on a more strategic approach, the sales promotion can have an impact on a brand or organisation's overall image (NB

Hoover). A strategic approach does not preclude the use of tactical promotions since it can provide a framework within which shorter-term tactics can be determined. In this way a sales promotion strategy makes the tactical planning easier and more productive.

(Julia Cummins)

Exhibitions should not be used as a one-off *ad hoc* activity. They can be used more effectively when (Smith, 1993):

- they are viewed as a possible series of exhibitions;
- they are integrated carefully with other communications tools;
- they are selected and planned well in advance;
- their effectiveness is constantly monitored.

Now consider how individual communications tools can adopt a strategic approach (as opposed to one-off *ad hoc* tactical tools). Here are some examples covering sales promotions, direct mail, public relations, sponsorship and exhibitions:

Sales promotion strategy – Pears Soap

Create a nationwide competition suitable for anyone in the country and which is capable of repetition, and which most importantly enhances Pears' caring family image.

Direct mail strategy – Woolworths

- To develop a database to expand the Ladybird franchise.
- To launch a free-to-join children's club – the Kids at Woolworth.
- To create exclusive branded characters to reinforce the merchandise link.

PR strategy – Hewlett-Packard

A two-pronged communications strategy was developed to position HP as 'the knowledgeable partner' and 'agent of change' for implementing IT solutions while using a creative theme, 'think again' (about computer systems), to help undermine a competitor's current advertising approach through a series of top-level conferences.

Sponsorship strategy – TSB

The sponsorship strategy briefly explains which types of sponsorship programmes are preferred, why a particular sponsorship programme is selected, how it will be exploited and integrated, and at what cost. To maximise the effect, sponsorship must be integrated with other elements of the communications mix, eg advertising, sales promotion, direct mail and public relations.

It should be explained internally and sometimes used internally as part of psychic income as a means of improving employee relations. Sponsor Melchester Rovers supported by a media relations campaign.

Exhibition strategy – Sedgewicks

To achieve the objectives (to reinforce Sedgewicks' position as the foremost European-based broker with the best European network; to demonstrate true pan-European expertise with a visible 'cohesive, one-company' European image; to improve internal communications) in a cost competitive manner by developing an outstanding pan-European exhibition involving a press conference and a press lunch, with senior speakers at the main conference dinner; by hosting a major dinner; and by an innovative exhibition crowd-pulling concept, all integrated into a creative theme – 'One Europe, 1st in Europe'.

APPENDIX 5.3: ADVERTISING STRATEGY, CREATIVE STRATEGY AND MEDIA STRATEGY

BMW: advertising strategy

Use advertising to build and enrich the BMW brand by:

- advertising core brand values of performance, quality, advanced technology and exclusivity;
- 'sniper' strategy of communicating many aspects of BMW values to different consumer segments in a large number of adverts;
- raising the brand's 'centre of gravity' to more advanced, expensive models;
- adopting a consistent tone of voice (cold, precise, technical).

(IPA Advertising Effectiveness Awards, 1994)

Häagen Dazs: advertising strategy

Can be split into a creative (or message) strategy and a media strategy.

Creative strategy
Build a brand leadership by creating a new language for ice-cream. Other ice-creams focus on ingredients or images of happy families. The new advertising instead talked about end benefits that are sometimes hidden deep below the surface of traditional and conscious feelings expressed about ice-cream.

Media strategy
Use weekend press to allow the ads to be savoured and enjoyed at leisure while the intimacy of the experience could be hinted at better through the more personal communication of the press (vs shared viewing of TV adverts).

British Airways: creative strategy

To position British Airways as an airline that more people around the world choose to fly: 'The World's Favourite Airline'.

Boddingtons Bitter: creative strategy

Focus on product truth of 'smoothness' executed in a straightforward and contemporary way.

Co-op Bank: creative strategy

To transform the bank's differentiating factors into a relevant and motivating proposition.

APPENDIX 5.4: OCCASIONALLY TACTICS ARE PREFERRED TO STRATEGY – A JUSTIFICATION?

Some organisations only see sales promotions as a short-term tactical tool to support what they call the more strategic communications tools such as advertising. Realistically, however, it is not always possible to achieve strategic goals if the client does not want them in the first place. Roger Hyslop of the Marketing Triangle gives as an example the retailer who says: 'I don't need this promotion to add to my brand image, otherwise I wouldn't be spending millions of pounds on TV. What I need is to bring 50,000 people in to see my store opening.' The difficulty is compounded by the fact that some strategic promotions may sometimes not generate maximum customer response in the immediate short term. Should the longer-term image-building capability of sales promotions be forfeited for the shorter-term tactical 'trial sales' objective?

DISCUSSION TOPICS FOR CHAPTER 5

1) Can a strategy build and reinforce brand image and increase user loyalty as well as tempt new customers all at once?
2) Do you ever need to have several strategies?
3) How are communication strategies different from advertising strategies?

REFERENCES

Engel, J, Warshaw, M and Kinnear, T (1994) *Promotional Strategy: Managing the marketing communications process*, 8th edn, Irwin, Homewood, IL

Govoni, N, Engell, R and Galper, M (1986) *Promotional Management*, Prentice Hall

Griffin, T (1993) *International Marketing Communications*, Butterworth-Heinemann

Moriarty, R and Moran, U (1990) Managing hybrid systems, *Harvard Business Review*, November–December

Schulz, D E, Tannenbaum, R E and Lanterborn, R E (1993) *Integrated Marketing Communications – Pulling it together and making it work*, NTC, Chicago

Smith, P R (1998) *Marketing Communications – An integrated approach*, 2nd edn, Kogan Page, London

Planning: the corporate, marketing and communications hierarchy

---

LEARNING OBJECTIVES

- Understand how corporate marketing and communications plans link.
- Use the SOSTAC framework and the planning hierarchy.
- Understand the stages of both strategic and operational planning.
- Use the product lifecycle to plan communications.

TOPICS COVERED BY THIS CHAPTER

The Overall Strategic Planning Process 96; The SOSTAC Planning Framework 97; The Planning Hierarchy 98; The Strategic Planning Stages of Marketing Communications 98; The Operational Planning Stages of Marketing Communications 99; Linking Marketing and Communications Strategy 100; Using the Product Lifecycle Concept for Marketing and Communications Strategy 102; Discussion Topics 108; References 108

THE OVERALL STRATEGIC PLANNING PROCESS

This book is concerned almost exclusively with both marketing communications strategy and planning. Yet marketing communications strategy cannot exist in isolation from marketing strategy which in turn is directly linked to corporate strategy. So at the start of this chapter we consider the simple strong relationships between the three levels of strategy shown in Figure 6.1.

Figure 6.1 The three levels of strategy

Planning can be carried out using a top-down or bottom-up approach, or preferably using a mixture of the processes at each of the three levels. This involvement of the different organisational levels implying a planning hierarchy immediately suggests that there is an effective sequence of planning in which the development of marketing communications strategy proceeds after a proper consideration of both corporate and business strategy. Ideally this should be the case. Undoubtedly, however, there are situations where marketing managers and their agencies do undertake some bottom-up planning. They are often called on to develop marketing communications strategies to a different timescale from corporate planning. In some cases their knowledge of corporate strategy may be limited. They therefore have to do their best in a given situation. However, in all situations marketing communications must be developed with an awareness of its fit within the overall strategic planning framework.

THE SOSTAC PLANNING FRAMEWORK

Whatever the level of the planning hierarchy the SOSTAC planning model – which is the basis of much of this book – can be applied easily (see Table 6.1).

It will immediately be obvious that it is possible to apply the SOSTAC model at each level of the planning hierarchy, that is SOSTAC applies equally at the corporate level, the marketing level and the marketing communications level. However, the choice made in this book is to apply SOSTAC particularly in the later case, that of developing an effective marketing communications strategy.

Table 6.1 The SOSTAC planning system

Stage	Strategic question
1) Situation	Where are we now?
2) Objective	Where do we want to be?
3) Strategy	How do we get there? (Broad direction)
4) Tactics	The details of strategy What communications tools should be used when?
5) Action	The details of tactics What steps are required to put each tool into action?
6) Control	How do we know when we have arrived?

THE PLANNING HIERARCHY

In the 1960s and 1970s a system of management was developed by the first British management consultancy company, Urwick Orr, now part of Price Waterhouse. The system, called 'Management by Objectives', became extremely popular and is still in use today. The principle of the system is that individual managers' objectives have to be linked into corporate objectives in a direct and distinct way. Each manager discusses and agrees with the next level of management above them over what action they will take in the following 12 months in order to contribute to achievement of the overall corporate objectives. This linkage into a hierarchy of objectives ensures that an organisation's main resource, its staff, are involved, integrated, motivated and, hopefully, rewarded as shown in Figure 6.2.

At each level it is possible to consider the two elements of objectives and strategy. Objectives are the end result and strategies are the means of achieving the objectives. This relationship is explored in more detail in Chapter 5. The whole process can also be seen as an end/means hierarchy. The means (strategies) at one level become the ends (objectives) at the next level down. Strategies cascade down to the next level of planning as an objective.

THE STRATEGIC PLANNING STAGES OF MARKETING COMMUNICATIONS

The details of Figure 6.2 have been redrawn in Figure 6.3 in the form of a flowchart showing how the objectives at the three planning levels – corporate marketing and marketing communications – are directed and linked to each other. In addition Figure 6.2 has been extended to form a triad of objectives,

Figure 6.2 The planning hierarchy

strategy and tactics. Tactics refers to a number of relatively short-term actions, but of course what is 'short term' is relative to the level of the organisation being considered. Corporate level planning could typically extend up to five years depending on the type of industry. Marketing planning would extend two or three years; marketing communications planning usually only looks at a one-year timescale. However, it should be noted that an organisation's branding strategy may be planned over a longer period of five years or more as this is of strategic importance.

THE OPERATIONAL PLANNING STAGES OF MARKETING COMMUNICATIONS

In Figure 6.4 the process is taken to a greater degree of detail and in particular the major resource constraint of money (budget) is introduced. At first sight it may seem odd that the marketing communications budget is estimated before detailed operational plans are drawn up. This, however, represents many real situations for both large and small companies. Small companies often budget to spend all they can afford, which is often too little. Large companies sometimes base their budgets on previous experience or use a

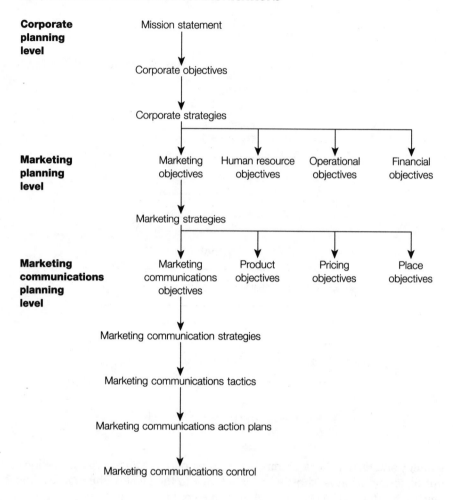

Figure 6.3 The strategic planning stages of marketing communication

formula such as the advertising to sales ratio. Whatever the situation, the budget level is indeed a broad starting point for making decisions on the most appropriate communication elements. After detailed planning it is then possible to submit a revised budget.

LINKING MARKETING AND COMMUNICATIONS STRATEGY

The previous sections of this chapter have asserted that marketing communications strategy should derive directly from marketing strategy which in turn derives directly from corporate strategy. This suggests that there is a strong body of knowledge and practice which provides a framework for making these linked decisions. In reality, although marketing theories and concepts are well developed across specific planning levels, their vertical integration is rather less developed. This is perhaps understandable on two counts.

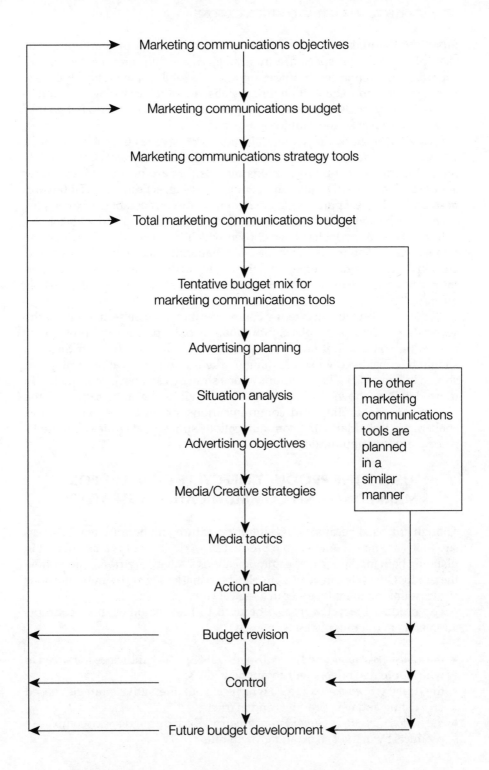

Figure 6.4 The operational stages of marketing communications

Firstly, individuals tend to specialise in certain areas of marketing. For example, those who specialise in strategic marketing are not necessarily experts in marketing communications and this inhibits the vertical linkages. Books either tend to be written for specialist areas, ie marketing communications strategy, or else they are written on a broader basis and do not go into detail on the specific communications aspect.

Secondly, the marketing communications strategy area is a complex one in which many factors play a part. This makes the development of the models more difficult. The communications models that are developed are either simple such as the AIDA (attention, interest, desire, action) and ATR (awareness, trial and repeat purchase) models, or they are considerably more complex such as the behavioural models of Engels (1994), and Wind and Webster.

In this book a model has been chosen which is intermediate between the two extremes. The model described in Chapter 2 is customer focused and encompasses customer perception, the buying activity, communications and the marketer's strategy. The process is integrated with the strategy of the whole business.

At the simplest level marketing communications can be seen as one of the seven Ps: product, price, place, promotion, people, process and physical, ie marketing communications is the promotional element. Each of these Ps should be considered when planning marketing communication strategy, as shown in Figure 6.5. The communications strategy can then be considered in more detail as shown in Figure 6.6. It is obvious that integrating all the elements for marketing and communications strategy is a complex and challenging task. Marketing communications strategy integrates all these Ps since every P communicates.

USING THE PRODUCT LIFECYCLE CONCEPT FOR MARKETING AND COMMUNICATIONS STRATEGY

Though criticised because of its simplistic nature and because real business situations are more complex, the product lifecycle concept is a useful tool in planning both marketing and communications strategy. Figure 6.7 shows how the product lifecycle can be used to plan both marketing and communications strategy, linking them together in a logical way.

The product lifecycle can also be used to link the other three concepts adopted in marketing planning, namely:

- the *diffusions of innovation curve* (Rogers, 1963) which indicates the speed at which potential buyers will accept new ideas;
- the *Ansoff growth matrix* (1957) which sets out alternative strategies based on existing and new products and markets;
- the *Boston Consulting Group portfolio matrix* which distinguishes a company's products by market share and growth rate.

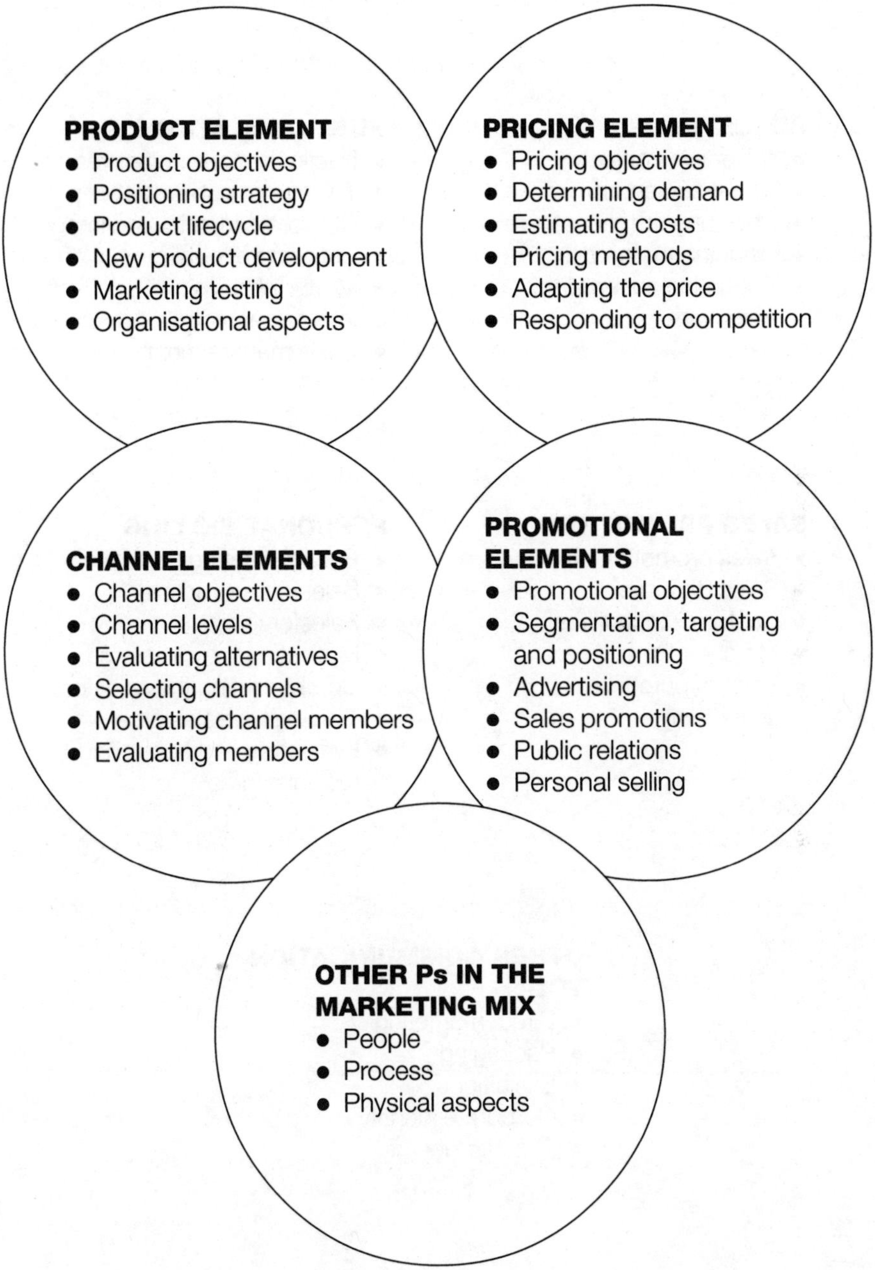

PRODUCT ELEMENT
- Product objectives
- Positioning strategy
- Product lifecycle
- New product development
- Marketing testing
- Organisational aspects

PRICING ELEMENT
- Pricing objectives
- Determining demand
- Estimating costs
- Pricing methods
- Adapting the price
- Responding to competition

CHANNEL ELEMENTS
- Channel objectives
- Channel levels
- Evaluating alternatives
- Selecting channels
- Motivating channel members
- Evaluating members

PROMOTIONAL ELEMENTS
- Promotional objectives
- Segmentation, targeting and positioning
- Advertising
- Sales promotions
- Public relations
- Personal selling

OTHER Ps IN THE MARKETING MIX
- People
- Process
- Physical aspects

Figure 6.5 The Marketing Mix variables to consider when formulating communications strategy

ADVERTISING
- Advertising objectives
- Target audiences
- Choosing the message
- Deciding the media
- Evaluating advertising effectiveness

PUBLIC RELATIONS
- Public relations objectives
- The role of public relations
- Corporate identity and image
- Definition of public
- Media relations
- Internal marketing
- Crisis management

SALES PROMOTION
- Sales promotion objectives
- Sales literature
- Customer incentives
- Merchandising
- Point of purchase advertising

PERSONAL SELLING
- Personal selling objectives
- Salesforce structure
- Salesforce size
- Motivating the salesforce
- Compensating the salesforce
- Training the salesforce
- Evaluating and controlling the salesforce

OTHER COMMUNICATION TOOLS
- Direct marketing
- Packaging
- Exhibitions
- Corporate identity
- The Internet

Figure 6.6 The Communications Mix variables to consider when formulating communications strategy

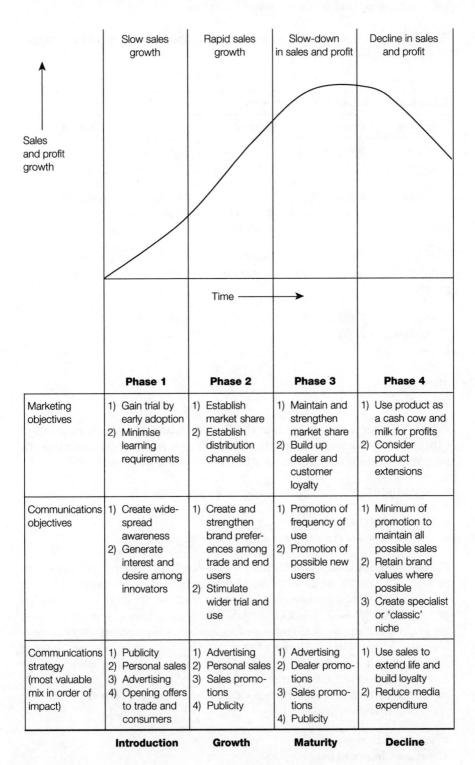

	Slow sales growth	Rapid sales growth	Slow-down in sales and profit	Decline in sales and profit

Sales and profit growth

Time ⟶

	Phase 1	**Phase 2**	**Phase 3**	**Phase 4**
Marketing objectives	1) Gain trial by early adoption 2) Minimise learning requirements	1) Establish market share 2) Establish distribution channels	1) Maintain and strengthen market share 2) Build up dealer and customer loyalty	1) Use product as a cash cow and milk for profits 2) Consider product extensions
Communications objectives	1) Create wide-spread awareness 2) Generate interest and desire among innovators	1) Create and strengthen brand prefer-ences among trade and end users 2) Stimulate wider trial and use	1) Promotion of frequency of use 2) Promotion of possible new users	1) Minimum of promotion to maintain all possible sales 2) Retain brand values where possible 3) Create specialist or 'classic' niche
Communications strategy (most valuable mix in order of impact)	1) Publicity 2) Personal sales 3) Advertising 4) Opening offers to trade and consumers	1) Advertising 2) Personal sales 3) Sales promo-tions 4) Publicity	1) Advertising 2) Dealer promo-tions 3) Sales promo-tions 4) Publicity	1) Use sales to extend life and build loyalty 2) Reduce media expenditure
	Introduction	**Growth**	**Maturity**	**Decline**

Figure 6.7 Using the product lifecycle to decide promotional strategy

Each of these concepts can be examined using the four phases of the product lifecycle as shown in Table 6.2.

Table 6.2 Several marketing concepts

Concepts	Phase 1	Phase 2	Phase 3	Phase 4
Product lifecycle	Introduction	Growth	Maturity	Decline
Diffusion of innovation	Innovation	Early adopters majority	Late majority	Laggards
Ansoff growth matrix	Product development	Market development	Market penetration	Diversification and alliances
Boston Consulting Group portfolio matrix	Problem child	Stars	Cash cows	Dogs

Phase 1 is represented by introduction (product lifecycle), innovation (diffusion), product development (Ansoff) and in high growth markets, problem children (Boston). Among the common characteristics are:

- new products;
- low sales;
- low market share;
- specific types of customers willing to buy the new products.

Phase 1 communications are then typified by creating widespread awareness at a reasonable cost while at the same time persuading innovators to try the new product. Public relations or publicity is used to gain additional coverage and personal sales to gain initial trials. Mass advertising is usually of less benefit at this stage because customers are limited in number and mass advertising would be wasteful. However, care must be taken to distinguish between consumer and industrial or business-to-business marketing situations. In consumer market situations there is often a good case for using mass advertising to introduce new consumer goods to a mass target audience.

Phase 2 is represented by:

- sales and profits growth;
- more widespread usage;
- development of the market;

- high market share;
- but increasing competition.

Phase 2 communications are then typified by creating and strengthening brand preference among both trade consumers and users. Advertising will be used to stimulate trials among a wider audience. Personal sales will continue to be important. Overall, the advertising budget will increase, in part to deter competition.

Phase 3 is represented by:

- market maturity and a slow-down in sales growth;
- conversion of late majority of customers;
- trying to increase market penetration and share.

Phase 3 communications are then typified by a continuing advertising spend, though not at the rate of the Phase 2 expenditure. More will be spent below the line in the form of promotions with both dealers and the end user. Ways will be sought to expand the market either by encouraging the frequency of use or by promoting new ideas.

Phase 4 is represented by:

- declining sales and profits;
- rationalisation in the marketplace through mergers, acquisitions and take-overs;
- some products will be milked for the profits;
- often products may need to be harvested;
- in a few cases product extensions can be developed.

Phase 4 communications are then typified by retaining brand value where possible. Promotional expenditure is reduced and what little remains is spent below the line in sales promotions. It may be possible to retain some loyal listeners by appealing to 'traditional' or 'classic' images.

The above descriptions have shown that it is possible to link marketing communications strategies in a logical way with marketing and corporate strategies. The last decade has seen a strong growth in the application of marketing concepts and theories to real-world situations. These concepts can be used to develop and justify the selection of particular marketing communications strategies.

This process of linking marketing and communications strategies must continue to be refined and improved in exciting ways in the future and creative ways as the 21st century unfolds.

DISCUSSION TOPICS FOR CHAPTER 6

1) Where does the marketing communications process fit within the overall strategic planning process?
2) At what levels of planning can the SOSTAC model be used?
3) What are the key elements of the planning hierarchy?
4) How can the SOSTAC model be used to plan advertising?
5) Why is it important to link marketing and communications strategy?

REFERENCES

Ansoff, I (1957) Strategies for Diversification, *Harvard Business Review*, September–October, p. 114

Engels, J, Warshaw, M and Kinnear, T (1994) *Promotional Strategy: Managing the marketing communications process*, 8th edn, Irwin, Herrewood, IL

Rogers, E M (1963) *Diffusion of Innovations*, Free Press, NY

Webster, F E and Ward, Y (1972) *Organisational Buying Behaviour*, Prentice Hall, Englewood Cliffs, NJ

SEVEN

Planning: writing marketing communications plans using SOSTAC

LEARNING OBJECTIVES

- Realise the full potential of SOSTAC.
- Use the pro formas to develop own plans.
- Use the pro formas to anticipate and analyse competitor plans.

TOPICS COVERED BY THIS CHAPTER

AN OUTLINE MARKETING COMMUNICATIONS PLAN: THE SOSTAC SYSTEM

There are many different approaches to building a marketing plan, or more specifically a marketing communications plan. There is no single common approach, but there are essential elements which every plan must have. The SOSTAC planning system shown in Figure 7.1 has been proved to be a generic, powerful and successful approach.

Situation: Where are we now?
Involves analysis which includes a company's past performance in terms of its marketing results, strengths and weaknesses and analysis of a company's environment, in terms of opportunities and threats. The key issues that affect the company's future must also be identified.

Objectives: Where are we going?
Mission; long/medium and short-term objectives; marketing objectives (eg sales and share); communications objectives (eg awareness; trialists; positioning) × timescales

Strategy: How do we get there?
Summary of how to achieve the above objectives – can include the 'marketing mix' target markets, spends/budgets/timescales, etc

Tactics: Details of strategy
What communications tools (communications mix) should be used? What is the sequence of tools, when will they be seen externally? How much will be spent on each one? A Gantt chart can help to summarise this kind of detail.

Action: Details of tactics
What steps are required to put each tool into action? What internal activities must occur in order for the communications tool to be created and delivered on time? This makes the development of each communications tool into a mini project which can involve critical path analyses and more detailed Gantt charts.

Control: Measurement and control
Knowing whether you're on target or not. Some form of monitoring to give you early indicators which let you adjust your plans before it is too late to maximise the results. Also includes various areas of market research (including testing)

Figure 7.1 The SOSTAC planning system

SOSTAC AND 3MS

The SOSTAC planning system was first mentioned in Chapter 4 on page 66 but Figure 7.1 here provides more detail. We can also modify the formula to 'SOSTAC + 3Ms'.

'SOSTAC + 3Ms' then is a simple *aide-mémoire* which helps managers to recall the key elements of a plan. Use this formula and you are well on your way to building a well structured and comprehensive plan. You can also use this approach to check other plans to see if they are comprehensive and cover the key items which every plan needs. Remember, you don't have to use the same terminology or even the same sequence, but SOSTAC should help the development of a logical structure combined with the key elements of a plan.

The 3Ms are the three key resources: men, money and minutes.

- *Men* means men and women, the expertise and abilities to do different jobs.
- *Money* means budgets – have we the money? This may also include cash flows, forecasted profit and loss and even return on investment generated by certain communications activities.
- *Minutes* mean time – what are the timescales, schedules or deadlines? Is there enough time?

One final question – where would you put target markets, marketing mix and positioning in the SOSTAC system? Remember everyone has their own style or layout of a plan. For example, some managers put target markets into the situation analysis, others put them into objectives and so on. Target markets are so important that once identified in the situation analysis, they drive the subsequent objectives, strategy and tactics. A summary of the current marketing mix and positioning should appear in the situation analysis under a 'review' section. The future mix and positioning and target markets are often summarised under strategy and explained in detail under tactics.

Below are some comments on SOSTAC from the experts, taken from the CD ROM *Marketing Planning* produced in 1997 by the Multimedia Marketing Consortium, London:

- Professor Kotler: 'SOSTAC is a system for going through the steps and building a marketing plan.'
- Sam Howe, Director of CATV Marketing Southwestern Bell: 'SOSTAC is a great approach for anyone going ahead and building a marketing plan.'
- David Solomon, Marketing Director, TVX: 'It appears that we are following the principles of SOSTAC.'
- John Leftwick, Marketing Director, Microsoft UK: 'We use SOSTAC within our own marketing planning.'
- Peter Liney, Concorde Marketing Manager: 'I think SOSTAC is very good in terms of identifying, if you like, major component parts of what you're doing in marketing.'

The short case studies in Chapter 8 show how easily SOSTAC works for products and services in both consumer and business-to-business markets: from Daewoo to Hewlett Packard, from the National Lottery and Gordon's Gin to United Airlines Business Travellers, SOSTAC lends itself to any type of outline marketing communications plan.

SOSTAC PRO FORMA WORKSHEETS

Marketing planning involves many complex variables and issues, even for a small business. These pro formas have been developed to help marketing managers cope with this complexity by prompting consideration of each variable and issue in a sequence, which will help to build a logical and effective communications plan. As marketing problems vary considerably from business to business, these pro formas will not solve every marketing manager's communications strategy problems, but they will ensure that the key components of communications strategy are developed in a way that will integrate the outputs of a wide variety of communications tools. The pro formas will also help marketing managers to achieve leverage across the communications tools. Leverage is a key tactic of integrated marketing communications, as it enables a variety of communications tools to be combined with synergetic effect (ie 2+2=5).

How to use these pro formas

1) Copy them and complete each one 3-4 times. This will give you a much better grasp of your marketing problems.
2) Give special attention to:
   - Stage 1.8 Issues Analysis – this could provide you with major new business opportunities.
   - Stage 4.3 Integrating the tools – this will help your communications tools to work more effectively with each other.
   - Stage 5.1 When you have developed your GANTT chart, go back to Stage 4.2 and check how different communications tools are supporting each other. This is a key basis for producing integrated marketing communications.
   - Stage 6.2 Use this as an opportunity to review all your marketing communications, and to assess how well they all work with each other.
   - Stage 6.3 3Ms – these are your major resources. Make sure that you have them available at the level you need for your marketing communications plan.

After all that, you will be able to write a logical, tightly argued, and cash flow-based plan to show what its costs and benefits will be.

The Six Stages of the SOSTAC Marketing Communications Plan

S	Situation	Where are we now?	Stage 1
O	Objectives	Where do we want to go?	Stage 2
S	Strategy	How do we get there?	Stage 3
T	Tactics	What specific tactics will fulfil the strategy?	Stage 4
A	Action	What detailed actions are needed for each tactic?	Stage 5
C	Control	How do we know we have arrived?	Stage 6

Now move on to Stage 1.1 over the page and start your situation analysis

SOSTAC © Smith, Berry and Pulford 1997, 1999

SOSTAC

Stage 1.1

SITUATION – PERFORMANCE

Main areas of marketing performance		Trend Increasing or declining?	Strength or Weakness (compare with competition)
PROFITS (last 3 years)	ROI; margins; net profit		
SALES (last 3 years)	sales revenue sales – units 80:20 rule applies? (Do we rely on just a few major customers? Do we have a large number of small-transaction customers?)		
MARKET SHARE (last 3 years)	Overall market share % (estimate if you do not have sales figures for the whole market). Are we the market leader or a market follower?		
POSITIONING	Against competition – how are we seen in the market-place?		
MARKET SEGMENT	What segments are we in? – List main current segments. – Are we attacking the same segments as we were 3 years ago?		
CUSTOMER SATISFACTION	Do we measure it? What is the current score?		

Summary Question: How are we performing?

Now move on to Stage 1.2 over the page to assess your company's competencies

SOSTAC © Smith, Berry and Pulford 1997, 1999

SOSTAC

Stage 1.2	SITUATION – COMPETENCIES		
Competency		**Trend** – are we getting better/worse	**Strength or Weakness** (compare with competition)
Marketing	Particularly good or bad? Better or worse than competition? Strong or weak brands? When did we last conduct a marketing audit? Has action taken place as a result?		
Production	Appropriate range of skills? Appropriate technologies? Learning curve – do we learn faster than the competition? More efficient production than competition?		
Financial	Cash flow OK? Do we get budget for marketing initiatives when we need it? Balanced product portfolio? % sales allocated to marketing (compared to competition)?		
Technology	Good quality database? E-commerce strategy?		
HRM	Constantly recruit good people? Training available? Reasonable compensation schemes?		

Summary Question: What are our distinctive competitive advantages (from a marketing perspective)?
Now move on to Stage 1.3 over the page to assess your current marketing mix

SOSTAC © Smith, Berry and Pulford 1997, 1999

SOSTAC

Stage 1.3	STITUATION – MARKETING AND SERVICE MIX		

Mix ingredient	How effective is our current mix?	Trend – are we getting better/worse	Strength or Weakness (compare with competition)
Product	Quality rating/score Portfolio/product range % new products in the portfolio Do the products create synergies?		
Price	Pricing strategy, eg skim/penetration Pricing options, eg lease/rental/purchase Scope for marginal pricing		
Place	Distribution channels % penetration into specific channels Point of sale support Pressure on margins from some channels		
Promotion	Branding – strong or weak? Share of voice in our markets Leverage across the communications tools		
People	Particularly good at the customer interface? Is staff turnover too high? When did the CE last serve on the counter?		
Processes	Efficient and effective front counter and back office processes? Are our processes up-to-date?		
Physical evidence	Buildings, uniforms look appropriate? Is it all clean & well maintained? Is design co-ordinated across everything in the business?		

Summary Question: Is our marketing mix right?
Now move on to Stage 1.4 over the page to assess your current customer mix

SOSTAC © Smith, Berry and Pulford 1997, 1999

SOSTAC

Stage 1.4	SITUATION – CUSTOMER MIX (Segment Mix)		
Describe each segment using several segmentation variables, eg – buying process; – geographic; – benefits sought, etc.	Segment size: – turnover; – no. units sold; – geographical spread.	Segment profitability: – prices; – levels of competition; – high sales & low cost; or – high sales & high cost.	Sales Current sales & potential sales – within each segment.	Segment attractiveness: – rank the segments in order; – least attractive 3; – most attractive 1.
Segment 1:				
Segment 2:				
Segment 3:				

Duplicate this table for any other segments

Summary Question: Are we competing in the best segments with the right type of customer?
Now move on to Stage 1.5 over the page to analyse the way you currently access your markets

SOSTAC © Smith, Berry and Pulford 1997, 1999

SOSTAC

Stage 1.5	SITUATION – ACCESS TO TARGET MARKETS (Chosen Segments)		
Describe each segment as you did at Stage 1.4	Distribution channels: – Have we penetrated all distribution channels for each target market? – Have we missed any?	DMU (Decision Making Unit which makes the buying decision): – List the key decision-makers – List the main influencers for each segment	Opinion formers – Who are the key opinion formers? – Can they be used to influence the market, eg press, trade bodies, etc	Communication channels – How can we communicate with the target audiences? – What tools and media are used? – Have we missed any?
Segment 1:				
Segment 2:				
Segment 3:				

Summary Question: Are we using the right distribution channels and communications channels?
Now move on to Stage 1.6 over the page to assess the uncontrollable variables in the market

SOSTAC © Smith, Berry and Pulford 1997, 1999

SOSTAC

| Stage 1.6 | SITUATION – EXTERNAL ANALYSIS OF UNCONTROLLABLE VARIABLES | | | |

General area	Specific area	Future uncontrollable events/trends	Impact – opportunity or threat?
Near or competitive environment	STEP 1		
	Structure/market		
	Trends in market		
	Economics (micro)		
	Power forces (eg dominant retailer)		

Far or wider environment	STEP 2		
	Sociological		
	Technological		
	Economic (macro)		
	Political		

Summary Question: What uncontrollable events or trends can impact my business?
Now move on to Stage 1.7 over the page and identify what you have learned from your markets

SOSTAC © Smith, Berry and Pulford 1997, 1999

SOSTAC

Stage 1.7

SITUATION – LEARNINGS

What have you learnt about your market-place this year?

List your five most important learnings.

These can be drawn from the external analysis (at Stage 1.6) or from more detailed market research findings about the perceptions our target customers have of our market offerings.

1	
2	
3	
4	
5	

Now move on to Stage 1.8 over the page and develop your key issues

SOSTAC © Smith, Berry and Pulford 1997, 1999

SOSTAC

Stage 1.8　　　SITUATION – ISSUES ANALYSIS

What are the five key marketing issues that have to be resolved?

These emerge from your extensive analysis already carried out both internally and externally.

For example, the 80:20 rule – over-dependent on one or two big customers? Weak brand? Low awareness of your brand in the market? Low profit contributions from some types of customers, either because they buy too little or because their costs are too high – should we sell more to them, or increase margins, or dump them?

| 1 |
| 2 |
| 3 |
| 4 |
| 5 |

Now move on to Stage 2.1 over the page and start defining your objectives

SOSTAC © Smith, Berry and Pulford 1997, 1999

SOSTAC

Stage 2.1	OBJECTIVES – SEPARATING MARKETING & COMMUNICATIONS OBJECTIVES		
Hierarchy of objectives	**Involves**	**Broad objective**	**Do you have clear objectives? ✔ or ✘**
Business mission	Overall vision and direction	Corporate positioning, leadership and values (including ethics)…	
Business objectives	All departments within the organisation	Survival; growth; ROI; acquisitions…	
Marketing objectives (eg Ansoff)	Market penetration	Grow sales; market share; distribution; penetration…	
	Market development	Enter new markets; new market segments…	
	Product development	Develop & launch new products; expand range…	
	Diversification	Move into new products/services and markets…	
Marketing communications objectives (here we follow AIDA)	Attention	Increase awareness…	
	Interest	Attitudes, preference…	
	Desire	Intentions to purchase, likelihood to…	
	Action	Repurchase, enquiries, trial purchase…	

Now move on to Stage 2.2 over the page and quantify your objectives

SOSTAC © Smith, Berry and Pulford 1997, 1999

SOSTAC

Stage 2.2	OBJECTIVES – TURNING OBJECTIVES INTO NUMBERS				
Broad objective	**Target market**	**From**	**To**	**When**	
eg To increase awareness	Among ABC1 women	From 20%	To 30%	Within 12 months	
eg To increase sales	Among large electrical engineering companies in Germany and Austria	From £15m	To £20m	Within 18 months	
To...					
To...					
To...					
To...					

NB Objectives should be $\boxed{\text{S-M-A-R-T}}$: <u>S</u>pecific (with numbers); <u>M</u>easurable (must be measurable so that we know whether we are achieving them); <u>A</u>ctionable (can we do it?); <u>R</u>easonable (reachable, attainable and not so high that staff get frustrated); <u>T</u>imescale (incorporating deadlines).

Now move on to Stage 3.1 over the page for the components of strategy

SOSTAC © Smith, Berry and Pulford 1997, 1999

Stage 3.1

STRATEGY (How to get there) – THE COMPONENTS

You have decided where you want to go (Objectives at Stage 2.2) but now you must decide how you are going to get there (Strategy). So how will you achieve the Objectives which you defined at Stage 2.2? Use the pro formas at Stage 3.2 and 3.3, to start to write a marketing communications strategy. Below is a list of some of the key components of a marketing communications strategy. The first seven come from the acronym STOP&SIT.

Segmentation

Is the communications strategy based on a mass market approach or should the market be broken up? How is the market segmented – what variables are used to segment the market?

Targeting

Does the communications strategy select specific target customers, DMUs and stakeholders who can also affect my results, eg shareholders and local community?

Objectives

Keep your eye on the ball. Will the communications strategy succeed, ie will it fulfil the objectives? Will it beat competition?

Positioning

Is there a clear positioning? Are our market offerings represented in the customers' minds by a unique set of values? Does the communications strategy support the overall positioning (which should have already been clearly defined in the overall marketing plan and marketing strategy)?

Sequence

Are there a number of stages or is there a sequence of events, eg mailshot, inbound telesales, follow-up field visit? Or does brand building advertising create a platform for more specific targeting activities such as direct mail? Does the strategy cover the many stages in the customer's buying process (repeat buying process)? Is it a multi-stage strategy?

Integration

Does the communications strategy naturally lend itself to integrated marketing communications? Does the strategy leverage itself across several communications tools?

Tools

Which of the 12 communications tools will be used? Are we going on TV or just mailings?

Sustainable competitive advantage

Does the communication strategy play to our strengths?
eg Cost leader/differentiate/focus/niche]. Are we learning faster than our competitors?

Resources Required

Can we afford the strategy? Television advertising might build awareness quickly but this is not realistic if the strategy goes way beyond budget. Maybe we need to create an effective but lower-cost strategy. The answer to this will probably lie in the use of a combination of lower cost communications tools rather than a full-scale advertising campaign.

Now move on to Stage 3.2 over the page to write your basic strategy statement

SOSTAC © Smith, Berry and Pulford 1997, 1999

SOSTAC

Stage 3.2

STRATEGY – THE BASIC STATEMENT

Now you're ready to generate a marketing communications strategy that will help you to achieve the specific objectives which you developed at Stage 2.2. First, copy the objectives from Stage 2.2:

Objective 1 ....

Objective 2 ....

Objective 3 ....

Objective 4 ....

Now decide how your marketing communications are going to achieve these objectives. Write down a marketing communications strategy by listing how many stages, which tools, and which other components (shown at Stage 3.1) might be included.

(i) Marketing Communications Strategy: TOOLS, STAGES AND COMPONENTS

SEGMENT 1		
How many stages in the strategy?	Which communications tools?	Any other components from 3.1?
(repeat for each segment)		

(ii) Now see if you can find an alternative communications strategy – Strategic Option (ii)

SEGMENT 1		
How many stages in the strategy?	Which communications tools?	Any other components from 3.1?

When you feel that a sufficient number and range of strategic options have been generated, use the matrix at Stage 3.3 to rank them as a basis for selection.

(iii) Now see if you can find another alternative communications strategy – Strategic Option (iii)

SEGMENT 1		
How many stages in the strategy?	Which communications tools?	Any other components from 3.1?

Now move on to Stage 3.3 over the page to select the best strategy from these strategic options

SOSTAC © Smith, Berry and Pulford 1997, 1999

SOSTAC

Stage 3.3 **STRATEGY (How to get there) – SELECT THE BEST STRATEGIC OPTION**

Strategic option [please repeat the strategic options]	Segmented	Targeted	Meet objective	Support positioning	Sequence/ no/ of stages	Integrated	Tools	Play to DCA	Resources	Rank the strategic options in order of attractiveness: – Least attractive 4 – Most attractive 1
(i)										
(ii)										
(iii)										

Now you have chosen the best strategic option, you are ready to move on to Stage 4.1 over the page and start designing your tactics

SOSTAC © Smith, Berry and Pulford 1997, 1999

Stage 4.1 TACTICS (the details of strategy) – WHAT HAPPENS WHEN?

SEGMENT A (B,C, etc). The same tactics will normally run across several product/service ranges.

Tool	Jan	Feb	Mar	Apr	May	June	July	Aug	Sep	Oct	Nov	Dec	Cost £000
Market research													
Packaging redesign													
POS preparation													
Advertising – TV – press – poster – cinema – radio													
Sales promotion													
Press launch													
Direct mail													
Sales conference													
Sales drive													
Exhibitions													
Web site													
E-commerce													
TOTAL SPEND													

Now move on to Stage 4.2 over the page to start integrating your tactics

SOSTAC © Smith, Berry and Pulford 1997, 1999

SOSTAC

Stage 4.2   TACTICS (the details of strategy) – DO THE TACTICS SUPPORT EACH OTHER?

You need to check that each communications tool identified on the previous page is used in a sensible, coherent and integrated manner. Remember the target market customers are influenced by the DMU (Decision Making Unit) and the wider stakeholder audience (investors, regulators, local community, etc). Finally, consider whether any of these methods (tools), media and messages can be combined across different market segments to produce extra leverage, maximum impact at minimum cost.

Method – Communications Tools (eg ads, sales promotion, exhibitions and sales force, Internet...)	Media – for each communications tool eg ads: TV, press, radio & sales promo. coupons, competitions, collectables	Message What is the message? (positioning, USP...)	Timing Any particular sequence of methods and media?

You may now need to reconsider your Gantt chart 4.1

Now you are ready to convert each tool into a mini-project requiring detailed action plans. Move on to Stage 5.1 and consider one such communications tool, direct mail.

SOSTAC © Smith, Berry and Pulford 1997, 1999

SOSTAC

Stage 5.1   ACTION – DETAILED ACTIVITIES REQUIRED FOR EACH COMMUNICATIONS TOOL

Each tactical communications tool needs to be planned as a mini project eg direct mail campaign

STAGE OF PRODUCTION	Who is responsible?	Wk 1	Wk 2	Wk 3	Wk 4	Wk 5	Wk 6	Wk 7	Wk 8	Wk 9	Wk 10	Wk 11	Wk 12	Cost £000
Creative & media briefing														
Database list preparation														
Laser printing														
Print production (brochure, envelopes)														
Letter shop (collating, folding, packing)														
Mailing														
Response monitoring														
Response action														
Follow-up sales call														
Evaluate mail shot														
TOTAL SPEND														

Each communications tool will need to be managed in the same way ie a mini-project.
Now move on to Stage 6.1 over the page to develop a control system

SOSTAC © Smith, Berry and Pulford 1997, 1999

SOSTAC

Stage 6.1	CONTROL – HOW TO MEASURE COMMUNICATIONS EFFECTIVENESS

Quantified objectives State each quantified objective and its time period	Means of measuring How will it be measured – survey, or sales…?	Frequency of measurement quarterly, weekly, daily?	Accountability – Who does it? = Who measures?	How much does it cost to measure?	Action? Who needs to be alerted if significant variances are found?

Now move on to Stage 6.2 over the page to check the integration of your marketing communications

SOSTAC © Smith, Berry and Pulford 1997, 1999

SOSTAC

Stage 6.2 — **CONTROL – SEVEN LEVELS OF INTEGRATION**

	Type of integration	Check	✔ or ✘	How do we ensure integration? What action do we need to take?
1	Vertical	Do the communications objectives fit with the marketing objectives and with the overall corporate objectives?		
2	Horizontal/functional mix	Do different departments and business functions incorporate marketing communications, eg trucks with logos? Finance invoices with messages etc?		
3	Marketing mix	Is the marketing mix consistent with required messages, eg low price versus top quality image?		
4	Communications mix	Are all the communications tools being used to guide the buyer through each stage of the buying process? Do they all give the same overall message (eg consistent positioning)		
5	Creative design mix	Is the logo, typeface, pantone colours used in a consistent manner?		
6	External/internal creative departments	Do all the external agencies (advertising, direct mail, PR) and all internal departments meet and plan together? Run monthly strategic and weekly tactical meetings, attend the same briefings…		
7	Financial	Is the budget being used in the most cost effective way?		

Now move on to Stage 6.3 over the page for a final resources check

SOSTAC © Smith, Berry and Pulford 1997, 1999

Stage 6.3

CONTROL – THE 3M RESOURCE CHECK

SOSTAC Stage 6: Control   6.3 the 3M Resource Check

SOSTAC + 3Ms – The Key Resources Required
Each tactic and action requires resources. Always check to see if the 3Ms are available

M	Men/Women	Human resource – Who will do it?	Notes:
M	Money	Budgets – How much will it cost?	Notes:
M	Minutes	Timescales – When will it happen?	Notes:
	Other resources required, eg database software		

Now, finally, move to the next page

SOSTAC © Smith, Berry and Pulford 1997, 1999

Congratulations Having answered the questions below you have now created
an outline for a marketing communications plan.

S Situation ⟹ Where are we now?

O Objectives ⟹ Where do we want to be?

S Strategy ⟹ How do we get there – broad direction?

T Tactics ⟹ How do we get there – individual tactical tools?

A Action ⟹ What are the specific actions required for each individual
tactical step? How do we get people to do them?

C Control How do we know we have arrived?

SOSTAC PLANNING SYSTEM

SOSTAC © Smith, Berry and Pulford, 1997, 1999

EIGHT

Planning: case studies of SOSTAC in use

LEARNING OBJECTIVES

- Reinforce the SOSTAC planning system.
- Appreciate the diverse approaches to using SOSTAC.

TOPICS COVERED BY THIS CHAPTER

The Use of the SOSTAC System 136; United Airlines 137; Gordon's Gin 141; The National Lottery Game 144; Daewoo 149; Hewlett-Packard's LaserJet Printer 153; etc limited: Human Resource Consultants 156; Invesco Fund Managers Limited 161; Discussion Topics 163; Further SOSTAC Cases 163

THE USE OF THE SOSTAC SYSTEM

In each of the cases which follow it should be noted that SOSTAC has been applied slightly differently, with different emphasis on different aspects. Despite this, the basic SOSTAC structure remains the same.

Obviously, in reality, a manager would draw up a much more detailed set of analyses and action plans. Although it is unusual, plans can be kept short with all the bulky details being confined to a series of appendices at the end of the plan. The following cases have been kept short partly for reasons of confidentiality and partly for ease of reading. In reality, the marketing communications plan is often part of the larger marketing plan. Either way, the marketing communications plan would contain much more detail whether in the appendices or in the main body.

The following outline plans help to reinforce how easily SOSTAC can be applied by a wide range of organisations.

CASE 1: UNITED AIRLINES

Stage 1: Situation

With a route network which spans the globe, a fleet of 2,200 daily departures to 140 airports in 30 countries, over 80,000 employees and 75 million passengers, United Airlines is the largest air carrier in the world.

Since its first biplane took to the skies in 1926 to deliver the US mail, United's area of operations for the first 60 years remained in the USA. However, the airline has since the 1980s expanded its operations first to the Pacific Rim, then to Europe and finally to South America. It now operates the only scheduled round-the-world service.

When United Airlines began operating out of London Heathrow in 1991, the company faced a simple problem. Nobody knew them. How could United Airlines establish themselves in a marketplace dominated by British Airways who in their home market and major hub were always likely to outspend the competition many times over?

Stage 2: Objectives

- To establish United Airlines' presence in the UK.
- To do this by shifting awareness of the airline among the key target group of Business Travellers, from negligible to a situation where United are always on the list of possible choices for transatlantic flights.

Once a traveller has flown a relationship marketing strategy turns trial into loyalty.

Due to the regulated nature of the transatlantic travel market United's share is relatively small. However, the London hub needs to show a return in its own right for United's employee owners.

Stage 3: Strategy

The UK is BA's home market, London Heathrow its major hub. Competing for share of voice using 'traditional' media is a non-starter as BA dominates the rest of the airline market in the UK and outspends UA 9 to 1. Also since UA only offers transatlantic flights, the message is of relevance to a discrete target audience.

It was therefore decided to analyse the process by which choice of airline is made and treat each influence or influencer within that process as a potential medium or 'contact point' via which a relevant message about United Airlines could be communicated.

Using a variety of communications tools, UA sought to put the thought of United Airlines into the minds of the target traveller at every opportunity. This involved thinking through how business travellers spend their day, who they speak to when booking a flight and even how they travel to the airport.

Given the multitude of different ways that customers might be reached UA needed to ensure that, however the traveller received a message about UA, the end result was always that they were more likely to consider the airline next time they flew.

The decision over which airline to use starts and ends with the traveller, but the person who books the flight, the agent who takes the booking and the travel policy maker within the company can all exert influence over the choice of airline.

For example, the travel trade needs much more detailed information about routes, schedules and prices than business travellers, since we want to ensure that an agent will be fully briefed about United if asked.

The core target is actually quite small in number – just over 100,000 people – and it was recognised that there are many other demands on their time and many other products and services seeking to capture their attention and loyalty. Unless UA practises integration in both planning and execution there is a real risk of being swamped. Research into the target and the way they spend their days allows UA to manage this relationship using a number of different contact points. Taking an integrated approach allows the communications budget to stretch much further than if UA were to limit itself to traditional media.

Stage 4: Tactics

Transatlantic business travellers tend to be concentrated around London and the South East. How can they be reached?

UA therefore decided to use one of the most recognisable images in London to convey their message – the black taxicab. They turned the front half of 175 cabs into yellow New York taxis. These are a constant presence on the streets of the capital and at Heathrow. The message is not limited to the outside paintwork. The inside of the cab carries information about the airline. The driver is briefed about the services offered and even the receipt is branded. It is calculated that 84 per cent of UK businessmen would, on average, see one of the 'UA taxis' 378 times.

Other Heathrow routes, such as the Piccadilly Underground line is also covered. Every day, so many times a day, a complete tube train liveried in United Airlines colours runs to and from Heathrow. Tube carriage panels carry specific messages about the airline. Even the seats carry the UA name. Business travellers read newspapers. Carefully selected titles are most effective at reaching the target audience and the aim is to build up over time a relationship with the readers by offering them something more than a straightforward sales message. In the *Daily Telegraph*, for example, UA ran branded supplements covering a series of topics close to many businessmen's hearts – the Ryder Cup, the Five Nations Rugby tournament, the World Cup, business travel. The desk-top PC provides another opportunity to reach the target, so a site in the Electronic Telegraph on the Internet has also been created.

Before leaving for work, the target audience is contacted via the letterbox. Working in partnership with a number of organisations such as the Institute of Directors, letters are sent out giving information about the airline to their members and inviting them to join UA's frequent flier programme – Mileage Plus. Mileage Plus members are by definition UA's most loyal travellers, but communications play a crucial role in keeping them informed about the airline and making them feel valued. The information captured also gives crucial insights into who is flying regularly, where they fly to, who has stopped, and what might persuade them to fly with UA again. So each subsequent communication is made more and more relevant to their personal needs.

Another way to reach the traveller is via an intermediary – the travel agent who actually books the ticket. UA wants to ensure that the trade has enough information about United's routes, services and schedules. UA wants to turn them into potential advocates of the airline and so treats them as partners. The Route 1 Plus programme has been created and members are recruited via trade exhibitions, trade advertising and direct mail. The Route 1 handbook is an agent's introduction to UA and via a series of regular updates, or the *Skylines* newsletter and Skyfax – a way of quickly conveying tactical information to the trade – UA manages to keep agents informed about news and developments of relevance to them.

A contact point is simply a way of reaching the target – it is a place or indeed even a person who can carry a brand message. Many of the traditional 'advertising' contact points will be dominated by competitors and so UA needs to think more broadly about ways to make contact in order to achieve its goal of putting United's profile in the mind of the UK transatlantic business traveller. How this has been achieved so far is summarised in Table 8.1.

Stage 5: Action

Managing this programme demands effective coordination. Whenever UA plan a communications 'hit', the team needs to consider all the communications channels which can be used when developing creative ideas. The objective is always to achieve consistency of message thus increasing UA's fluency. Each communications task is managed using carefully planned project management techniques identifying key release dates, artwork preparation dates, artwork approval dates, creative briefing dates, etc.

Stage 6: Control

Effectiveness is measured by tracking awareness and image, by measuring the response rate to all direct mail, and of course by looking at sales revenue.

Table 8.1 United Airlines marketing communications strategy

Communication tools	Timing
Advertising – theme	Year-round presence on taxis, liveried tube and tunnel site at Heathrow. Presence upweighted using press whenever the airline has something new to announce, eg inaugural flight of the Boeing 777.
Advertising – route	Press outdoor used to carry route specific message. Used both to announce a new destination and for promotional activity. Timing is dependent on market/promotional circumstances.
PR	Ongoing in both consumer and trade press.
Direct	Activity integrated in communications 'hits' with advertising. Focus has been on data capture and recruitment using cold lists. Mileage plus members receive regular membership mailings.
Travel agents	Regular newsletter (*Skylines*) keeps agents up to date with the airline every two months. Skyfax enables the airline to respond overnight to competitive developments. Frequent bookers rewarded with incentive scheme linked to flights/holidays.
Corporate travel organisers	Regular contact with the salesforce. Also receive *Skylines* and information relevant to their needs via Skyfax.

CASE 2: GORDON'S GIN

Stage 1: Situation

The Gordon's brand is owned by United Distillers, the multinational spirits company wholly owned by Guinness plc.

Gin and tonic is a middle-class icon, and Gordon's dominates the market with a share of about 70 per cent of all gin consumed in pubs and clubs, and about 40 per cent in grocers and off-licences. However, gin is in long-term decline, its band of ageing drinkers dwindling in number. And Gordon's has declined with the market.

UD therefore has a choice: withdraw investment and milk Gordon's for profit as the gin category volume falls, or invest to expand the category by recruiting new drinkers.

Stage 2: Objectives

- To have halted the brand's decline (*circa* –7% pa) within 12 months, returning to positive growth within 18 months (*circa* +2–3% pa).
- To recruit a new generation of drinkers.
- To reposition Gordon's as one of the most exciting and rewarding drinks available.

Stage 3: Strategy

The task is to recruit a new generation of drinkers by repositioning Gordon's in young people's minds from a middle-class, middle-aged drink typically drunk by their parents to one of the most exciting and rewarding drinks available.

> To focus on the fantastic experience you get when you drink Gordon's gin and tonic: its crisp, clean, aromatically effervescent taste scintillates on to your palette and slices cleanly, like a blade, straight through your taste buds, refreshing every fibre of your being.

So uniquely refreshing is the taste and effect of a Gordon's and tonic that a new word has been coined to describe the experience: 'Innervigoration'.

The successful implementation of this strategy depends on addressing each of the following tasks:

- *Task A:* Conveying the Innervigoration Experience.
- *Task B:* Owning the Innervigoration Experience – especially in pubs and bars. (Marshall McLuhan famously said 'the medium is the message', and the way to own the Innervigoration Experience is for Gordon's to be seen delivering it.)

- *Task C:* Making it clear that *only* Gordon's can truly deliver the Inner-vigoration Experience.

An alternative strategic approach?

An alternative strategic approach would be to tackle Gordon's dull image – convincing young people that, far from being boring and old fashioned, Gordon's is in fact fun and contemporary. While this approach would improve the brand's personality, it fails to offer non-drinkers any reasons to go out and try a Gordon's and tonic, ie a new generation of drinkers will be recruited if – and only if – they believe in the excellence of the drinking experience.

Stage 4: Tactics

The communications mix comprises activities to address each task:

Task A

The Innervigoration Experience is best conveyed in communications via dramatic, highly involving advertising executions. The creative challenge is to use the senses of sight and sound to evoke in the viewer the sense of taste and the sensation of feelings associated with the drink.

A mix of media are being used: cinema for its tremendous impact on a small but captive audience; TV for its potential impact on a huge audience; posters to take the message to the streets (which is obviously where the pubs and bars are); and highly targeted press to keep the message in front of the young target audience, constantly reminding them of the uniqueness of the Gordon's experience.

The Internet also provides an opportunity to create a virtual Innervigoration Experience which net users can explore vicariously using their PC.

Another, albeit less orthodox, communications vehicle has been created via line extension. Analogously, if the Innervigoration Experience was another type of product, what could it be? One possible answer is a Gordon's and tonic sorbet. UD have developed, and are now distributing, just such a product using it to put focus on and strengthen the brand's associations with stimulating refreshment.

More generally, *all* other Gordon's communications play a supporting role by reminding consumers of the Innervigoration Experience (ie whether via a direct mail pack or an ice bucket, the experience will be in some way conveyed).

Task B

Owning the Innervigoration Experience requires it to be delivered consistently and branded clearly.

In part this is being achieved by retraining in pubs and bars and by providing point-of-sale merchandising.

Retraining is necessary to reduce the number of poor quality drinks all too often experienced in the on-trade (a Gordon's and flat tonic, mixed with a soggy bit of old lemon and a few melted, watery slivers of ice, all served unceremoniously in a warm wine glass).

Merchandising items in pubs and bars (eg attractive drinks coasters, tall elegant glasses, ice bucket scoops, etc) help orchestrate the mixing and serving of the drink, thereby enhancing to the fullest the drinker's experience. This also brands the experience 'Gordon's' (eg by branding the coasters, glasses and ice buckets, etc plus impactfully branded items like Gordon's fridges).

In off-licences point-of-sale materials (eg price strips, special offer shelf-barkers, etc) can also be used to remind shoppers of the link between Gordon's and the Innervigoration Experience.

Finally, as well as conveying the experience, the Internet site can also list bars which serve a perfect Gordon's and tonic, provide guidance on how to mix one for yourself, and can link the Innervigoration Experience firmly to Gordon's.

Task C

Two main approaches are being taken to explain why only Gordon's can deliver true Innervigoration, each geared to a particular group of consumers.

A detailed explanation is principally of interest to consumers who already have a propensity to consume gin. One of the most efficient means of communicating with known likely gin drinkers is to use direct mail (eg by collecting names from bought-in mailing lists). This efficiency is reflected not only in minimising media wastage (ie not trying to communicate with disinterested people), but also in the amount of detailed information that can be included in a direct mail leaflet (eg the history of the Gordon's secret recipe, product stories such as Gordon's use of more and better quality juniper than any other gin, etc).

For younger non-drinkers of gin, 'expert' brand ambassadors are more likely to impress. The programme of retraining bar staff is thus a means of enrolling them into the brand, using them as a communications medium through which to talk to consumers directly about why Gordon's is better than other gins.

Additionally, the Internet site provides an opportunity to describe the history of Gordon's and relate the brand's various unique product quality stories.

And more generally, public relations can seed stories in appropriate media about Gordon's heritage and superior taste.

Stage 5: Action

A series of project management teams have been set up to manage the development and delivery of each of the communications tools. This means that the advertising, direct mail, merchandising, sales training, etc has to be planned as mini projects but all tying in to the overall timing of the total marketing communications plan.

Stage 6: *Control*

All activity is carefully and extensively pre-tested. Results achieved are monitored continuously using a mix of sales tracking (ex-factory, retail audit and consumer research) and intermediary tracking (eg brand awareness, advertising recall and communication, brand image profile, etc). Key performance indicators have been agreed and are reviewed formally at quarterly intervals. Provided the results monitored stay on track, investment behind the programme will grow.

CASE 3: THE NATIONAL LOTTERY GAME

Stage 1: *Situation*

Camelot was awarded a licence by Parliament to run a National Lottery in the UK in May 1994. This meant developing a name, a logo, a positioning and a fully integrated communications plan for a product that was to be a completely new concept to the British public, so Camelot appointed Saatchi & Saatchi Advertising to help them with this task. Initially there would be no direct competition in the form of another national lottery game; however, there would be vigorous competition in a broader gaming context. This competition was likely to be in the form of low-stake gaming products such as the football pools, bingo, raffles and high street betting. It was estimated that the UK gaming market at the time was worth approximately £14.14 billion annually. Other competition for discretionary expenditure was expected to come from low-value entertainment and leisure products such as cinema and fast foods.

Stage 2: *Objectives*

The fundamental business objective for the National Lottery Game is to maximise the funds raised for the five 'Good Causes' designated by Parliament, which are Sports, Heritage, Charities, the Millennium and the Arts. To achieve this, a new national institution that would appeal to all adults in the UK had to be created. The marketing objectives set for the game were divided into the following phases: pre-launch, launch and ongoing.

Pre-launch:

- Build awareness to 39 per cent.
- Generate agreement that the National Lottery is 'good' for the UK.
- Create widespread predisposition to play.
- Develop an enthusiastic and motivated retailer base.

Launch:

- To reach 100 per cent adult awareness.
- To establish the correct values for the game (via agreement with a series of attitude statements).
- To achieve universal understanding of where to play.
- At least 60 per cent agreement that the National Lottery Game is easy to play.
- To reach 60 per cent trial during launch week.

Ongoing:

- To maintain awareness levels.
- To maintain the image and appeal of the game as the market becomes more competitive.
- To maintain consumer interest and excitement.
- To build trial to 80 per cent.

Stage 3: Strategy

The communications strategy of a regular *chance* of winning large amounts of money was identified as having the greatest and most universal appeal to the British consumer. It was also important that the brand was positioned as being accessible, fun, honest, harmless and for everybody. The idea of the 'Hand of Good Fortune' and the line 'It Could Be You' was found to be the most motivating and appealing way of communicating this. The *chance* strategy also generated the 'crossed fingers' design for the National Lottery logo and informed the way media channels were selected and used.

Strategic options
The idea of *chance* was not the only one that had been identified as a potential creative strategy. The options that were considered and researched were:

Strategy	Explanation
The chance	Every player has a chance to win
The spending	Players having millions to spend
The playing	The fun of participating

The 'chance' creative strategy was chosen essentially because the idea of *chance* allowed consumers' imaginations the most scope. By not referring explicitly to what might be done with the winnings, the *chance* strategy was not restrictive. It allowed people to have their own individual dreams about what they would do if they won. It also capitalised most strongly upon the anticipation and moment of winning.

The integrated communications strategy

The *chance* of winning had to be at the heart of all of the communications for the brand. The communications were intended to be 'total advertising'. The strategy was deployed across all communication channels including television, press, posters and radio advertising, but also in-store material, merchandise, even ticket receipts and retailer signage. A single-minded strategic thought at the core of all activity allowed for synergistic and integrated communications.

Stage 4: Tactics

All mass market media and a comprehensive range of point-of-sale materials have been utilised within the mix since launch (see Table 8.2). The ongoing media selection is based on the message to be communicated, the environment it needs to be communicated in, and the reach and the frequency that is required for those messages.

Communications were deliberately planned to commence very close to the actual launch date of the National Lottery Game so as not to create a huge demand too far in advance of the tickets going on sale. Prior to launch a road show was set up to travel around the country educating people to play the National Lottery followed by a door drop leaflet to 20 million homes in the UK providing further education. Approximately one week before launch national advertising broke on television (see Figure 8.1), press, posters and radio, occurring simultaneously with the unveiling of point-of-sale materials.

Stage 6: Control

A comprehensive programme of market research and sales data is in place to continuously monitor communications against the set objectives. Media activity is constantly being reviewed in a programme of testing and refining to ensure maximum impact and effectiveness. The campaign as a whole is also constantly being reviewed and refined in the light of both qualitative and quantitative research findings. All objectives set for pre-launch, launch and ongoing have been exceeded with approximately 70 per cent of the adult population playing the National Lottery Game weekly.

Table 8.2 Tactics: The National Lottery Game

	1994						1995											
	Jul	Aug	Sep	Oct	Nov	Dec	Jan	Feb	Mar	Apr	May	Jun	Jul	Aug	Sep	Oct	Nov	Dec
Advertising					X	X	X	X	X	X	X	X	X	X	X	X	X	X
Public relations	X	X	X	X	X	X	X	X	X	X	X	X	X	X	X	X	X	X
Retailer training			X	X	X	X	X	X	X	X	X	X	X	X	X	X	X	X
Retailer manual				X														
Point of sale					X	X	X	X	X	X	X	X	X	X	X	X	X	X
Door drop					X													
Road show				X	X													
Radio promotion													X	X				
Trade communications															X			

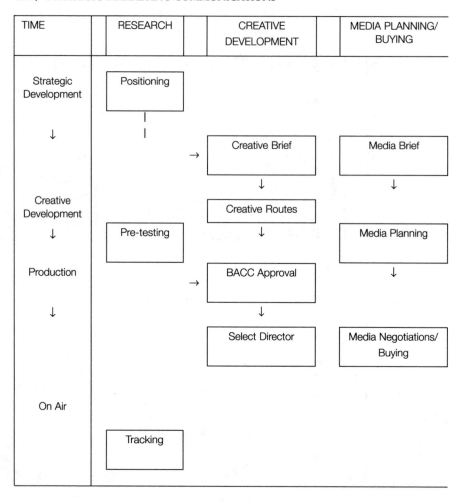

Figure 8.1 The National Lottery Game: project management schedule to launch TV commercials

CASE 4: DAEWOO

Stage 1: Situation

Globally Daewoo is bigger than Procter & Gamble and manufactures a vast range of products but it was unknown in the UK for some time before becoming the fourth Korean car importer.

The UK car market is oversupplied. It peaked in 1988 with over 2.3 million new registrations. Since then the trend has been downwards (to 1.8 million) and manufacturers have been ruthlessly cutting prices to maintain market share.

Consumers are very brand influenced. They map the mainstream brands qualitatively. These qualitative perceptions match volume very closely. So, in order to rapidly achieve high market share, Daewoo had to build a strong differentiated brand from nothing, fast.

Stage 2: Objectives

Daewoo's objectives were to enter the UK car market quickly and become a mass market brand with 1 per cent market share as quickly as possible, ideally within a year. To put this into perspective, Mazda after 24 years have 1 per cent, Hyundai after 13 years have 0.7 per cent and Proton after six years have 0.5 per cent. Daewoo needed to do this while selling two sizes of unpretentious but high specification, high value cars based on two earlier GM models already withdrawn from sale by Vauxhall in the UK.

These two cars gave Daewoo access to only 35 per cent of the car market by model type, engine type and body style.

Stage 3: Strategy

3.1 What was the communications strategy?
Daewoo and their advertising agency Duckworth Finn Grubb Waters felt that there was an opportunity to position Daewoo as *the most customer-focused car company in the UK*.

This would be achieved not by claiming it directly, but by demonstrating it imaginatively to get around consumers' cynicism.

3.2 Were other strategic options considered?
Most Far Eastern car manufacturers entering the UK market sell their cars on low price, a positioning that eventually becomes a trap because only a limited number of people will buy a car with no brand image. And with so many cheap car brands in the market (including three other Korean companies) even the cheap price sector looked overcrowded.

Clearly it would have been impossible for Daewoo to achieve any of its ambitions unless the company managed to radically differentiate itself and offer UK car buyers something completely unique. This ingredient would not come from the cars themselves.

3.3 Why was 3.1 chosen?

All the research in this area points to a vast gap in the market. While UK car buyers are broadly happy with increasingly reliable, comfortable, modern cars they remain overwhelmingly resentful of car dealers. The car may be good but the buying and ownership experience is frequently a miserable hassle. Daewoo could own customer service because they are:

1) *big* – Daewoo needed to convince people that it was a serious player with the scale to back up its promises;
2) *new* – Daewoo had no heritage of disgruntled customers to live down;
3) *Asian* – Far East Inc was seen to be setting the pace in the car market and Daewoo sounds Far Eastern. (Its specifically Korean origins researched as neither positive nor negative.)

Too many car companies claim to be customer focused. Daewoo's research told it that motorists had become cynical of these claims. Dealerships don't deliver marketing's promises. They seem to have a separate agenda. In fact, cynicism is so high that motorists regularly ignore car companies' assertions of customer focus. Daewoo needed to be different in everything it did if it was to be believed as offering something different (genuine customer focus).

Therefore the chosen strategy necessitated integration throughout marketing communications and operational implementation. To ensure complete control of all customer contact, Daewoo decided to engineer the company around the customer. This led it to operate through wholly owned outlets rather than dealerships. This ensured that the strategic vision was not just a marketing campaign but was central to everything Daewoo did.

3.4 Does the strategy help integrate all the marketing communications?

Yes, because being truly customer focused requires direct contact with potential and actual customers. Consequently, advertising builds brand awareness and directs people into Daewoo's telemarketing database system.

3.5 Selection mix

The scale of the task Daewoo had set itself necessitated the use of a vast range of marketing and communication disciplines including retail design, interactive point-of-sale technology, sales promotion, direct marketing, database construction and management, PR and advertising. Each element was rigorously tested through a continuous programme of qualitative and quantitative research.

Television was used as the primary medium. It confers greater scale on an advertiser, and by harnessing both audio and visual imagery it builds brands quicker.

National press and specialist motoring magazines have been used to add greater opportunities to see the campaign and to develop more detailed messages. National press adverts were not placed in the weekday news sections which many car companies use but in weekend review sections of mid-market and upmarket titles. Daewoo has a consistent presence, rotating nine separate full page executions.

In areas where Daewoo had opened stores it used poster sites and local press, and took its offer out into the community using Daewoo road show displays at major shopping centres. These were especially important as they could fill in gaps in the wholly owned network as it was being built.

3.6 Timings

Although Daewoo wasn't able to sell any cars until April 1995 it planned an innovative pre-launch phase starting in October 1994 to ensure it hit the ground running.

Daewoo's chosen strategy was to plan and execute the campaign in three main phases:

1) *Corporate credibility building*. TV and motoring press ads in October 1994 showed the range of high technology and heavy engineering products that Daewoo manufactures. This phase introduced 'The biggest car company you've never heard of...'
2) *The Daewoo dialogue* campaign between November 1994 and February 1995 asked people to tell Daewoo what they liked and disliked about car ownership and what they wanted it to do differently. To incentivise response Daewoo offered a chance to become one of 200 guinea pig Daewoo drivers who would be given a free car for a year's extended test drive. This exercise had the twin objectives of being seen to consult customers (showing Daewoo was customer focused) and built a database of 200,000 to ensure rapid sales growth when the cars went on sale.
3) *Brand launch*. Daewoo is a different kind of car company because it is customer focused. The brand launch was creatively the most difficult phase of the campaign. Because Daewoo had built genuine differentiation into their offer, it had 22 distinct messages to communicate. None of them was a showstopper in its own right but the cumulative effect was very impressive. It's very difficult to get across a series of individual messages in advertising (particularly TV which Daewoo needed to use for speed of brand building). The risk was that people might get lost in the detail.

The creative solution was to divide the messages into four 'commitments' each of which was allocated a 40-second TV commercial. The adverts were placed two per break across two consecutive TV breaks to ensure viewers got the whole story but in manageable chunks.

The commitments are: (1) *Daewoo sells direct*: the absence of dealers gives consumers permission to believe in the Daewoo difference; (2) *Hassle-free* buying, pleasant showrooms with free coffee and children's areas, no commissioned salesmen and no hidden charges; (3) *Peace of mind*: three-year comprehensive warranty, three years free servicing, three year total

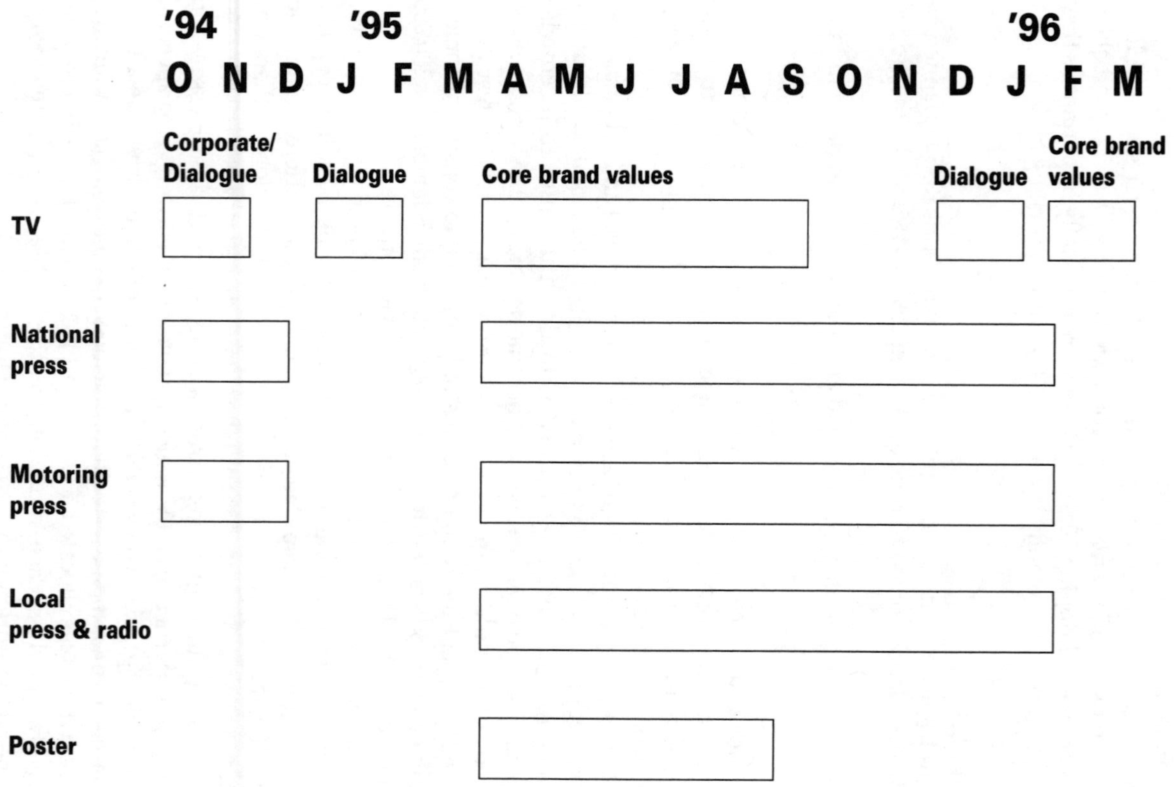

'94   '95   '96

O N D J F M A M J J A S O N D J F M

	Corporate/Dialogue	Dialogue	Core brand values	Dialogue	Core brand values
TV					
National press					
Motoring press					
Local press & radio					
Poster					

Figure 8.2 Daewoo 1995 advertising plan

AA cover, (4) *Courtesy servicing:* free courtesy car and free pick up and return of your car when it's serviced.

They were combined with a fifth shorter advert that ran at the end of the second break, inviting telephone responses.

Stage 4: Tactics

See Figure 8.2.

Stage 6: Control

Marketing activity is measured by:

1) *Sales data, Daewoo's own figures and SMMT figures.*
2) *The Daewoo tracking study* (through Millward Brown). Lord Leverhulme (founder of what is now Unilever) is reputed to have said: 'Half the money I spend on advertising is wasted: I just don't know which half.' The Daewoo tracking study is invaluable in the light of this statement. It doesn't just measure how well the advertising is doing, it allows the campaign to be fine-tuned. Is the whole message coming across? Are the right people noticing it?
3) *Daewoo Dialogues* (Guinea Pigs I in 1995 and the Maltreated Dialogue in 1996). Daewoo's consumer dialogues (for example, the Maltreated campaign) allow it to understand issues such as consumer dissatisfaction with the process of buying and owning a car, both in an overall sense, and in finer detail. All these variables can be sifted and studied, *and the results acted upon.*
4) *Qualitative research.*

CASE 5: HEWLETT-PACKARD'S LASERJET PRINTER

Stage 1: Situation

Hewlett-Packard invented and brought laser printing to the market in 1984. The standard technology in the market at that time was dot-matrix. Hewlett-Packard LaserJet printers were revolutionary in their technology and brought the customer benefits of quick, quiet, quality printing. In the last 15 years, Hewlett-Packard has continued to represent the standard by which competitive products are measured, both by manufacturers and industry experts. Research into HP LaserJet brand equity indicates that, in its role as undisputed leader of the laser printer market, HP LaserJet owns the generic category benefit of high print quality and all its associated benefits.

HP LaserJet had a European market share of 53.1 per cent. Although none of HP LaserJet's competitors could claim over a 25 per cent share of the laser sector, a number of them represented a substantial threat to the brand in certain countries and sectors, particularly Canon, Epson, Oki and (IBM) Lexmark in the economy sector of the market.

InkJet technology, whose combination of low prices, colour capabilities and ever increasing speed and network capability, was proving a major threat to the more traditional laser technology.

Stage 2: Objectives

The primary objective was to grow market share within the laser printer market. In order to do this in an extremely competitive market, the communications strategy needed to concentrate on increasing preference among consumers. (While total awareness of Hewlett-Packard in the laser printer market was already extremely high at 75.3 per cent preference for the brand stood at 48.8 per cent.) This was particularly crucial for the low-end products, where competitors offering cut-rate prices could potentially switch customers at the point of purchase.

Stage 3: Strategy

The role for the creative work was to dramatise the core strategic thought of:

> No matter what business you're in, HP LaserJets can make it look even better.

It was imperative that the new creative idea provided a clear demonstration of quality output (the very tool that would enable businesses to look their best), reflected the new, more approachable and lively HP LaserJet brand image, and was sufficiently flexible to work across all elements of the promotional mix.

The campaign that was developed focused on the idea that it requires real skill to produce great looking objects. The art of origami is a prime example of one such skill which, when correctly applied, can produce beautiful objects. Similarly, it is a great skill to create great looking documents and presentations. HP LaserJet's capabilities are such that it can provide you with all the tools to do just this. By enabling you to craft your output, HP LaserJet can help you produce outstanding documents, which in turn will enable your business to present a more professional and competitive image to the outside world.

The origami creative device encapsulated this key in an impactful and visually stunning way. The HP LaserJet brand was successfully portrayed as warm and approachable, while the all-important 'quality output' message was communicated by making the printer output the hero of each individual execution. The origami animals also allowed additional customer benefits of individual printers in the range such as speed or affordability to be highlighted in a visual way.

Executions:	'Parrot'
Core message:	'Get your business looking better in the new year with HP LaserJets.'
Desired response:	'I never realised my company could afford to own an HP LaserJet. Now we can *really* do our best work.'

Reasons for the communication strategy

Recent pan-European research into the HP LaserJet brand equity proved that Hewlett-Packard could no longer rely solely on reactional benefits about product-related benefits to increase preference. It was found that consumers also respond to a brand on an emotional level, and their buying choices are increasingly driven by these benefits. The research illustrated that, while HP LaserJet's four-year strategy based on *resetting standards in print quality* was strategically sound, the brand's emotional appeal, which was based on aspiration, prestige and a solid company image, could be made more dynamic and convey an increased sense of warmth. Importantly, this increased emotional appeal would also enable the HP LaserJet brand to become accessible to a broader range of people across a wider spectrum of business.

The communications strategy that was chosen as retaining the quality output message, but to modify the way in which this was communicated to consumers, by presenting a more approachable and lively brand image. The intention was to ensure that consumers gained a more personal, vested interest in the brand, which would be more difficult to dislodge by rational means such as competitive prices or promotional offers at the point of sale.

The communications platform that was developed as a result of this strategy was as follows: 'No matter what business you're in, HP LaserJets can make it look even better.' This platform would be used to develop the overall brand campaign, and also as a framework which could accommodate all other HP LaserJet activity.

The strategy was broad enough to form a platform from which to launch a fully integrated campaign including press, posters, sales lists, direct mail and POS. In the case of the Parrot, the execution was used through the line for press ads, retail marketing hits and POS.

The media objective for the HP LaserJet brand was to generate maximum awareness of the advertising message, thereby increasing preference for the brand (NB brand awareness levels were already very high).

These objectives were to be delivered via a strategy of prioritising frequency over coverage as far as possible within the available budget.

The role for press was to deliver the required coverage of all the above audiences: specialist small business and PC magazines for the boss-enthusiasts, business and general news publications to reach user-managers, and for the technical audience, computer magazines.

Posters were also recommended to 'kick-start' campaigns, ie to generate awareness of the new creative theme, focusing on major conurbations or areas of high sales potential.

Stage 4: Tactics

This was dictated, as is normal for all HP business, by the quarterly business reporting structure the company operates. Budgets are issued quarterly, and media plans are thus prepared quarterly also. This tends to dictate the shape of the campaign, ie three or four bursts throughout the year.

PR activity commenced on 1 March, a month before the product launch, to generate interest. POS was in-store by the date of the product launch while press activity began two weeks before the product launch and ran for a month.

Local markets

Media planning was flexible in that each local market conducted their own, according to the guideline of using print and posters. Markets were free to recommend other media, provided that a rationale was offered to justify these other media.

January	February	March	April	May
		PR		
			POS	
		Press Adverts		
			Product launch April 1st	

Figure 8.3 HP's tactics – the details of strategy

CASE 6: etc limited: HUMAN RESOURCE CONSULTANTS

Stage 1: Situation

etc limited is a relatively young company (set up in 1992 by four founder directors, all of whom still work within the organisation). It was set up to provide human resource (HR) consultancy services, management development courses and training venues within which that training could take place. It has a turnover of £2 million and now employs 30 staff at three sites in central and south London.

The organisation's weaknesses upon starting up were significant:

- The recession was still in progress (or at least organisations *felt* it to still be in progress) and budgets for HR consultancy had been slashed. Companies had got used to *not* buying such services.
- etc limited's client base was small and heavily overweighted towards the public sector (reflecting the background of the founder directors).
- Most importantly of all, beyond a few personal contacts the organisation had no market presence, and selling consultancy services to service management teams without a significant brand franchise is a thankless task.

Stage 2: Objectives

Maintaining cash flow and increasing the turnover were obviously of crucial importance if etc limited was going to thrive and grow quickly. The marketing programme as a whole was given the goal of increasing sales from £250,000 in 1992 to £1 million by the end of 1995. Simultaneously, in order to create a better balance for the client mix, a target was set of having a minimum of 50 per cent of sales and profits generated by private sector clients. Specific communications objectives were: to raise awareness of etc limited (from a standing start), to increase the target audiences' understanding of the product range on offer (itself an important factor when selling relatively abstract and discretionary purchases), and to create an external image which reflected the internal values of ethical behaviour, professionalism and dedication to delivering value to clients.

Stage 3: Strategy

The communications strategy eventually adopted was relatively modest in scope and very focused in terms of targeting; although 'unglamorous' it has, as we shall see, delivered results.

The crux of the strategy is the interplay of two key premises:

- a relatively small organisation such as etc limited should play to its strengths rather than attempt to be all things to all people;
- the number of clients required to achieve etc limited's objectives is relatively small.

If both of these premises are accepted, then the communications strategy becomes clear: that etc limited should focus on communicating its strengths and proven track record in a few key sectors (in this case the marketing services industry, health service, local government and financial institutions) and, given the small numbers required, concentrate on developing relationships with a few key decision-makers within each sector. Internally, the strategy was known as *Client Relationship Communications*: the internal communications focus was no coincidence. It was central to the success of the communications programme that all staff played their part: in the final analysis all relationships are attributable to *people*, and internal communication to energise staff was a central part of the exercise.

Strategic options

Perhaps not surprisingly, the decision to have a Strategy of *Client Relationship Communications* (which has proved to be extremely successful) was not the first attempt or even the most obvious option. Firstly, an attempt was made to address, in textbook fashion, the key issues underlying certain problems with regard to the corporate brand of etc limited, namely *awareness* and an *educational process* to raise understanding of the products on offer. Both previous attempts floundered.

The 'awareness raising' strategy failed primarily because etc limited could not afford to make enough noise to be heard: available budgets for advertising and media relations were never sufficient to create the level of momentum required, and without that momentum further spend was ultimately being wasted.

The 'educational' strategy failed also, not because of a lack of interest *per se* from target audiences but from a failure to be able to convert that relatively abstract interest into consultancy projects.

Thus, when etc limited published a book on growing small to medium-sized businesses, there was a great deal of interest but little linkage to convert that interest into a business relationship.

Integration of the communications mix

The successful strategy, that of Client Relationship Communication, integrated a small selection of communications tools:

- Advertising was discarded as being too expensive to allow sufficient momentum to be established and too diffuse in nature given the size of the target audience.
- Media relations (part of PR) coverage was generated primarily so that it could be recycled by direct mail, on the assumption, once again, that left to its own devices it would not generate sufficient momentum to be of value.

Instead the strategy used only those communications tools which could be harnessed *directly* to establishing and building client relationships over the long term:

- database marketing;
- seminars on issues of topical interest to audience segments;
- media relations activity in the trade press of targeted sectors;
- more general media relations activity (eg in the management pages of the national quality press), but recycled through direct mail to key targets;
- corporate literature tailored for key sectors;
- sales drive.

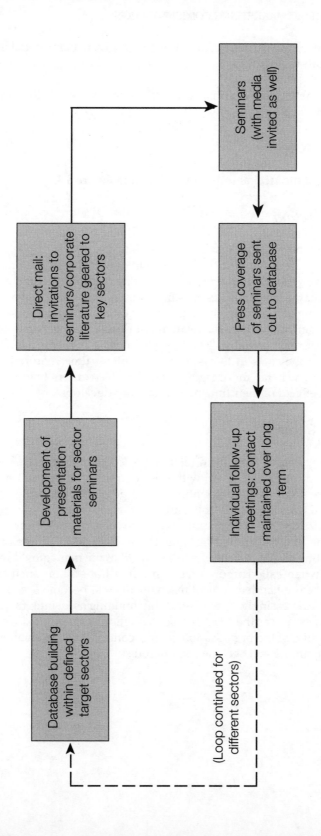

Figure 8.4 etc limited: stages of the tactical roll-out

And so on. The main criteria for using a given part of the marketing communications mix was:

Will this help create or enhance a *relationship* between etc limited and its target markets?

Stage 4: Tactics

The stages of the tactical roll-out are shown in Figure 8.4.

Stage 5: Action

The key to the strategy's success was that *everyone* was responsible: all consultants were given specific responsibilities with the programme and were required to do their part in terms of cultivating relationships and maintaining contacts over the long haul. Responsibility for organisational matters was given to a marketing and communications manager (organising databases, seminars and direct mail) and to a media relations working group, acting in conjunction with an external specialist. The bought-in costs involved were relatively modest, but the costs in terms of the consultant time required to develop relationships was far more significant, with fee-earners being expected to spend 15 per cent of their time on relationship development.

Stage 6: Control

The strategy has, to date, been relatively successful in terms of assisting in meeting marketing objectives, with sales currently riding at £1 million plus and private sector work accounting for 40 per cent of consultancy income. Control and tracking is time-consuming but essential and is primarily geared towards ensuring that consultants live up to their responsibilities within the programme in a disciplined fashion. The individual in charge of control is the marketing manager, with the full support of the managing director being available when called upon. Over time it is hoped that such simple but relatively heavy-handed control mechanisms will become less necessary as consultants increasingly view relationship building as an integral part of their working lives, and as the process assumes a more 'organic' texture within the day-to-day life of the organisation, so the 'control' and 'motivational' aspect of the programme will become less onerous.

CASE 7: INVESCO FUND MANAGERS LIMITED

Stage 1: Situation

INVESCO is one of the world's leading independent fund management companies. With the recent merger between INVESCO and the AIM corporation in the US, INVESCO is now ranked within the top five global investment management companies in the world. Assets under management are over $90 billion and worldwide INVESCO employ over 1500 people.

The company operates out of three US centres – Atlanta, Denver and Houston. In Europe, London and Paris are the centres for operations covering the UK, Continental Europe and the Far East.

In 1990, INVESCO (then known as MIM Britannia) were one of the leading investment managers in the UK and had control of over 15 per cent of the PEPs market and a 5 per cent share of the total mutual funds market in the UK.

However, over the next four years INVESCO suffered a series of major regulatory, financial and management problems that resulted in market share falling to under 1 per cent. The resulting PR was both negative and hostile.

Since then a number of fundamental changes in the business have taken place that have focused INVESCO's retail business. INVESCO now has top quartile performance in all key funds, has restructured the sales team, repositioned the advertising and embarked on a corporate identity programme. This internal business shift has been greatly helped by a shift in external perceptions, brought about by a refocused and re-energised communications strategy.

Today INVESCO can benefit from its independence, a global network of offices and distributors, and the strong performance of its funds in the UK, Europe and South East Asia.

Stage 2: Objectives

There are four key objectives.

The key objective of the communications strategy was to raise the awareness and profile of INVESCO to potential and existing distributors and the general public. The communication process was essential in order to change perceptions and to provide a complete and consistent story about the progress and performance of the company's products and future developments. It was intended that INVESCO reclaim part of the market lost to competitors, especially in PEPs. All products will then produce a reasonable level of return on expenses and be packaged in part as a result of research and distributor need.

Stage 3: Strategy

Strategy

The key to our communications strategy is targeting and focus: focusing on intermediaries rather than the general public, and within the great mass of intermediaries targeting those with the greatest potential benefits for INVESCO.

The strategy is to coordinate our advertising campaign aimed at conveying the core messages of proven fund performance and expertise to the key business generators, and to support that communication through an integral mixture of PR, sales support material, direct mail and presentations. This campaign is generated through consistent advertising in selected national newspapers and intermediary 'trade' magazines. The advertisements contain the same 'core' elements and are consistent in appearance. However, key messages differentiate the ads depending on the target audience.

Strategic options

INVESCO was faced basically with two options. In the face of a (generally) hostile press it could either stop all forms of communication and 'keep quiet' or it could regroup its operations and, when in place, roll out a coordinated platform of communications across a number of different media.

The essential first stage was to rebuild the investment management process in order to provide tangible evidence that INVESCO provided a credible fund management service. Leading on from this an out of focus sales and marketing team was then reconstructed with the key objective of emphasising key products and rebuilding relationships with *selected* intermediaries.

The word 'selected' is important in this context. Previously INVESCO had been selling (or attempting to sell) all its products to all intermediaries. Under the new strategy it could target resources on those intermediaries who were most likely to maximise business potential for INVESCO.

The important second stage was to get the sales team back on the road with a story and a range of products that were better than most of the competitors. As this stage was being planned an integral support programme was introduced consisting of direct communication in the form of literature and performance information to key distributors.

Stages 4 and 5: Tactics and actions

To support the sales team and to widen the message to the selected intermediary audience INVESCO started a programme of seminars. These half-day programmes were aimed at offering intermediaries the opportunity to 'sample' the 'New INVESCO' at first hand.

In the next stage INVESCO undertook extensive research among key potential and existing business introducers. This research was instrumental in deciding to change the advertising propositions and product offering, and emphasised the need for regular personal contact.

The importance of PR was not overlooked. As we have seen, INVESCO's past relationship with the press had been very poor. Once it became clear that it had products that were credible and had initiated the relationship building stage INVESCO began to actively contact the press and rebuild relationships with them. This strategy was quick to produce results and the positive PR began to translate into positive enquiries from intermediaries who for years had not 'trusted' the INVESCO brand.

Finally, when the stages above had been put in place INVESCO began to work on an extensive campaign of advertising. The structure and content of this campaign was partly driven by the impetus of the unfortunate Morgan Grenfell story (Europe became its platform), partly from the research results, and partly from its own intuitive feel for what the market wanted.

INVESCO chose this strategy as it felt this would have the most impact, and each stage would be self-supporting and interactive with each of the others. This has been proved to be correct.

Stage 6: Controls

All marketing expenditure was and is closely monitored. Each stage in the communications plan has been carefully costed and the results measured against the income generated and projected volumes. Each advert is coded so that conversions to actual business can be reported. The effect of close monitoring is to be able to react to placements that work and those that don't. In this way INVESCO can direct its resources to produce the best results and make the case for additional expenditure if it does.

Since the communications strategy was introduced late in 1995, sales have improved substantially, with a year on year increase by December 1996 of just under 115 per cent.

DISCUSSION TOPICS FOR CHAPTER 8

1) How can the SOSTAC model be applied to any marketing communications plan?
2) Choose a successful communications campaign and apply the SOSTAC model to analyse it.
3) Use the SOSTAC system to plan your own marketing communications

---

FURTHER SOSTAC CASES

Further examples of successful marketing communications plans analysed using the SOSTAC system can be found in the 1996 Institute of Practitioners in Advertising Effectiveness Awards Case Manual, IPA, London (tel: 0171 235 7020).

NINE

Planning: how to integrate marketing communications

LEARNING OBJECTIVES

- Understand what is meant by integrated marketing communications.
- Analyse the seven levels of integration.
- Apply the ten golden rules of integration.
- Achieve integration using SOSTAC.

TOPICS COVERED BY THIS CHAPTER

THE DEVELOPMENT OF INTEGRATED MARKETING COMMUNICATIONS

Although integrated marketing communications have been practised for many years the specific term 'integrated marketing communications' has come to have greater significance in the last decade of the second millennium. This chapter explains the significance in terms of the rapidly changing marketing environment. It is our assertion that these changes are not simply evolutionary but that a combination of factors has caused a quantum transformation. Integrated marketing communications as presently conceived is not some temporary fashion but will be of lasting significance in the practice of effective marketing.

A number of books published in recent years have recognised this significant change and sought to improve the understanding and practice of integrated marketing communications. P R Smith in 1993 published *Marketing Communications – An integrated approach* which has been widely used in undergraduate and professional marketing teaching. Also in 1993 Schultz, Tannenbaum and Lauterborn published in America what was a landmark book titled *Integrated Marketing Communications - Pulling it together and making it work*. This book challenged organisations to confront a fundamental dilemma in today's marketing – the fact that mass media advertising, by itself, no longer works effectively and efficiently.

In the United Kingdom in 1995 two similar practitioner books were published: *Integrated Marketing Communications* by Ian Linton and Kevin Morley, and *A Practical Guide to Integrated Marketing Communications* by Tom Brannan. The first of these two books arose out of the then controversial decision by the Rover Car Group, now part of BMW, to move all its marketing support and communications programmes on to one agency – Kevin Morley Marketing. This highlighted the benefits of integrating above the line and below the line marketing communications. This is sometimes called the 'through the line approach'. The second book, by Tom Brannan, who was Chairman of the Chartered Institute of Marketing, sets out to give practical advice on how the successful interaction of each aspect of marketing communications is vital if organisations are to gain maximum effectiveness from a given marketing budget.

DEFINITIONS OF INTEGRATED MARKETING COMMUNICATIONS

Although integrated marketing communications has become increasingly well known in the 1990s on an international scale, there is not yet a common understanding of its full scope nor of its exact definition. This is in spite of the individual words 'integrated', 'marketing' and 'communication' being relatively clear. Table 9.1 illustrates some important elements of a range of definitions.

Although Definition 3 is the most comprehensive there are common elements to all three definitions. The main elements are:

- a reference to all marketing communications;
- the description of a strategic management process;
- the reference to an economic, efficient and effective process;
- it is clear also that the process can be applied to any type of organisation.

Table 9.1 Definitions of integrated marketing communications

- Definition 1:

   The management and control of all market communications.

- Definition 2:

   Ensuring that the brand positioning, personality and messages are delivered synergistically across every element of communication and are delivered from a single consistent strategy.

- Definition 3:

   The strategic analysis, choice, implementation and control of all elements of marketing communications which efficiently, economically and effectively influence transactions between an organisation and its existing and potential customers, consumers and clients.

The first question arising from these definitions then is: 'What are marketing communications?' Marketing communication is a term whose widespread use is comparatively recent. It is now taken to mean all elements of communication that occur in the marketing context. The main elements can be shown in the marketing communications wheel in Figure 9.1.

* Direct marketing covers a number of communication methods including direct mail, telemarketing and direct response advertising.

** Corporate identity is projected through all points of public contact including buildings, signage, uniforms, vehicles, literature and invoices.

Figure 9.1 The marketing communications wheel

However, it can be quickly seen that this wheel represents only those key elements of which can be described as the promotions mix. It is now commonly accepted that all the elements of the marketing mix, that is product, price and place besides promotions, also communicate in important ways. Indeed the elements of the service mix – people, process and physical evidence – also communicate. The combined elements of efficiency (best use of resources), effectiveness (maximum achievement of results) and economy (minimum cost) are illustrated in Figure 9.2.

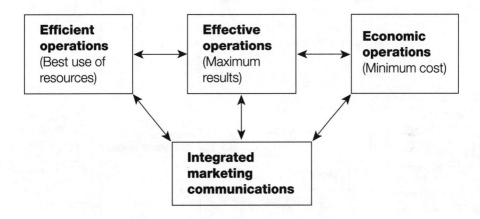

Figure 9.2 Efficient, effective and economic communications

It can be argued that marketing research is part of any effective two-way communication process. All these elements of the marketing mix, the service mix, the promotions mix and marketing research are shown in Figure 9.3 which illustrates the complete integrated marketing communications process. Figure 9.3 also illustrates that integrated marketing communications is part of a deliberate management process. The marketing planning and control model used in this text is the SOSTAC model which was described in more detail in Chapter 7.

THE SEVEN LEVELS OF INTEGRATION

In order to understand the full meaning and process of integrated marketing communications, it is important to define what is meant by the word 'integration' in this context. In the same way as the use of other apparently simple English words can cause confusion, so can 'integrated'. Each author and reader may have a different understanding of the meaning of the word. Careful thought has been given to this problem and we suggest the use of the powerful tool illustrated in Checklist 9.1 which shows integration as occurring at one or more of several levels.

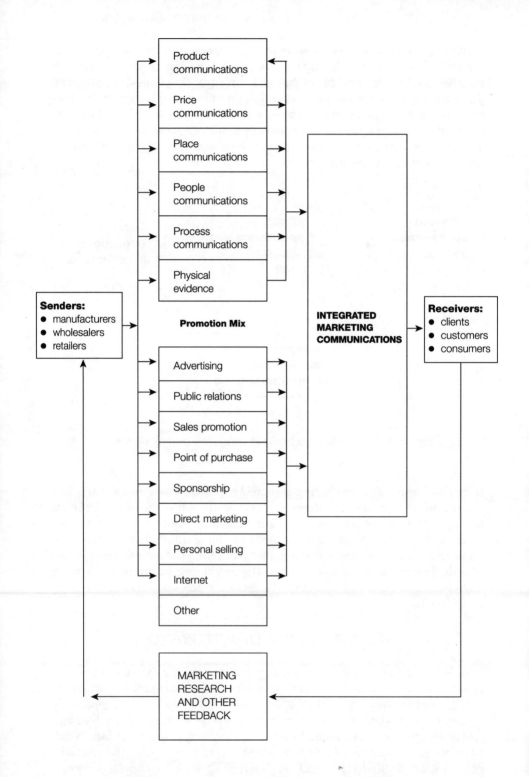

Figure 9.3 The integrated marketing communications process

Checklist 9.1 The seven levels of integration

Level of integration	The degree of integration	Score your organisation out of 10
1. Vertical objectives integration	Do the communication objectives fit with the marketing objectives and with the overall corporate objectives?	
2. Horizontal/ functional integration	Do the marketing communications activities fit well with the other business functions of manufacturing, operations and human resource management?	
3. Marketing mix integration	Is the marketing mix of product, price and place decisions consistent with the required communication messages?	
4. Communications mix integration	Are all the 12 communications tools being used to guide the customer/ consumer/client through each stage of the buying process? Do they all portray a consistent message?	
5. Creative design integration	Is the creative design and execution uniform and consistent with the chosen positioning of the product/service?	
6. Internal/external integration	Are all internal departments and all external agencies employed by the organisation working together to an agreed plan and strategy with regular progress meetings?	
7. Financial integration	Is the budget being used in the most effective and efficient way ensuring that economies of scale are achieved and that long-term investment is optimised?	

Level of integration: Total
(Total score possible 70)

Of these levels perhaps the most important and most fundamental is that of the vertical integration of objectives and activities as described in Chapter 6. The initial conclusion is that it is not possible to have an effective marketing communications objective which is not directly linked to specific marketing objectives and ultimately to specific relevant corporate objectives. All of course come under the umbrella of the corporate mission. This process of integration is cascaded downward through strategies, tactics, actions and control which is the basis of the SOSTAC model (see Chapter 7).

ANALYSIS OF DRIVING AND RESTRAINING FORCES

So far we have assumed that there is an almost natural force which is moving organisations to consider implementing integrated marketing communications. Although the net effect of a combination of a number of factors may be the same it is important to analyse and understand each of these factors in turn. In Checklist 9.2 these driving forces are described. Conversely there are a series of restraining forces and these are illustrated in Checklist 9.3.

MEANS OF ENSURING INTEGRATION

It is possible to use the analysis of the driving and restraining forces for your organisation to plan the most effective manner of ensuring integration. This can be done in stages.

Stage 1 Check the driving forces that apply to your organisation (see Checklist 9.2). Add any additional ones that exist at present.

Stage 2 Check the restraining forces that apply to your organisation (see Checklist 9.3). Add any additional ones that exist at present.

Stage 3 Rank the driving and restraining forces in order of magnitude.

Stage 4 Consider ways of increasing the existing driving forces or adding completely new ones.

Stage 5 Consider ways of decreasing existing restraining forces or of completely removing some.

Stage 6 Remember that it is sometimes easier to gain a small amount on a number of fronts rather than concentrate on the big push in one area.

Stage 7 Remember, especially for large forces, there can be an opposite and nearly equal reaction (Newton's Laws of Motion).

A helpful set of 'ten golden rules of integration' (Smith, 1996) are described in Figure 9.4 which show how managers can ensure that they become integrated and stay integrated in their marketing communications planning.

Checklist 9.2 Forces driving towards integrated marketing communications

Driving force	The strength of these forces	Score your organisation out of 10
1. Pressure on marketing communications budgets	Often the first budget to suffer in times of economic difficulties and falling profits. There is constant pressure for cost savings and increased performance.	
2. Fragmentation of the media	There are literally thousands of media from which to choose. How can effort be concentrated and not fragmented?	
3. Growing international communications	With satellite television and global publications there is an international choice.	
4. Development of electronic communications	Millions of people throughout the world are now connected beneficially through the Internet.	
5. Increasing power of computers	The use of such techniques as databases, data warehousing and data mining have all become possible because of the power of computers.	
6. More sophisticated marketing managers	Marketing managers have now mostly undergone professional training and have become more dominating.	
7. Move from mass advertising	A combination of several of the above factors has stimulated the move from mass advertising to one-to-one marketing.	
8. Economies of scale, synergy of effort	Economies of scale in the choice and use of communication media is yet another driving force towards integration.	
9. Increasing understanding of integrated marketing communications	As integrated marketing communications becomes better defined marketing managers are beginning to understand its power.	
10. Increasing evidence inte-grated marketing communications works	The proof that integrated marketing communications works is a powerful driving force towards its successful use.	
11. Add your own driving forces	There may be circumstances special to your organisation which are driving IMC.	

Strength of IMC Driving Forces: Total
(Total score possible 110)

Checklist 9.3 Forces restraining the move towards integrated marketing communications

Restraining forces	The strength of these forces	Score your organisation out of 10
1. Resistance to change	In most human endeavours there appears to be resistance to change.	
2. Old planning systems	Such systems maintain the status quo in which communication methods are not integrated.	
3. Traditional/rigid organisations/ functional managers	In traditional organisations some managers representing only part of the communication process may inhibit effective integration.	
4. Tight, autocratic control	Integration requires a significant amount of flexible planning and cooperation which may be inhibited by tight, autocratic control.	
5. Specialist external agencies	Agencies have in the past tended to specialise in only one form of communication such as advertising or public relations. Integration has been made more difficult.	
6. Not invented here	Moves to integration are often resisted because the ideas did not originate within the department being required to cooperate.	
7. Turf wars	IMC may be prevented by different departments jockeying for power.	
8. Initial investment in time	IMC does require a significant investment in managerial time. Some managers may not be prepared to commit this time.	
9. Add your own restraining forces	There may be circumstances special to your organisation which are restraining IMC.	

Strength of IMC Restraining Forces: Total
(Total score possible 90)

1. Get senior management support

Get senior management support for the initiative by ensuring firstly that they understand the benefits of integration, and secondly that they support its implementation.

2. Practise vertical and horizontal integration

Put integration on the agenda for meetings of different levels of management and different types of meetings – whether creative sessions or annual reviews. Ensure that it is implemented horizontally, that all managers, not just marketing managers, understand the importance of a consistent message, whether on delivery trucks or through product quality. Ensure also that advertising, PR, sales promotions and other communications means meet and work together and really integrate their message.

3. Use design manual and brand book

Ensure design manual is used to maintain common visual standards for the use of logos, typefaces, colours and the brand book is used to maintain a consistent brand personality across all communications.

4. Focus on a clear marketing communications strategy

Have crystal-clear communications objectives and positioning statements and link core brand values into every communication. Ensure that all communications reinforce, reiterate and add value to (instead of deleting) the brand. Exploit areas of competitive strength and advantage.

5. Start with a zero budget

Build a budget and the communications plan around what you need to do to achieve your objectives. Then practise what simply has to be done.

6. Think customers first

Identify the stages a customer goes through before, during and after a purchase. Develop a sequence of communication activities which will help the customer more favourably through each stage. Design communication around the customer's buying process.

7. Build relationships and brand values

All communications should help to develop stronger relations with customers. Ask how each communication tool helps to do this. Customer retention is sometimes given more importance than customer acquisition. Ensure that each communication strengthens the brand value.

8. Develop a good marketing information system (MkIS)

The MkIS should define who needs what information when integrated marketing communications encourages the development of a system which defines, collects and shares vital information. A customer database, for example, can help direct mail, telesales and the salesforce to help each other.

9. Share artwork and other media

Consider how artwork for one communication tool (eg advertising) can be used in mailshots, exhibitions, point of sale, packaging, new releases, newsletters, Christmas cards and even the Internet.

10. Learn from experience

Be prepared to change it all. Constantly search for the optimum integrated communications mix. Test and improve each year.

Figure 9.4 The '10 golden rules of integration' (Source: Smith, 1996)

THE BENEFITS OF INTEGRATION

In the same article containing the '10 golden rules of integration', Smith (1996) describes the benefits that can accrue to any organisation setting out to really adopt a positive approach to integrated marketing communications. It helps to create competitive advantage and boost sales and profits, and it helps customers while strengthening relationships and simultaneously saving time and money and even stress for the busy marketing manager. So even though integrated marketing communications requires a lot of careful thought it delivers many benefits as described below.

Integrated marketing communications helps to move customers through the various stages of their buying process – before, during and after. It helps an organisation or a brand to consolidate its image, develop a dialogue and nurture a relationship which, ultimately, builds a bond between buyer and seller. This bond can protect the customer from the inevitable onslaught of competition thereby keeping the customer for life (not just for Christmas). This is a very powerful advantage.

Integrated marketing communications also increases profits through increased effectiveness. At its most basic level, a unified message has more impact than a disjointed myriad of messages. A consistent, consolidated and crystal-clear communication strategy has a better chance of cutting through the 'noise' of several thousand commercial messages which bombard individuals every day. At another level, initial research suggests that images shared across advertising and direct mail campaigns boost advertising awareness and, simultaneously, increase response to the mailshot.

Integrated marketing communications can boost sales by stretching messages across both communication tools and business functions to create more awareness for customers to become aroused and, ultimately, buy a product or service on a repeat basis. Carefully linked messages help buyers by providing them with timely reminders, relevant information and, where necessary, special offers which move them more comfortably through the stages of their buying process, reducing the misery of choice in a complex and busy world.

Integrated marketing communications also make the range of messages more consistent and, in turn, more credible. This reduces risk in the mind of the buyer which then shortens the search process and helps to dictate the outcome of the brand comparisons.

Unintegrated or disintegrated communications, on the other hand, send disjointed messages which dilute message impact and sometimes confuse, frustrate and arguably arouse anxiety in some customers. In contrast, integrated communications present a reasoned sense of order. Consistent images and relevant, useful messages help nurture long-term relationships with customers. This is where customer databases can identify which customers need what information and when – throughout their whole buying process.

Integrated marketing communications also save money as they can eliminate some duplications in areas like graphics and photography which can be shared across, say, advertising exhibitions and sales literature. Agency fees may be reduced when using a single agency for all communications. But even with several agencies, time can also be saved in meetings, whether strategic, tactical or just briefings, which bring all the disciplines together. As well as fusing bright minds into synergetic sparks, multi-disciplinary meetings reduce repetition which in turn reduces workloads and subsequent stress levels.

Lastly, the internal benefits of integrated marketing communications should not be forgotten. Integration can continue beyond communications to all the other elements of the marketing mix decisions such as product decisions, price decisions and place decisions, so that the customer is presented with a complete, comprehensive and consistent pattern. In turn the marketing mix decisions will be better integrated with the other business functions. (For a discussion of the principles of Integrated Marketing Communications see pages 65–70.)

INTEGRATION USING THE SOSTAC MODEL

Chapter 7 has described the SOSTAC planning model and its application in some detail. The power of the model is its widespread application. At its most basic level the separate steps of:

Situation
Objective
Strategy
Tactics
Action
Control

represent a generic and systematic planning process. Application of the model in its entirety will lead to a well thought-out solution. Almost by definition this solution will be an integrated one. The integration will arise naturally out of the process of carefully considering each stage in turn. Getting the strategic SOS stages (situation analysis, objective setting and strategy development) will lay the firm foundations for an integrated marketing communications plan. The operational stages of tactics, action and control will then lead to an integrated action plan. The control methods ensure that integration is working in practice, with necessary improvements being made in the light of experience.

DISCUSSION TOPICS FOR CHAPTER 9

1) What is meant by the term 'integrated marketing communications'?
2) What elements comprise the 'marketing communications wheel'?
3) Debate the seven levels of integration. Do they add to an understanding of effective integrated marketing communications?
4) What forces are driving towards integrated marketing communications?
5) What forces are restraining the move towards integrated marketing communications?

REFERENCES

Brannan, T (1995) *A Practical Guide to Integrated Marketing Communications*, Kogan Page, London

Linton, I and Morley, K (1995) *Integrated Marketing Communications*, Butterworth-Heinemann, Oxford

Schultz, D E, Tannenbaum, R E and Lauterborn, R E (1993) *Integrated Marketing Communications – Pulling it together and making it work*, NTC, Chicago

Smith, P R (1996) 'Benefits and barriers to integrated marketing communications, *Admap*, February

Smith, P R (1996) *Marketing Planning* (CD ROM), Multimedia Marketing Consortium, London

Smith, P R (1998) *Marketing Communications – An integrated approach*, 2nd edn, Kogan Page, London

T E N

Strategic issues: the Internet

LEARNING OBJECTIVES

- Understand the rapid nature of IT change.
- Understand the concept of the Internet.
- Grasp how the Internet can help marketers.
- Grasp how the Internet can hinder marketers.
- Consider developing online strategies.

TOPICS COVERED BY THIS CHAPTER

CHANGE AND THE CHANGING NATURE OF IT

Everything changes including products, people, organisations and technology. Shorter product lifecycles, faster NPD cycles, agile new competitors, mobile global organisations, more mobile workforces, changing social values, new desires, new pressures, new needs, new markets and technological shock-waves – these create change. Are they sources of insecurity or of opportunity? Customers move on, change jobs, die. Companies grow, merge and go bust. Where are Tom Peters' 'excellent' companies now? Change is constant. It needs to be monitored, harnessed and exploited.

Information technology (IT) changes very quickly. The pace of IT change is accelerating, and IT arguably changes everything. It is important to recognise this change and adapt accordingly. Rapidly changing IT brings advantages and disadvantages to society, businesses and marketers in particular. From confusion and anxiety created by information overload, to 'dumb-down' individuals who rely on intelligent agents to search for specific information, IT is changing the way we think, the way we read, the way we move, our manners, our friends, in fact our whole social fabric. Some researchers insist that IT can now even create life – completely artificial organisms which can respire, reproduce, mutate, react to their environment and live or die according to the principles of natural selection. Perhaps they could breed captive customers as opposed to virulent viruses. Now there's a challenging thought for marketers – creating your own customers, payment systems and consumption patterns!

Others argue that tomorrow's digital shanty towns and the 'IT underclass' will be countered by new problem-solving digital communities. On top of this, shifts in customer buying power through consumer IT will be countered by vast accurate marketing databases held by mega corporations. IT is forcing marketing organisations like advertising agencies to reconsider their existence. As media fragment and websites proliferate, the concept of the advertising agency as we know it today may become redundant. Whether it is competitive paranoia or an appreciation of the IT opportunity, marketers are moving towards digital marketing. Information technology, and the Internet in particular, present more than new media opportunities. The Internet offers marketers a diverse range of features some of which can help and some of which can hinder.

It is currently argued that tomorrow's industrial winners will be those firms that seize and exploit technology as a strategic weapon. One clear implication emerges: marketers have got to learn and relearn IT every three years. As always, we can learn from history since the Victorians had e-mail, virtual museums and cyber crime over a hundred years ago. This chapter looks at all of this in more detail as well as the specific problems and opportunities facing marketers in this new web-wired marketing environment. We first consider IT-driven 'change' in some more detail. The world of information technology is a rapidly changing one. This chapter attempts to capture this feeling of change by presenting a series of carefully selected information 'bites' and information 'chunks' drawn from a wide variety of sources.

Recognise IT change

Change can creep up seemingly slowly. The unaware can miss out. Often, it is the normalisation and quiet acceptance of news about change that makes it unworthy of conversation or even observation. News about cloning and artificial intelligence appear normal because the news is delivered by the same news readers wearing suits instead of Star Trek uniforms. It is easy to miss out and not recognise change that will affect an organisation's future, eg:

> 'I could have travelled the length and breadth of this country and talked with the best people, and I can assure you that data processing is a fad that won't last out the year.' Editor in charge of Prentice Hall Business Books, 1957.
>
> *(Screen Digest*, quoted in *New Media Age*, 27 June 1996, p 8)

IT grows rapidly

> All the technological knowledge we worked with in 1992 will represent only 1% of the knowledge that will be available in 2050. If you're retired by then so 10,000% increase is not relevant... but within five years you will have 1,000% increase in IT power.
>
> (World Futurist Society)

IT creates information overload – 'information fatigue syndrome'

> Data proliferation seems to be rampant. Everyone has too much reading to do. Too much information can be as dangerous as too little information. Managers drown in a sea of information. Too much information can cause mental anguish and even cause physical illness among managers while simultaneously strangling the individual's ability to make good decisions. '...unmanageable choice can lead to information overload, confusion and anxiety. The confusion arising from an excess of choice can therefore leave consumers feeling out of control – an apparent contradiction we call the consumer in/out of control paradox' (Henley Centre for Forecasting).
>
> (Dwyer, 1997)

1,000 books a day:

'Almost 1,000 books are published daily around the world.'

(Source: Hubbard, 1996)

A lifetime in a day:

'A weekday edition of the *New York Times* contains more information than the average person was likely to come across in a lifetime in 17th-century England.'

(Source: Wurman, 1996)

IT creates 'dumb-down humans'

Intelligent agents are, some say, both 'wrong and evil'. Others suggest that they are an issue of real consequence to the near future of culture and society, while others say that intelligent software makes people stupid.

(Dwyer, 1996)

There are three classes of agents: 'fetch it' agents will collect and assemble information according to a pre-assembled template, 'do-it' agents who will deliver messages and update recipient files, 'watchdog' agents who will scan traffic until a pre-defined pattern triggers an alert and a report.

(Coulson-Thomas, 1996)

Intelligent agent based on neural networks will learn from selections the user makes of its initial searches, and will refine future searches to take into account its user's behaviour.

(Dwyer, 1996)

No more stumbling across golden nuggets of knowledge discovered when browsing through papers and magazines. When we need to know the population of Fiji, we will just ask the computer, 'What is the population of Fiji?'

IT changes the way we think

The warm bath effect of reading your favourite newspaper has gone and the atmosphere is more alert, more cynical, sharper. Over this lies the long-term effect of the way the information explosion is changing the way people think.

(Watts, 1995)

IT changes the way we read

A pilot scheme in schools discovered that CD ROMs can create a new condition for literacy. Children began to use information books better as a result of their experiences with CD ROMs where they learned to use the index. As they got more used to using the index they transferred this skill to books. Now they use information books better.

(Marshall, 1996)

IT changes the way we watch

As TV stations and websites proliferate, those with the buttons or the mouse seize power. The zap factor emerged when TV remote controls appeared many years ago. Whoever had the button seized control over a family's viewing – at least momentarily. Even individuals engaged in solus viewing got caught up with the habit of zapping as attention spans decreased and restless non loyal viewers zapped continually in search of fulfilment. Split screen TV emerged to show a second station simultaneously in a corner of the main screen. Multiscreen TV may yet become popular as several stations' programmes are shown in sections of the same TV screen.

IT changes what we watch

The introduction of hundreds of channels will lead to fragmentation of audiences and the arrival of various forms of interactivity will engender different types of relationships with consumers... TV might exist without advertising at all... next year Rupert Murdoch could well be transmitting 100 channels rising to 500 or more over the next decade... Thus it will be necessary to develop a total communications approach which can be extended from television advertising through to sponsorships, informercials, Web sites and so on.

(Sheldon, 1996)

IT changes the way we move

From washing machines, to bleepers, to talking diaries and now 'hyperinstruments' at MIT Laboratories which can be played without touching them.

Small electric currents that run through the body will jump across a smaller air gap to electrodes on the surface of these instruments, so the electrodes become sensors for monitoring hand position... Some instruments can even be played as invisible piano keys in the air. The same technology is used to move a cursor on a computer screen just by pointing at it, or to flip pages of an electronic newspaper by hand gestures.

(Libbenga, 1996)

IT changes manners

A decade ago, if you telephoned a friend and reached an answering machine, you probably thought 'how rude'. Today you are more likely to be miffed by your thoughtless friends who refuse to buy one.

(Fortune, 20 March 1995, p 60)

IT changes friendship

We may be moving into a world in which even notions of friendship change. If workplaces are always changing and work is always changing as well as house moving, you can't even hold friendships together.

(Hutton, 1995)

IT fuels love

Hot Badges are programmed to find a partner. The badges glow when another wearer with similar likes and dislikes comes within range. And IT can go a step further, with virtual presents. Lovers can send each other cyberspace gifts which can range from flowers to Hawaiian holidays to pet elephants. A virtual thought from virtual presents (http://www.virtualpresents.com/). Valentine poems (http://valentine.chadwyck.co.uk) and of course blind dates are also available (http://www.blinddate.co.uk).

IT might change our capacity to love, weep, steal and then to feel shame

Arthur C. Clarke, author of *2001: Space Odyssey* and the more recent *3001: The Final Odyssey*, believes that technology could 'alter our capacity to love, to weep, to steal and then to feel shame, I think that in the long run, yes, they may. Modern technology separates us from everyday reality'.

(Clarke, 1997)

IT becomes sociable?

How do we make electronic transactions a satisfying social experience? Going to a museum, a store or a movie is a tribal experience. There is already evidence of community spirit on the net. People are generally happy to help and to share information if the request is sensible, relevant to the news group and presented within the basic rules of etiquette for the net (netiquette).

IT creates new problem-solving communities

It has been said that society could not build today such things as the pyramids, because we have lost a sense of 'collective' intelligence and co-operation; with such developments as the Internet and multimedia, could we see a collective approach to problem solving, a massively parallel society, so to speak?

(Negroponte, 1995)

IT creates digital shanty towns

There is a danger that digital communities will more resemble shanty towns than friendly villages. The danger arises if the growth of new private media channels delivering targeted content to fragmented audiences is not counter-balanced by public sources of content... What is required of it so that citizens are in control of information and not 'disempowered, misled or overwhelmed'? By analysing the economics of information, Graham believes that there will be a gap between high quality private information and poor quality public information... High fixed costs and low marginal costs characterise the production of information (eg CD ROMs).

(Graham, 1997)

IT creates an underclass

The world of information technology is a world made for a very fortunate few, maybe 20% of the population; the people who are called these days the 'symbolic analysts', who can work with numbers and ideas, who live in a little leafy suburb surrounded by high spiked gates and guards; who sit with their little computers and their telephones and deal with ideas and information all over the world. And they don't venture downtown, and they don't use the public transport system, and when they do travel its in the front parts of international aeroplanes. And they'll have a nice life. And then there will be the rest, who don't have access to this kind of technology, who don't know how to use it, who don't know how to make products out of it. And they live downtown, and they use public transport, and they'll have a tough time. And this is the underclass.

(Handy, 1995)

> *The collapse of governments under (or over) the weight of wires:*
>
> 'I like the unapologetic conviction with which he (Louis Rossetto, co-founder of *Wired* magazine) speaks about the great millennial *Wired* enchilada: the collapse of governments and economies under the weight of gajillion interconnected, deregulated fiber-optic strands; the rise of the global village; the triumph of one-to-many communication; the demise of the clueless press.'
>
> (Source: Quittner, 1996)

IT changes buying power

While the Internet will increase the power of buyers (to shop around globally), MIT's Nicholas Negroponte, tells the story of a woman who was turned down when she wanted to buy a $20k Ford for $17k. She subsequently asked a discussion group on cars whether anyone else was interested in this car for $17k. She got 20 positive responses. She then explained that she still wanted the car at $17,000 but that she also wanted 20 of them. The salesman couldn't have been more pleased to oblige. On the other hand massive marketing databases may tip the power back into the hands of sellers.

Online auctions and online sales sell help buyers by offering an alternative route to purchase. Some industrial buyers make extensive electronic purchases, e.g. General Electric has a Web-based Trading Process Network which will account for about $1 billion of its purchases during 1997.

(Stipp, 1996)

IT changes the way we buy
Automated shoppers or 'BOTS' will increasingly help shoppers to find what they need. Unfortunately, many 'BOTS' will search for the cheapest price while perhaps ignoring other criteria such as quality.

IT changes ad agencies

'We cannot assume we are going to continue with the same structure.' William Eccleshare, strategic planning director at JWT.

'HHCL dropped "advertising agency" from its name last year. One creative idea must now fit into all forms of fragmented media – from televisions to CD ROMs.'

IT changes clients

Back in 1995, P&G's chairman, Edwin Artz, told agencies that unless Madison Avenue agencies get their interactive act together, companies like his will find other ways to tell consumers about their products. But brand advertisers also need network distribution – just like their products need shelf space at Walmart far more than they need colourful packaging. Could P&G build a global brand without a single TV ad? What about a national brand? How about a line extension?

(Schrage, 1995)

Marketers feel that very few ad agencies are equipped to help them market via the information superhighway (*Advertising Age* 95 Survey of 280 top US executives). Nearly half say they will not need an agency at all if the infobahn allows them to communicate directly with their customers via shopping channels, CD ROM catalogues, multimedia kiosk and online services.

(Arden, 1995)

IT fuels competitive paranoia

Managers feel that their business will be threatened by a competitor's use of the Internet. 59% feel that competitor's use of the Internet will become threatening. 76% stated that their competitors were already using the Internet. Threat will come from UK competitors (25%), competitors abroad (21%), or global competitors. 79% believe their career opportunities will be enhanced by having personal expertise in electronic commerce. (Media In Retail Group Survey of commercial use of the Internet.)

(New Media Age, 13 June 1996)

IT changes the nature of competition

Smaller organisations with high quality Web sites can compete head on with larger organisations. The Internet knows no geographical boundaries. Audiences know only what they see, hear and experience. Web sites can position an organisation in the mind of an audience. Borders and barriers disappear as the Internet offers global accessibility instantaneously. The size of organisation may be less relevant than quality of Web site.

IT creates life?

Create a completely artificial organism – which can respire, reproduce, mutate and react to its environment, and live or die according to the principles of natural selection.

...So if a computer virus can be 'alive' why not try and engineer an organism that offers more practical benefits? The creatures have a lifespan of around 40 hours, depending how well they are cared for. They fulfil all biological criteria for life: they eat, breed, compete for natural resources and adapt to their environments. ... each creature has a virtual blood stream and a virtual endocrinal system with sex drive 'hormones' ... these are segments of code that become active in its blood stream when the creature reaches puberty, they accumulate over time to create a sex drive – a motivational situation – that makes the brain tell the creature to go off and, er, have a bit of fun, which then reduces the drive. Similar principles hold true for urges like hunger, thirst and even boredom. When the creature mates (a tasteful off-screen affair – 'like a firm handshake') their genetic code is combined to create an entirely new offspring.

(Toor, 1996)

Keep IT in perspective – we're born, we live for a brief moment, and we die

It's been happening for a long time. Technology is not changing it much, if at all. Things don't have to change the world to be important. The web is going to be very important. Is it going to be a life changing event for millions of people? No. I mean, maybe. It's not an assured Yes at this point. And it'll probably creep up on people. It's certainly not going to be like the first time somebody saw a television. It's certainly not going to be as profound as when someone in Nebraska first heard a radio broadcast. It's not going to be that profound...

We live in an information economy, but I don't believe we live in an information society. People are thinking less than they used to. It's primarily because of television. People are reading less. So I don't see most people using the web to get more information. We're already in information overload... When you're young, you look at television and think, there's a conspiracy, the networks have conspired to dumb us down. But when you get a little older, you realise that's not true. The networks are in business to give people exactly what they want. That's a far more depressing thought. Conspiracy is optimistic!

(Jobs, 1996)

Seize and exploit IT

'The *Industrial Winners* will be those firms that *seize and exploit technology* as a strategic weapon.'

(Booz-Allen & Hamilton)

Got to learn IT every three years

Change is happening very fast. The things that were right five, three, two years ago won't work well enough in two, three, five years time to come. So we have got to learn new things not once in a lifetime, but every three or five years. And if we don't, we're missing out on some part of the possibilities of the new technology. Now that's very exciting, but very demanding. Some people can keep up, but others can't.

(Handy, 1995)

Learn from history – the Victorian 'Great Highway of Thought'

The Victorians were familiar with, in their own way, e-mail, virtual museums and cyber crime. Transatlantic cable 1858; 3-D tangible e-mail – pneumatic tubes were used in big cities to carry messages over short distances to district post offices. (Still used for cash today.) Compression and encryption emerged with a form of data compression called Philips code which substituted letters for whole phrases (like BTW – by the way!); hackers cut wires. Samuel Morse, the American Telegraph pioneer who invented Morse code – and who had visions of distant husbands communicating with their wives by telegraph, and lovers exchanging clandestine messages over the wires – referred to the telegraph as the 'Great Highway of Thought'.

(Standage, 1996)

What is the Internet?

The Internet is just an international network of computers linked together. Once you're hooked up and plugged in you can rocket around computers across the world, drop into discussion groups, read bulletin boards, and share ideas, photos, videos, articles, news and games. Visit virtual shopping malls, buy products, tour Universal Studios, the Louvre in Paris or watch the Rolling Stones play a concert. The Net has a unique combination of anonymity (who knows who you really are?) and intrusiveness (junk e-mail). Estimates suggest that hundreds of millions of customers will be moving out of the market-place and into market space – cyberspace – the new electronic frontier. Marketers have to try to identify which industries will be impacted 'first, last, hardest and lightest'.

The Internet provides an endless array of both useful and useless types of information. You can: discover how many cans of Coke are left in a Coke machine on the other side of the world; watch live coffee being brewed in a coffee pot; hear President Clinton's cat; make contact with old and new friends; tour a museum; and explore libraries and encyclopaedias, all online.

Baebhen Schutte is alive

Baebhen Schutte is alive because of the Internet. At just five days old, she is the youngest ever recipient of a transplanted organ. Her parents found the information that led them to King's College Hospital in London on the Internet. Her parents live in Dublin. The day after I read about Baebhen I heard a radio report which stated that French police had arrested 49 people in connection with an Internet-based paedophile ring.

(Source: *Nua Surveys*, March 1998)

There is no doubt about it – from ethical, moral and social perspectives the Internet has both good and bad aspects. Equally in marketing, the Internet has its positive and negative features. Before exploring how the Internet can firstly, help marketers and secondly, hinder marketers, remember that:

- the Internet is still largely misunderstood;
- cybermarkets are much faster changing than traditional markets, eg Netscape established a seemingly unassailable lead (over 80% market share) by flooding online with free copies of its browser software. Internet Explorer is attacking it vigorously and eating into Netscape's market share;
- cybermarket models have extreme polemic changes – there is no 'norm' model, eg AOL (America On Line) used to pay ABC News for content. Now ABC pays AOL to place its content on AOL pages. 'Old World businesses' may struggle to keep up with the third millennium business models;
- cybermarkets require new marketing marriages (alliances) – whether paid for or pure alliances, new marketing partnerships open up huge cyber opportunities. The BBC's record breaking Web cast for golf's Ryder Cup was based upon the BBC providing the content, Progressive Networks providing the technology and various ISPs (Internet Service Providers) providing the backbone;
- the Internet impacts different markets at different levels. Find out what proportion of existing and future customers have access to the Internet, and what they would like to do with it.

Despite the fast-changing uncharted waters and overall unstable nature of the Internet, it can help marketers in more ways than one. Both the organisation's own Web site and those of other organisations and associated technologies can help marketers in many ways, from gathering market research, to database building, relationship management, customer service, new product development, internal communications, cost reduction and last but not least, promotion, selling and distribution.

HOW CAN THE INTERNET HELP MARKETERS?

1. Marketing research

Market information
Competitor information
Customer information
Miscellaneous information
Collect cost-saving ideas

2. Database building

World-wide club
Dynamic relationship marketing

3. Customer service

Self-servicing customers
Self-service customer abuse
Self-service cost savings

4. New product development

Collecting new ideas
Tailor-made products
Accelerating NPD

5. Internal communications

Intranets
Extranets

6. Cost reduction

Print and distribution
Phone calls
Customer service
Collecting cost-saving tips
Revenue generation

7. Distribution

Products
Services
Purchases

8. Selling

Few fairytale sales stories
New markets
Small value, big turnover
Sales management tool

9. Promotion

Have a presence
Interactive advertising
Creative sponsorship
Sales promotions
Public relations
Database marketing

1. Marketing research

There is a lot of marketing research that can be collected on the Net, ranging from market analysis to customer interviews, through to creative ideas. The Net provides a bountiful channel for customer research.

As with any marketing intelligence and information system, the defining of what information is needed is the crucial first stage. The next stage is finding or sourcing the information and logging these sources for future use. Next is filing it – a skill not taught in universities. Finally, the information is used to reduce risk and make better decisions. The problem is that there is more information available today than ever before. The Internet adds a huge resource, so huge that some feel that the Internet, alongside other new sources, provides too much information for the average manager to cope with. Having said that, the Net still provides a fast and sometimes free resource. It is worth getting to know what is available. Keeping a log of useful sources is essential.

Filing it or flinging it? Lost file = lost business

'It is increasingly important to find critical ones (documents) quickly. Bruce Duff, Information Dimensions vice-president, cites the case of US airline Valuejet, whose grounding after a series of crashes was prolonged because the company could not find the required documents held within the company.'

(Source: *New Media Age*, January 1997)

Searching for information on the Net can be simplified by using intelligent – or 'Web-savvy' – agents. 'New products like Surfbot and WebCompass can gather information from your favourite sites while you sleep and deliver you a personalised newspaper every morning' (Dibbell, 1996). WWW Wanderer, Wandex and WWW Worm systems allow users to insert a keyword and wait for a list of what is available. Some intelligent agents are being developed to cope with specific questions like 'What is the population of Fiji?' It is worth asking friends and business colleagues for the addresses of any useful user groups, news groups, mailing lists and Web sites devoted to your speciality or particular area of interest.

Building natural selection into intelligent agents

'Pattie Maes, MIT, designed a programme to keep abreast of the flood of news on the Internet. She pitted slightly different retrieval agents against one another for the user's approval. Those that brought back the most interesting articles were permitted to pass their "genes" on to the next generation, some making precise copies of themselves, some introducing small mutations, others reproducing "sexually" by swapping patches of code with fellow agents. The net result: a self-adapting news feed that proves as flexible and fine-tuned as evolution itself.'

(Source: *Time Magazine*, 1 July 1996)

Market information

The Internet provides a rich resource for research. From government reports and statistics to tourist boards, newspapers to journals, a vast amount of background market information is freely available. Commercial sources also offer a wide array of information which must be purchased. It is possible to tap into news groups and discussion groups asking if anyone knows where specific types of information might be found. Members are usually happy to help their Net colleagues by pointing them in the right direction. Although the Net is a quarter of a century old, it is still in its relative embryonic state, and so a sense of goodwill still prevails in cyber communities as long as visitors maintain reasonable standards of good manners or 'netiquette'. Many newspapers, journals and press clipping services offer search facilities so that articles about specifically named companies, brands, products, industries and individuals can be tracked. Some services are currently free and others charge for certain sections. The first 'port of call' for any job candidates who want to know more about their potential employers should be the potential employer's Web site (followed by its competitors' Web sites).

Competitor information

Whether about your own company or a competitor's the Net reveals all. Well, as much as an organisation wants to reveal when it puts up its own site on the Web. An organisation's Web site provides useful information. The first port of call for competitor information is often the competitor's Web site as it reveals something about the organisation, its employees, its culture, internal newsletters, new products, new visions and sometimes hard information such as financial results. Carrying out word searches for brands, competitors or even your own organisation can reveal what others are saying about your organisation. Some organisations constantly monitor relevant news groups and discussion groups for any comments about their brands/organisation. There are also several information organisations online who charge per enquiry for delivering an organisation's financial results and analysis of results online. Monitoring an organisation's own Web site's visitors can also reveal which competitors visit which pages of the site. Incidentally, monitoring the most popular pages may reveal product preferences among customers and therefore give clues about which products might be worth supporting with heavier promotional spends.

Customer information

Online feedback from customers visiting a Web site provides the opportunity to carry out a continual focus group. Imagine running a year-long focus group to really find out what makes customers tick. The Net can provide a continual dialogue between customer and company (eg MTV have year-long focus groups running through their Web site). This does not replace regular face-to-face focus groups but it does add a rich layer of information. The Web visitors become collaborators in the creative process, eg a McDonald's online visitor's question: 'Why didn't I get a shamrock on St Patrick's Day?' prompted a possible new promotional idea for next year. The power of good branding on the Net is apparent, particularly when more McDonald's customer feedback revealed 'seeing your logo on the Net made me hungry' (a classic stimulus–response model suggesting that humans can also be conditioned to salivate upon receipt of certain stimuli, just like Pavlov's dogs).

> *'It's as if they worked here. No, it's as if they lived here.'*
>
> This is how MTV feel about their online discussions from customers at their Web site.

There are commercial information suppliers on the Net who can also supply specific information at a price. Another Net source is discussion groups covering a particular interest area – whether it's ballet or beer, politics or pinball, churches or charities, discussion group members often help by pointing an enquirer to a new source. It is worth asking colleagues about useful sites and sources on the Net.

Miscellaneous information

Online research can collect information and ideas about new products, new promotions and even cost-saving ideas. These are all discussed later.

Spies on the Net

The National Computer Intelligence in the US reports that redundant US spies have given up traditional spy gadgetry and are using the Net to compile information on a scale that is unprecedented.

(Source: *Nua Surveys*, September 1997)

2. Database building

With thousands, hundred of thousands and sometimes millions of interested visitors entering a particular Web site, several opportunities arise: trapping their data on to a database and developing a dialogue, which support a strategy of relationship marketing. The dialogue can be both online and offline, with real or virtual Christmas cards, catalogues, special offers, loyalty schemes, etc. The full details of the visitor are usually captured either through registration (when entering the site) or other form-filling activities required for competitions, free gifts and further information.

World-wide club

Today's database and relationship marketing techniques help to build sophisticated membership clubs. As Mike Elms says, 'In today's global village there is something intensely satisfying about forming a part of a world-wide club and discovering shared interests with someone on the other side of the planet... tribal instincts are still strong... we still all want to share a sense of society and community'. (See Appendix 10.2 for more on creating virtual communities.) The Internet provides this opportunity. The Internet Sky Blue Army is one such example of just how satisfying it can be.

Coventry City FC & Virtual Houdini

A Coventry City Football Club user group decided that although their beloved club was regularly found languishing around the relegation zone, it was a truly amazing escapist feat. The Houdini T-shirt listed the last-day escapes from relegation – all 10 of them. An online committee was formed. Various members used their own Web sites to display their proposed T-shirt designs. An online vote decided which design was preferred. A T-shirt company was sourced online, the design passed down the line and 150 T-shirts were printed, bought, despatched and worn very proudly by the CCFC fans and regularly applauded by opposition fans when seen.

(Source: Paul McFarland, 1998)

Dynamic relationship marketing

There is now the opportunity for dynamic relationship marketing to move away from mass images towards tailored messages (mass customisation) and direct feedback, delivering a dreamlike dialogue between the brand and the customer. It has been suggested that brands should be seen as places; open-ended, multimedia and based on a sense of community (eg the community feels creative when bringing in a bottle for a refill at the Body Shop). Discussion groups, member involvement and speedy responses all help to create a sense of involvement and a type of 'active ownership' of the brand itself. Whereas brand equity may have been traditionally visually driven, in the online world brand equity may be driven by interactivity, easy accessibility and immediacy. The relationship may also be nurtured by mixing online and offline activities, such as a synchronised call-back system available to all Web site visitors.

Dynamic relationship marketing encourages mass customisation, which not only reduces operating expenses, but offers a permanent advantage. The first competitor to implement 1:1 marketing will steal an advantage. And if the relationship is invested in and nurtured carefully it will be extremely difficult, if not impossible, for the losers in this competition to catch the winners.

3. Customer service

Self-service customer service

Well designed Web sites can offer around-the-clock service for customers who have access to the Internet. In fact customers can service themselves. Most customer service departments deal with recurring questions that can be easily solved with simple and friendly advice. FAQs (Frequently Asked Questions) can be answered online instantaneously, clearly and in a polite, friendly and personal manner (see Carol Mickleborough, below). It is possible to build in personalised messages to the customer to check that everything is now all right. Any problems which cannot be solved online must be acknowledged and followed up by the customer service team within what the average customer considers to be a reasonable period of time.

Who is Carol Mickleborough?

'She writes 10 million letters to customers a year. To many of the 600,000 British Airways Executive Club members her name means something. One in three customer complaints is addressed to her. One in 10 customer phone calls requests Carol by name. Research reveals that one in 10, a staggering 60,000 people, already believes they have a personal relationship with Carol.'

(Source: David Haigh, *Marketing Business*, March 1997)

Self-service customer abuse

Any customer service facilities can damage customer relations if the responses are slow, ineffective or non-existent. The problems are aggravated, however, when already agitated customers with problems cannot get through or cannot get a clear or friendly answer. This is particularly true of the Internet. A *Computerworld* magazine survey tested the customer service response times of the Fortune Top 50 companies. The response to enquiries made through their Web sites varied enormously. On the Internet expectations of speedy responses are high. Only one third of the companies bothered to respond within 24 hours, and some, including Mobil, Nike and US Airways, didn't bother to respond at all. Their Web sites have generated dissatisfied customers because the problems of the latter had apparently been ignored. You don't have to be abusive to customers to insult them, a lack of response will suffice. However it isn't hard to improve as most organisations are starting from a relatively low level of customer service on the Web.

Self-service cost savings

Self-servicing customers save the organisation time and money. For example, Sun's round-the-clock technical documents facility, which allows customers to help themselves, has decreased customer calls by 20 per cent. Paul McFarland reinforces this idea by adding a 'zero cost way to promote a Web site to an absolutely key target audience' – use the recorded message on the switchboard's automated operator system. When calls are intercepted before reaching the operator the system tells callers which numbers to press for various departments. The Web address should also be given out and callers advised that they can also send an e-mail, order brochures and annual reports, request press information and find answers to FAQs on the Web site if preferred. A proportion of callers will hang up and hit the Web. Those who don't will get ahead in the queue and their calls will be answered more quickly. Result: 'those who hang up and those that hang on will both be satisfied'. Results may be particularly positive when a switchboard is jammed by a crisis, a product launch or a press announcement.

4. New product development (NPD)

Given that all markets constantly pull away from all products because of the underlying change factors, whether they be political, economic, social, technical, ethical or demographic, it follows that products and services have to be constantly improved, revamped and replaced. Many successful companies have NPD policies which ensure their long-term survival, eg Gillette require 30 per cent of their annual sales to come from new products (which are defined as being launched within the last five years). Other organisations are less rigorous in their approach to NPD. Whichever approach is taken, the Internet can help. But first, a word of warning: before encouraging customer suggestions, ensure there is a system in place to cope with the receipt, acknowledgement, analysis, selection development and feedback. This 'thinking overhead' must not underestimate the myriad responses that may emerge.

Collecting creative ideas

Whether for sales promotions or for new products, the Web site provides a fruitful source of ideas from customers visiting it. For example, the underwear company, Jo Boxer, asked customers via a bulletin board to submit their favourite underwear stories. They got over 10,000 responses, the best of which will be published in a book. They also created a nice mailing list, which could be turned into a proper database if future responses are collected and filed carefully. And, of course, the online focus groups (discussed in the marketing research section) as well as discussion groups can generate new ideas for tomorrow's products and services.

Tailor-made products

A reasonably sophisticated database can identify which customers want what. For example, it is possible to identify which customers: (a) like all advertising; (b) hate all advertising; (c) like some advertisements. An online newspaper can tailor the paper accordingly. It can even probably enjoy special advertising rate cards.

Accelerating NPD

Rosabeth Moss Kanter (1996) feels that NPD will be quickened by online feedback. Dr Kanter suggests that online feedback can directly affect both product development and new product development, facilitating much quicker NPD.

5. Internal communications

Intranets

The Internet is also used for internal communications as an internal Internet or 'Intranet' among staff nationally and internationally – sharing expertise and information, preparing presentations, pitches and simply communicating with colleagues around the world. This private network facilitates improved internal communications by distributing marketing, management and human resources information. The Intranet broadens the use of a company's resources and helps it to become more horizontally focused, embracing business processes rather than just vertical functions that tie up resources into rigid divisions.

Customer information can be shared with the sales team, who in turn can use e-mail, transfer documents, maps, press and TV advertisements, live links for presentations, conferences and product updates. New business pitches can be improved as case studies, research reports, biographies of consultants, graphics, photographic images and videos can be downloaded and incorporated within a new presentation. Some companies use the Intranet to encourage and facilitate a sharing of expertise and resources already developed.

The Intranet also helps in more mundane matters like maintaining and distributing an up-to-date telephone directory by making it accessible to any employee with a Web browser. Immediate benefits can be enjoyed since these internal directories are expensive to produce and out of date by time they are delivered.

Extranet

Paperless operations can also improve efficiencies when the Intranet is extended outside the corporate 'firewall' and into a limited number of external partners to form an 'Extranet'. The Extranet can be used in other areas like purchasing, where approved suppliers or tenderers have access to stock levels, job specifications and purchase order numbers through it. GE estimates it sourced $4 billion worth of goods and services in 1998 by using its Extranet. FT's Geoffrey Nairn believes that Extranets may represent 'the future of business to business commerce, particularly for high-volume transactions which account for 80 per cent of most organisation's purchasing activities'. Third millennium business models may see the emergence of vertical portals, creating new perks for employees. A portal is a gateway or entrance to the Web – often Netscape or Explorer or a company's own specially designed portal. Some portals may have links to privileged suppliers who offer their products and services to the employees at a special rate.

6. Cost reduction

Developing, designing, servicing and maintaining a Web site costs money. Even without a Web site, the Internet costs money to access, but it can also save money. Cost-saving ideas can be collected from the Internet when particular customer suggestions are listened to and acted upon. As mentioned in New Product Development above, resources are required to acknowledge, analyse, select, develop and respond to suggestions made.

Print and distribution savings

Annual reports, sales and technical literature and more can all be distributed on CD ROM (discs) or down the line through the Internet. This not only saves print costs (and trees), but it also saves distribution costs (and pollution). Catalogue companies pay $2 per CD ROM against $10 per catalogue. Sun saved $250,000 last year by distributing its annual report on the Net (and other electronic means).

Customer service savings

On the Internet, customers can serve themselves, as text and illustrations (and occasionally video clips and sound) combine to help them move through the required steps of self-servicing. Customer service costs can be reduced with a well-designed series of Web pages which answer as many anticipated FAQs as possible. It is estimated that every Dell Computers customer query answered on the Web instead of via the freephone number saves Dell $7. This then frees up customer service staff to get on with more productive and profitable work. Federal Express claim to save between $2–$5 per customer call by allowing customers to track their packages themselves through the Web (generating a total saving of £4 million a year plus more satisfied customers). Cisco Systems save $250 million a year by encouraging customers to specify and order computers through the Web instead of by phone and fax.

Stock/inventory savings

Using their Extranet, Ford aim to save billions of dollars in current inventory by manufacturing the majority of their vehicles on a demand basis (with a two-week delivery time). To do this Ford have to link more of their 15,000 dealers around the world into their Intranet (Extranet).

Collecting cost-saving tips

The dialogue with customers can generate an array of useful suggestions, hints and tips direct from the market-place. Those organisations that pay heed to the market-place can find money-saving ideas falling out of cyberspace. Silicon Graphics estimate that the tips that users exchange via its news group save the company $4–$5 million a year in customer service calls. Remember customers should be rewarded when they disclose information and ideas.

Cost reduction/additional revenue generation

Popular Web sites attract big audiences. Big audiences attract advertisers. Popular sites can sell advertising space on their Web pages. A really popular Web site could also charge Internet access providers that link users to the service, eg ESPN. This is similar to the business model from cable TV where local operators pay to carry ESPN.

Phone calls savings

E-mail messages can be more efficient and less time-consuming than making phone calls if used in a disciplined manner. And of course, they can be composed and read offline. This means that the user only goes online live on to the Internet to collect or send a whole batch of messages. Having said that, phone bills can bulge if users spend a lot of time browsing the infinite range of the Internet.

7. Distribution

It has been said that the crunch will come when the focus of activity on the Internet changes from marketing to distribution. Physical distribution, or place, is sometimes considered to be the dullest of the elements of the marketing mix, perhaps because it is not as exciting as developing new products, or as much fun as developing television advertisements. But without distribution even the best product or service fails. Author Jean-Jacques Lambin (1993) believes that a marketer has two roles: firstly to organise exchange through distribution, and secondly to organise communications. Companies like Coca Cola see their expertise in distribution as a very serious source of competitive advantage.

Products delivery
Newspapers, journals, books, films, television, photo libraries, real libraries, records, software packages and more can all be digitised and delivered by cable or telephone wire through the Internet. This may create channel conflict as manufacturers skip retailers and offer direct sales to customers. New marketing issues will arise. Take the music industry, where online sales are forecasted to grow rapidly (see Sales, page 200). The music industry traditionally promoted the artists and not the record companies. In the online world, record companies may start to brand and promote themselves to attract visitors to their Web sites for direct sales. The resulting channel conflict between manufacturer and distributor/retailer is compounded by the global reach of the Internet, where customers shop around between countries, distributors and manufacturers (see Global complications, page 214).

Online production

FujiFilm has launched FujiFilm Fotonet, an Internet photo print service (www.fotonet.com). Any PC or Mac with Internet connection can send digital files direct to FujiFilm for production.

(Source: *New Media Age*, 24 July 1997)

Services delivery
Already medical, legal and technical advice services are exploiting the digitised distribution trend. In fact, many services that are totally intangible lend themselves to delivery through the Internet. The Internet can both promote and distribute services on a wider scale. Take the Tate Gallery. It expects the Internet to double its visitors from 2 million to 4 million within two years but it may well be that many more millions of visitors will eventually make virtual visits, thereby bringing (or distributing) galleries and museums to a much wider market.

Products and services purchasing
Although not necessarily delivered through the Internet almost any other product or service can now be bought through the Internet. Groceries, travel,

hotels, airlines and car hire are already becoming popular purchases through the Internet. In a sense, the Internet is just another way for customers to access a company. If a product is readily and easily available through as many channels as economically possible, then it increases its likelihood of sales. The Internet, in this case, is just another channel for customers to find a particular brand. Not all customers have the same media and shopping habits. Some customers even change their media and distribution habits – the Internet can accommodate this potential new media habit. The whole buying process can be transacted digitally, from product awareness and education to product trial, product purchase and finally after-sales service, repeat purchase reminders and helpful suggestions on how to use the product or service etc. Certainly, the Internet gives access to new customers in markets previously ignored (see Selling, below).

8. Selling

Few fairytale sales stories
On average, the Internet does not currently provide a major flow of income from sales generated (through a Web site). Most organisations do not find pots of gold profits lying at the end of the electronic rainbow. Perhaps this is because very few companies have clear Web strategies (McKinsey's 1998 UK Internet Survey). Although some virtual shopping malls and virtual exhibitions are getting busier, there are still relatively few companies currently making profits from sales generated through their Web sites. However, it may be more than we think as actual sales may be made over the phone while the previous stages (in the buying process) were nurtured on the Internet. Online attraction may develop into offline transactions. The relatively low online sales situation may change. There are already a few organisations who are starting to sell well in cyberland. Dell computers sell $5 million worth a day, while IBM are enjoying reported online revenues of $1 billion a month. Amazon, with its 1 million customers spread around 160 countries is estimated to sell $130 million worth solely through the Internet. BMW estimate 40 per cent of their 'day-to-day enquiries' come from the Internet.

Music sales explode

Internet research consultancy, Jupiter, predicts that online music sales will rise from $47 million in 1997 to $1.6 billion in 2002.

(Source: *FT*, 11 August 1997)

Selling into new markets
The Internet can certainly help an organisation to penetrate new markets, since as it crosses borders with ease, it extends the reach of the organisation across

the world within minutes. For example, International Sports' world-wide Web site in Japanese allows it to get closer to its most distant market. 4,000 Japanese customers already use it by phone and fax, with a lot more expected via the Internet. Small companies become virtual companies. In a sense the Internet moves a company closer to its customers. Even in existing markets, it can help companies to reach customers whom they may have missed for some reason.

Small value, big turnover

Digital transactions do not have to be large as in the case of stock market trading companies or bank transfers, they can be for smaller sums, even coins. Some record companies are investigating the distribution of tracks from albums for the price of loose change (or new forms of 'digi-cash'). Multiply this by a growing mass global market and the sales revenue becomes significant. New instant selling opportunities are available on the Internet, eg when listening to a radio station online (through the Internet) there will be a constant 'option' or opportunities to 'buy now' whatever record is being listened to at that particular time (or for that matter, any time in the show as play lists will also be published).

Sales management tool

The Internet can also help management to communicate with sales people, providing them with customer updates, company news, product updates, competitor promotions, sales analysis, presentation packages, graphics, pictures, etc.

9. Promotion

Some industry analysts have said that businesses that are not on the Internet within the next couple of years will be out of business by the end of the decade. They say that running Pizza Hut without the Internet in the year 2000 may be like trying to run Pizza Hut without a telephone in 1999. The current size of the world-wide Internet population is small – 100 million +. It is expected to grow to 200 million within a few years. And it will continue to grow as customers move out of shops, the market-place, and on to the Internet, the market space. A whole new wave of customers is going to be out there, zipping around from Web site to Web site on an array of electronic back roads. Trading outposts (Web sites) need to be established on this new electronic frontier.

Having a presence

At this stage, it is useful to have a presence on the Internet for several reasons: (1) for the small percentage of customers who currently want to access you through the Internet; (2) for all audiences to see your Web address carried on all communications tools, eg letterhead, advertisements, product literature, etc gives an impression of an up-to-date organisation; (3) for managers to learn about the Web, what works, what doesn't, what it costs, how to integrate it with other communications tools, etc. Eventually to develop an Internet strategy which helps to exploit the opportunity. On top of this, in the cluttered world of the Web, a recognisable brand can deliver a reassuring sense of order, familiarity and powerful appeal. Having a presence on the Internet does not necessarily require a Web site. It could involve having a page on a partner's site or placing banner ads, interstitials and subverts (see page 203) on other sites. Widely distributed screen savers offer another form of electronic presence.

'No strong media brand will be complete without an active Web site and news group enabling its audience to interact directly with it and with each other all over the world.'

(Source: Mike Elms, *Marketing Business*, March 1996)

Interactive advertising

Advertisers now have an unprecedented opportunity to tailor their messages more precisely to a more fragmented audience. Amid the seemingly endless surge towards market maturation, fragmentation, globalisation and communications saturation (up to 1,500 messages aimed at an individual each day) the Internet allows more precise audience selection, interaction, engagement and involvement through interactive advertising. For example, interactive stories based on characters in advertising campaigns can be developed on the Internet. Today we see 'Context Sensitive Advertising' where the software tracks a visitor's Web activities and changes the banner ads accordingly, eg if searching for car sites the banner ads will deliver car ads. The challenge, of course, is how to attract and retain a sizeable audience in the diffuse landscape of cyberspace.

Interactivity will bind advertising into the consciousness of our culture

'Interactive is a derivative, as are all new mediums initially (eg early films looked like theatre). By the end of the millennium, interactive will have its own identity, and come into its own as an art form. Interactivity will bind advertising into the consciousness of our culture like nothing else that has gone before, but its success will be dependent on ideas, the imagination of creatives and their ability to strike up a conversation between brand and buyer.'

(Source: Phil Dwyer, 1997)

The range and type of online advertising is increasing. New advertising ideas blossom all the time: from the cheeky icons and graphical bursts of the I-Candy quasi Web sites to intelligent banner ads (capable of harvesting data from users), from 'traditional' banner ads to 'in your face' interstitials (which greet customers for 10 seconds before other content requested arrives), to the 20-second brand experience of the subverts. Chapter 11, Branding examines these in more detail.

Normal advertisements may not be so effective, particularly when online, as customers want a reward for accessing your advertising, whether entertainment, new experiences, knowledge acquisition, or payment. It may well be that one day audiences will have to be paid in some manner, shape, or form for watching a customised advertisement. Payment might be in the form of an incentive, voucher, free gift, or competition entry. The traditional advertising model is changing. One extreme example of this 'model change' is the screen saver. These selected advertisements are pulled down from the Internet (or from a CD ROM) by audiences on to their screens. Downloaded screen savers become advertisements for whichever brand is shown on the screen saver. Every time the machine is left unused the moving advertisement (screen saver) kicks into action. The advertising agency does not receive a commission on this new media, no one buys the space, only the audience makes an active choice and allows its privately owned media space (PC screen) to be used for the advertisement. Guinness's screen saver, 'Anticipation', was downloaded 100,000 times. Guinness estimated that this screen saver was on 500,000 screens at any one time, because people were encouraged to copy it.

Integrated screen saver advertisements

'When Guinness advertised their screen saver the number of requests went up by 260 per cent in two days... the idea is that as people are leaving the office, the last thing they see is the Guinness screen saver, and they think, 'Actually, I do fancy a pint.'

(Source: Mandy Sowter, Guinness, 1998)

The traditional advertising models are changing. Take banner burn-out. Once an individual has seen a particular advertisement twice, there is little point in repeating it. NetGravity's Jitendra Valera claims that 'Internet users tend to go back to their favourite sites much more often than glance back through magazines. To have a really effective campaign, you will need to advertise on a site which can manage the rotation and scheduling of ads on an individual customer basis.' Advertisements can be rotated dynamically according to the gender of the user (assuming the user has voluntarily registered this information earlier). Valera believes in the uniqueness of the Web. 'No other medium allows you such tight control of placing the right ad, in the right place, at the right time for the right person.'

Parasite aliens take over the Web

Unilever are reported to be making ads which suggest aliens are trying to contact Web users. Linked to the creative space theme for the Lynx fragrance, Apollo, users are taken from a quirky, deliberately vague banner ad to a 'strange audio-visual experience which plays weird sounds to the user. Unknown to the user, his/her software is being almost instantaneously interrogated to find out which Web page the user came from, and then makes an exact copy with several keywords replaced with garbled computer code and alien-like graphics so that when the user clicks on the back button to go back to the start page the user finds aliens attempting to send a message through the text on the apparently 'same page' with a garbled, interference-filled radio message.'

(Source: The technique is called 'Parasite', by interactive agency Lateral)

Advertisements can be blocked by Internet filtering systems which effectively block Web site advertising from Web sites. Software, like cybersitter which was originally designed to block objectionable material from Web sites can now also be used to block unwanted advertisements. Filtering increases the speed of downloading, but as connection times and downloading times quicken, the filter may become less used.

Direct mail

The Internet is a relatively new communications tool – a discrete form of promotion which can provide an engaging dynamic dialogue. This non-linear interactive tool can engage customers. It is a way of extending, enhancing and strengthening the brand values in both an interactive and truly integrated way and not in a 'mass intrusive and unsolicited way' (Smith, 1996). Despite the tempting offers of 30 million names for $99, it should not be used for mass unsolicited e-mailings.

Unsolicited mass e-mails (known as 'spams') are violently rebuked by audiences in the cyberworld (see 'Mass mailers are flamed', p 205). Mass e-mailing spammers are sometimes closed down by the Internet service suppliers who want to protect their subscribers from unwanted junk e-mail. For example, Cyber Promotions is 'teetering on bankruptcy' since its server removed the company from its Internet service because of junk e-mail. Internet servers like CompuServe and America On-Line are reported to have implemented blocking services which hope to protect their subscribers and 'further prevent cyber promotions and companies with similar spamming techniques from distributing unsolicited commercial releases online' (*Ragan's Interactive Weekly*). Other Internet service providers are prepared to take spammers to court for abusing the system.

Spammers sued

A Texas court fined a Californian spammer US $13,000 and ordered the spammer to pay US $5,000 in legal costs when the Texas Internet Service Providers Association and a number of individuals decided to sue for damages. The case was brought under the laws of nuisance, negligence, trespass to personal property, conversion and harmful access by computer.

(Source: *Nua Surveys*, 1998)

Some companies claim to have large e-mail databases of people who are happy to receive commercial e-mail. These companies build their lists through partnerships with other Web sites (sometimes tens of thousands of Web sites) where visitors can sign up to receive mail on subjects that are of interest to them. This is in fact an 'opt in' approach similar to direct mail when you are asked if you would like to receive further mailings (as opposed to 'opt out' where the user gets these mailings unless he or she ticks the box to opt out of any further mailings).

The safest route is of course to collect your own customer names and details to build your own customer database. The nurturing of a dialogue with individuals who have voluntarily agreed to be mailed is different from spamming and is of immense value. One-to-one marketing is proving itself as marketers move customer retention up the agenda beyond customer acquisition. Developing Online Strategies (page 219) considers database marketing in more detail.

Mass mailers are flamed

Unsolicited business propositions, like e-mail shots, breach netiquette (the code of etiquette on the net). Response: Flaming... 25,000 hate mail messages sent to two US solicitors who sent out an unsolicited e-mail shot.

Public relations

The Net can widen the distribution of news releases. Text, photographic and video news releases can be distributed over the Net and into news editors' electronic baskets. Busy journalists requesting a news update, pictures or comments can be referred to the Web site press room, or news release section, for speedy downloading. Digital press kits can help journalists. Buena Vista's recent film *Starship Troopers* had an innovative press kit – a ready-made mini-Web site packed with material related to the film which could be incorporated into any media partner's, distributor's agent's or promoter's own Web sites.

Several larger corporations monitor newsgroups regularly to see what is being said about their company or brand. The Net allows an organisation inside opinion forming, live as it happens. London-based Information Hyperlink Ltd developed a new product called Netscanner, designed to scroll the Internet and search for defamatory comments about customers or their products.

Essentially the Net can accelerate word of mouth. The Net also helps with crisis management. For example, the Intel debacle, in which customers raged about their flawed Pentium chips, could have been averted if the company had responded quickly online.

A quick game of tag

'A group of students recently began sending messages to several news groups berating a technical education company, DeVry Inc., who, thanks to regular news group monitoring, spotted the problem almost immediately. To balance the argument, De Vry then attached their reply to these messages so whoever got the negative message also got De Vry's positive response.'

(Source: *Ragan's Interactive Weekly*)

Ironically, this new communications landscape could weaken the 'gatekeeper' role of PR executives. As the press will have access directly into an organisation's Web site, they can skip the public relations executive and his or her gatekeeping role of managing the press. One bold approach is to publish negative publicity on the corporate Web site. The company under attack regains some control by attaching its response to the criticisms. Shell used this tactic during the heavy criticism it received about Nigeria a few years ago. The 'double-sided argument' gained Shell some credibility and equipped it to quash some of the cries of 'cover up' from the conspiracy theorists.

Sales promotions

If the Web site is considered to be a new medium, then, just like any other media, it can carry all sorts of sales promotions, ranging from competitions to collecting electronic coupons with each visit. Again, mainstream traditional sales promotions should be leveraged across the Web site. In a sense a URL address (Web address) listed on a piece of FMCG (Fast Moving Consumer Goods) packaging containing a sales promotion should invite the audience to check out the Web site. Web specific promotions can also attract a percentage of an organisation's customers who are cyber orientated. Trapping that database may reveal an interesting customer profile which may, in turn, trigger new ideas.

Sponsorship

The Internet can facilitate imaginative sponsorship – a whole Web site can be co-sponsored. A particular page (within a Web site) with a particular theme can be sponsored or co-sponsored if it attracts the right kind of audience. A

Web event can be created and held on the Web site – these of course can be sponsored or co-sponsored. So marketers can sponsor another organisation's Web site, specific page or event. They can also create their own forms of sponsorship events on their own sites. Sun operated a series of information servers in conjunction with sporting events. For example, way back in 1994, during the World Cup, its main server in LA was accessed over 3 million times. It has also linked up with the Rolling Stones to create a server which gives fans access to a database full of Stones information, concert dates, video and audio clips and a library of photos. And of course any traditional mainstream sponsorship should be leveraged across the Web site so that visitors are reminded of other external sponsorship activities.

Exhibitions

Virtual exhibitions now bring suppliers, competitors and customers under one virtual roof. Without leaving their office, or home, customers can reduce the exhausting tedium of massive exhibitions by visiting specific shows at any time, day or night. They can then go to the virtual stands, examine products and services and leave their details for future quotations.

Virtual exhibitions, like Virtex, now bring suppliers, competitors and customer under one virtual roof

HOW CAN THE INTERNET HINDER MARKETERS?

Information technology, and technology in general, creates advantages and disadvantages. Technology can be used, abused, misused, misunderstood, mistaken and maltreated. Before exploring IT's wide range of hindrances, consider technology as simple as the washing machine. It was created as a great labour-saving device. But then standards of hygiene and expectancy started to rise which eventually meant that clothes had to be washed more frequently which in turn meant more work, despite the technological labour-saving leap. Is it possible that the vast new information capacity (provided by the Internet) will constantly be filled by an even greater number of bits and bytes as well as improved search engines so that whenever you search for something, an ever increasing amount of data comes back to you? As networks and information grow can they become self-fulfilling systems, breeding and supplying each other in an uncontrollable digital spiral? Parkinson's law of bureaucracy observes that when you create larger bureaucracies, the tasks available strangely expand to match the resources available. Can this Internet technology create more work or less work? This can obviously hinder marketers from their tasks. The Internet can also hinder marketers in many other ways. Here are seven of them.

HOW THE INTERNET CAN HINDER MARKETERS

1. Failed expectations

Slow downloading and slow access
Slow response – poor customer service
Sloppy sites

2. Security

Credit card fraud
Infiltrators and vandals
Viruses

3. E-nasties

Fakemail
Hate mail
Mail bombs
Unwanted enrolment
Net rumours

4. Global complications

Branding
No PR gatekeepers
Compliance

5. Cyber squatting

Trademark hijacking
Killer clicks

6. Audiences

Exhausted
Unaudited
Dumbed down

7. Miscellaneous

Spam
Cyberlibel
Cyberskivers

1. Failed expectations

Slow access (getting online), slow downloading, incomplete sites, slow customer service responses, combined with a plethora of useless information, create a certain sense of disillusionment and an overriding feeling of failed expectations. The Internet, currently, does not live up to its promise.

Slow downloading

The lack of cable infrastructure (providing larger band width) combined with the lack of high-speed modems and super-fast PCs means that many users cannot download information (receive information into their PC) quickly. It can take up to 90 minutes to download three minutes of music. Digitised photographs can take three minutes to download onto a PC. On top of this, the explosion in users and the subsequent growth of traffic is threatening to clog the system, making it difficult to access popular pages at peak times, or even get onto the Internet in the first place.

A lot of excitement and interest has now burnt out as viewers are disappointed by the vast quantities of poor quality material as well as the difficulties of downloading images and video clips, and even accessing popular sites. Do people go online for information or entertainment? Neil Postman of *Time* magazine says that 'people go online for information, not for entertainment. They're more targeted. More focused. We're in danger of amusing ourselves to death'.

There is a lot of incorrect, libellous, malicious and useless information out there. Who needs to hear President Clinton's cat, watch coffee being brewed or count the number of Coke cans left in a vending machine on the other side of the world? There is also a lot of genuine entertainment and education (edutainment) out there, hidden in the vast regions of cyberspace. But if there isn't enough production talent or inventiveness to fill 500 TV network stations, what hope is there for the hundreds of thousands of Web sites?

Slow service

Creating a Web site is a bit like creating a new corporate identity in so far as they both raise customer expectations. If a new corporate identity is only cosmetic, customers may be disappointed with whatever had previously satisfied them, since a new identity heightens expectations of an even better company. Similarly, a new Web site sends messages to customers. As the Web is synonymous with speed and fast response, customers expect fast responses when leaving e-mail enquiries. An acknowledgement at least is expected almost immediately. Simple, automated, personalised response systems are often ignored and worse still, real customer enquiries, queries and problems are allowed to go unanswered (see page 195 which reveals slow responses from the Fortune Top 50 companies). A 1998 survey of 50 top German companies revealed that only 25 responded to e-mail enquiries within four days. Many, including Adobe, Apple, Epson, HP, Netscape and Novell didn't respond at all, while Intel and Lotus e-mails were undeliverable.

Sloppy sites

Certainly the plethora of incomplete Web sites with pages 'under construction' and slow access combined with slow downloading means many users are switching off and not renewing their subscriptions, and therefore increasing the 'churn' rate (customers not returning). There is a real lack of 'Net savvy', with lots of poorly designed Web sites built without any underlying instructional design blueprints. Many Web consultancies have flawed Web sites.

2. Security

Credit card fraud, infiltrators and vandals, database abuse, rogue sites, viruses and confidentiality issues all present problems to marketers.

Credit card fraud

Because of the apparent security risk involved in giving credit card details over the Internet, many customers are hesitating and not following their electronic enquiries right through to purchase. The fear of safer software being hacked into by some digital criminal (who will steal their credit card details) is still rampant. Perhaps the Internet gives rise to new unfounded fears since many customers are happy to release their credit card details over the phone. Other customers are happy to give their cards to strangers who take the cards away and remain out of sight for several minutes at a time (waiters in restaurants). Although a Web site with sensible systems built into its architecture (secure firewalls, passwords and regular policing) is safer than many assume, nothing is 100 per cent secure. There are other innovative safe solutions to online payment. In conversation with one of the authors, Web consultant Paul McFarland suggests that premium priced 0891 numbers can act as a method of payment. Web visitors wanting to make a purchase are asked for their telephone number, given a password and told that they will pay a premium price (equal to the cost of the item being purchased) on their telephone bill when they telephone a particular number. Without having to use a credit card the customer makes a purchase and is billed the premium rate by the telephone company, who subsequently pay the 0891 owner the premium (effectively the price of the items purchased).

Infiltrators, hackers and vandals

Digital hackers and saboteurs have been around a lot longer than the Internet. Digital genius Kevin Mitnick figured out how to intercept and over-ride the microphone used by clerks at fast food drive-up windows. Mitnick used to sit in his car and listen as a customer shouted his order. Then Mitnick would take control of the speaker system, pose as the food server, and curse the unwitting diner for 'eating such slop'. Information technology has always been vulnerable to sabotage.

Even before the emerging popularity of the Internet, in the early days of direct marketing and database marketing, security problems loomed. A few words keyed in here and there can cause mayhem, insult customers, lose sales and generate a public relations crisis. A sacked employee once changed the salutation on several thousand letters going out to top-spending credit card holders to: 'Dear Rich Fat Bastard'.

Free beer and live sex

A UK national daily newspaper, *The Daily Telegraph*, reported that a group of British hackers called Digital Anarchists had infiltrated the Labour Party's publicity site. 'The first attack promised free drugs and beer to young voters, and the Labour leader's formal response to the Budget was replaced with a live sex show of women wearing "demon eyes" masks seen in the Conservative advertising campaign.'

(Source: *The Daily Telegraph*, 12 October 1996)

Today's saboteurs and hackers can break into a site and change the content, put up a rogue site or satirise your Web site. With a click, hackers can copy a Web site into their directory and alter words, logos or images. Users might mistakenly access the satirical site when looking for the real site. For example, a user could be looking for Bell Canada and end up with Hell Canada.

Virus attack

The big worry for anyone using the Internet is catching a virus that will eat into their files and destroy everything. Downloading information, pictures, video clips, music, speeches or multimedia presentations open up the receiver's computer to the dangers of collecting a virus. A virus can wreak havoc with a computer's system, destroying files and sometimes hiding until it is released later at a specific time. In fact, some can wait six months and then start copying your private data back to its author. There are many virus checkers available. These need to be updated regularly as new viruses come out all the time.

A virus a day

For every 10 PCs a company can expect 4.6 virus infections a year at a cost of 22 person days.

(Source: National Computer Security Association, 1998)

---

3. E-nasties

There are other nasties out there on the Internet, including fakemail, hate mail, mailbombs, unwanted enrolment and viruses.

Fakemail

Fake e-mail messages may seem humorous but can have a devastating effect on the recipients. Fakemail messages can come from Bill Gates (see Net rumours), Bill Clinton, the Prime Minister, your local clergyman, the Lottery, or even God. The recipients are informed that they have won, been promoted, sacked, seconded… etc. Typical fakemail has included: job offers from Bill Gates; an admonishment to stop reading alt.sex and start studying from Bill Clinton; a proposition from supermodel Cindy Crawford; an invitation to the Second Coming from the Supreme Being; and an invitation to eternal damnation from Satan. Suicides have resulted, which have driven families, lawyers and IT experts to track down malicious mailers and seek full prosecutions in the courts.

Stressful distractions

A 43-year-old Bostonian who thought he was having a fling with a 23-year-old woman discovered to his dismay that 'she' was an 80-year-old man in a Miami nursing home. As people we need a tactile reference to make a complete bond.

(Source: *Time*, 19 February 1996)

Hate mail

Nasty messages, or hate mail, are not quite the same as the 'traditional' fakemail since hate mail is real e-mail sent by very angry people to very real people, for example, the unsolicited business propositions sent by two US solicitors generated a 'flaming' response of 25,000 hate mail messages returned to the solicitors. Some users even write a 'cancelbot' program which traverses the Internet deleting any messages that a targeted firm tries to post.

Mail bombs

Worse still are the mail bombs. One hundred megabytes of messages and mail bombs (equivalent to 100 copies of Tolstoy's *War and Peace*) brought one organisation's computer system to its knees and led to the organisation's Internet supplier suspending its access. Pressure groups previously used 'snail mail bombs' (when many thousands of members mail a dozen different items each, the recipient's traditional mail system becomes clogged and sometimes real, serious mail gets lost in the mail mountain). In the US mobilised pressure groups have acted similarly to clog all telephone lines going into a targeted organisation.

Unwanted enrolments

Possibly the most frightening of all are unwanted enrolments. Philip Elmer-DeWitt, Senior Editor, *Time* magazine, woke up one morning to find that he had been enrolled in a Barry Manilow fan club, a Mercedes owners discussion group, a Fiji Islands appreciation society and 103 other Internet mailing lists which he had never heard of. He knew that any one of these lists could generate 50 messages a day. 'To avoid a deluge of junk e-mail, I painstakingly unsubscribed from all 106 – even Barry Manilow's – only to log on on Monday morning and discover I'd been subscribed to 1,700 more. My file of unread e-mail had swelled to 16 megabytes, and was growing by the minute. By Monday the e-mail was pouring in at the rate of four a minute, 240 an hour, 5,760 a day' (*Time*, 18 March 1996).

Net rumours

Bad news travels fast and on the Internet it travels even faster. Witness Intel's Pentium problem and the speed at which it spread. Even apparently good news can travel fast, as in the case of Net rumours circulating about Nike and Microsoft. The Nike factory in Wilsonville, Oregon has been receiving thousands of pairs of smelly sneakers as a result of a rumour whizzing around the Internet that Nike would replace old Nikes with new ones free of charge if the old ones were returned. When it started in February 1998, Nike hoped it would just fizzle out. By June 1998 they had received over 5,000 pairs from all over the world, including Ireland and Asia. Microsoft have also suffered from a fakemail supposedly from Bill Gates, claiming that he had written a program to trace e-mail and requesting recipients to forward the message to everyone they knew. It promised everyone $1,000 or a free copy of Windows

98 once the message reached 1,000 people. Gerber baby food company have also been hit with a false rumour, with parents sending in their baby's birth certificate and expecting a $500 bond in return.

If in doubt check the company's own Web site. Hoax tracking organisations such as the US Department of Energy now have a site which tracks hoaxes: ciac.llnl.gov/ciac/CIAHoaxes.html.

4. Global complications

The global nature of the Internet presents two problems for marketers: firstly, global branding and secondly, compliance.

Branding

Moving into new media requires more than placing an existing brand on a Web site. Some images simply don't work as well online as off. Consequently some organisations now include the Internet in any briefings for any communications tools so that anything produced will also work well on the Internet (for example, light resolution brand images). Global complications pose more problems, particularly if there are regional differences in the branding, eg when Pepsi Cola had blue cans in the UK and red cans in the United States. The Web can smash through global boundaries and expose local differences.

In the United States Harvey's Bristol Cream is a fashionable drink with a predominantly young market. In Britain it's seen as being drunk by great-aunts. Harvey's had two Web sites, which were eventually merged into one with a return to Harvey's cultural heritage. Allied Domecq group media manager Patrick Barton says: 'People in the United States feel remote from Harvey's. Hispanic groups are our main US consumers. So we've moved it towards its cultural roots, which are in Europe, especially Spain. You'd expect a Harvey's site to be European.' The result was Harvey's Relaxation Station, which basically combines the look and feel of the US site with the British content and adds in more entertainment: music, comedy, art, a stress test, horoscopes, games, competitions and links to other esoteric locations. In the UK Tia Maria is all about girl power and is targeted at 18–24-year-old young women. In the Netherlands it is drunk neat by old age pensioners. And beyond the image differences, products with non-global packs (eg Pepsi can) and non-global branding create problems for Web sites that are accessed on a global scale.

Surfers cannot be relied upon to keep within the content kingdom of a regionalised section of a Web site.

No PR gatekeeper

Customers and competition are watching you! Different audiences can access the same message. Different audiences or 'publics' have access to the same information on most Web sites. This means that a pressure group has access to the same information that the shareholders might like to see, unless the site has exclusive or 'members only' areas that are only accessed by member passwords. This demands new thinking on the part of the public relations team, who previously could act as an information gatekeeper and tailor messages specifically for the local community, employees, customers, shareholders, pressure groups, regulatory bodies, etc. On top of this the Web allows scrutiny from a global audience. Inconsistent policies from subsidiaries around the globe are ruthlessly exposed by inquisitive pressure groups and journalists. A European PR manager who previously dealt with European stakeholders may now find inquisitive eyes from the other side of the world watching an organisation's locally produced Web site.

Compliance

As regulations, safety standards and pricing can vary across different markets, the Internet poses new problems for marketers. Regional pricing is difficult to maintain when local customers shop globally. Why buy, say, a BMW locally if you can buy it 20 per cent cheaper on the other side of the world and pay 10 per cent for shipping and customs? Complications grow when there is no global compliance of policies and regulations. What is deemed to be safe in one country may be dangerous in another. Even packaging standards are very different around the world. Does having a Web site and therefore a global presence mean an organisation is suddenly offering its goods and services in an array of differing markets with their differing regulations, legislation and taxation systems?

5. Cyber squatting

New threats are emerging on the Internet: trademark hijacking and killer clicks.

Trademark hijacking

Internet domain names have a country of origin attached to them, eg addresses ending in 'uk' and 'ie' are the United Kingdom and Ireland respectively. So Microsoft will register their 150 domain names (one for each country). Companies that don't register their names complete with the country of origin suffix leave themselves vulnerable to local laws of name ownership. Turkmenistan has become another country keen to sell Internet domain names. Many major players, including Esso and Cellnet, have now bought back their own names with the Turkmenistan suffix, '.tm'. Other names currently in reserve in Turkmenistan are digital.tm, microsoft.tm, dell.tm, bigmac.tm and surprisingly, guinness.tm. Not all countries allow this kind of trademark hijacking. The High Court in the UK found two individuals guilty of trademark 'passing off' when they applied to register such titles as Sainsbury's, BT, Virgin and Marks and Spencer. The judge ordered the two offenders to have the disputed names assigned to the complaining companies and pay £65,000 legal costs. The court further ruled that 'any person who deliberately sought to register a domain name with a view to eventually offering it for sale to a commercial concern of the same name would be injuncted'.

Killer clicks

A new form of potential trademark infringement has emerged in the guise of 'killer clicks'. It works like this: when someone is looking for a particular brand name on the Web the brand name is keyed into a search engine located on a particular portal such as Netscape or Excite. Immediately, a banner advertisement for a fragrance counter pops up on screen while the search presents its results. Inertia may kick in and the busy buyer may be more likely to next click on a fragrance counter and be taken away from the original brand request to another site altogether. This is known as the 'killer click'. If it happens to many thousands of searchers then it becomes a potentially significant form of lost revenue. Estee Lauder is reportedly suing some major portals for this new type of trademark infringement.

6. Audiences

Online audiences are exhausted and unaudited and may eventually become 'dumbed down'.

Exhausted audiences

Information fatigue is all around us. In fact information fatigue syndrome contributes to stress which increases illness and ultimately poor performance and absenteeism. There is too much information out there. Almost 1,000 books are published daily around the world. A single edition of the *New York Times* carries more information than an average 17th-century Englishman would have found in a whole lifetime. How to find the relevant information, the accurate information, the easily updateable information is now compounded by 'information addiction'. A Reuters survey revealed a new hazardous digital trend – a growing proportion of Internet users who find themselves addicted to information and the Internet. Over 50 per cent said they didn't have the capacity to assimilate the information. . . they were being overwhelmed by it. In the vast, vast cyberworld with its sea of hyper links and endless exploration, users can eventually get lost, confused, frustrated and increasingly anxious. Uncluttered interfaces, concise and clear Web sites and simple signposting can all help the weary cyber traveller to find what is required and attain satisfaction.

Unaudited

As with any medium, marketers are interested to know about the audience. Measuring audience size currently presents marketers with a problem: many sites report the number of 'hits' (the number of times an icon or a page is clicked, or opened). The problem is that one person can roam all over a particular Web site and register a click for each page, even registering a click if they go back to a page already opened. Measuring user hits can be misleading, since one user counts as multiple hits when accessing multiple files or pages on the same site. New research tools are aiming to track individual users, where they go, how long they stay at various Web site locations, and their movements from one site to another. On top of this Web site owners' claims of numbers of visitors visiting their sites need to be verified or audited independently, particularly if they are selling advertising space (for Web banner advertisements). The Audit Bureau of Circulation (ABC – traditional press audience verifiers) have a similar audience measurement service for online publications and their 'busy' Web sites. They offer to deliver 'certainty in a virtual world'. Not all sites are ABC-audited so advertisers need to exercise caution before buying banner space on unaudited Web sites.

Dumbed down humans and dumb search engines

It is feared that the overuse of intelligent agents and 'push technology' (which pushes e-mails and information at selected audiences) will cause the emergence of the 'dumbed down human' who does not peruse papers or actively evaluate or carefully select anything, from presents to programmes, as intelligent agents can do all that 'donkey work'. Intelligent agents will scour the world for the best deal, the best price, the most accurate information that best fits the question criteria. Whether it is 'What's the population of Fiji?' or 'Where can I buy the cheapest Jaguar car?', the intelligent agent will attempt to find it. Of course quality issues will be ignored unless these are built into the search criteria but few users know how to specify quality.

Search engines can be fooled, for example, when searching for a particular brand, person, item or subject, a user can call up a search engine and key in a word. Some search engines search according to the number of references a particular site might have. So, if a company wanted to grab all the Internet traffic aimed at its competitors, they could, in theory, insert thousands of tiny words almost invisible to the eye. The tiny words could be laid out to form an overall pattern or image which looks innocent but in fact used their competitors' names on their site. Another naughty approach is to insert a word repeatedly in the background in the same colour as the background colour, thereby becoming invisible to the eye but visible to some search engines.

7. Miscellaneous

From spammers to cyberlibel to cyberskivers, there are many other hindrances that the busy marketer must deal with in the online world.

Spammers

Research commissioned by Novell and carried out by Benchmark Research in 1998 revealed that spam (unsolicited junk e-mail) could cost British and Irish businesses up to $8.2 billion pa. The majority (75 per cent) of the 800 employees in the IT firms interviewed said that they received up to five junk e-mails a day each which cost them 15 minutes every day to read, decipher or file. Fifteen per cent spent one hour a day dealing with junk e-mail. Specialised software may have to be employed to intercept incoming junk mail. Some spammers, like the US lawyers on page 205, get 'flamed' with a plethora of e-mail replies, some as hate mail and some as mail bombs (see page 213). The Anti-spam organisation, EuroCAUCE (European Coalition Against Unsolicited Commercial E-mail) is a sister organisation of the US CAUCE (it is estimated that 95 per cent of spam originates from the United States). It will be interesting to see whether the deregulated nature of the Internet can sort the spamming problem out or whether governments will attempt to pass laws to stop it.

Cyberlibel

The Chevron corporation was reported to have paid $2.2 million following a sexual harassment case involving, among other things, sexist jokes on e-mail. Morgan Stanley were also involved in a $60 million racial discrimination lawsuit where racist jokes were allegedly circulated by e-mail. Back in the UK, Norwich Union paid medical insurers Western Provident £450,000 over comments circulated on Norwich Union's internal e-mail system. Although e-mail is fast and convenient it carries risks as it is the employer's legal risk. Although e-mail has the informal feel of a chat it has the permanence of a fax or memo.

Universities are sitting on landmines. A certain London physicist, who for reasons of privacy shall be called Mr X, now has several outstanding lawsuits against US universities whose students added their own defamatory messages to other negative comments being circulated about him. Mr X rubbed someone up the wrong way with his political commentaries and started receiving nasty messages. Eight separate e-mails listed as coming from one Philip Hallam Baker, a physicist in Geneva, smeared Mr X's career history and previous job performance. They also made criminal accusations about his personal life. Mr X became worried that his students, many of whom were active on the same 16 million-user chat group, would see the postings, and announced that if the messages didn't stop he would seek legal action. He eventually started legal proceedings and the issue was finally settled out of court.

Cybersex ends in court

Diane Goydan, from New Jersey, is being sued by husband John for the extreme cruelty of conducting an affair by news group. Mrs Goydan stands accused of conducting a virtual affair by exchanging explicit cybersex messages with a partner known only as the Weasel. The two had been having long, sexy online chats that left nothing to the imagination. Mr Goydan found and saved the messages on disk and filed for divorce. Mrs Goydan and the Weasel had never met, according to divorce papers filed in a New Jersey court, although the two were planning consummation in the honeymoon suite of a hotel in New Hampshire just as her husband made the discovery. But Mrs Goydan claims the affair was no more than a 'romantic day-dream' and promptly counter-sued for making the alleged affair public as she felt she had every right to expect these messages to remain private.

(Source: *Multimedia Futures*, 12 February 1996)

Cyberskivers

Surfing, browsing and wandering around the Internet can cost time and money – executive time and phone bills as well subscription bills. Kavanagh (1996) suggests that a company with 50 users on modest salaries of £15,000 is wasting £94,000 a year, excluding overheads. A different study by Nielsen Media Research revealed that employees from Apple Computer Inc., AT&T and IBM collectively spent 350 eight-hour work days visiting the soft porn Web site, Penthouse, in one month.

DEVELOPING ONLINE STRATEGIES

An online strategy is determined by the objectives (or reasons for going on-line) and the resources available. The strategy guides the overall instructional design of the Web site (structure, complexity, level of interactivity, look and feel) and its integration both with other communications tools and with overall business operations. The strategy must be developed and agreed before any actual home page (opening screen) is designed for the Web.

The marketer must know what the priority objectives are, eg is it simply to have a presence, help sales or build a database? If it is to help sales then the site should be built in such a way that it facilitates the customer moving through the various stages in the decision-making process from several different angles, routes or entry points. The other Web site functions can also be built in but it is likely that the site will need to satisfy some specific, quantifiable objective. Year one may prove difficult, but with each subsequent year it will become easier to quantify the objectives as the manager moves up the learning curve.

Even busy sites don't make profit:

'Even companies whose Web sites are frequented 100,000 times a day aren't profiting.'

(Source: Forrester Research, Cambridge, Mass. reported in *Fortune*, 1 May 1995)

So the online strategy will state whether the site is simply to have a basic presence or to become the world's best Web site and develop a prestigious 'must see' status among Web explorers. The strategy will state what kind of resource will be invested in it, the objectives it will satisfy and how it will reinforce both communications objectives and operational objectives. Use the marketing communications strategy checklist to check whether the online strategy adequately covers the key components of strategy: segmentation, targeting, positioning, sustainable competitive advantage, type of purchasing process, sequence and timing, communications tools, integration, scale, lifetime customers, brand enhancement, etc.

Before attempting to develop an online strategy a number of questions should be asked as follows:

Purpose and audience understanding

- Why go online? Is it just competitive paranoia or are there other operational and communications reasons?
- What are the objectives or functions of the Web site?
- How can the site support the overall marketing communications objectives?
- How can it support the required positioning?
- Define the brand, usage and the user imagery – how can the site support this?
- What is the brand's unique selling proposition – how can the site support this?
- What is the organisation's sustainable competitive advantage – how can the site support this?
- Define the target audience.
- How can a Web site help them?
- How can the target audience be rewarded?
- What will attract high traffic on to the site?
- Can we lock out competition from sponsorable domains?

Strategic dynamism

- Will it be able to merge with core systems, eg direct mail and telesales, invoicing, etc.
- Is the site dynamically planned, eg can it transact?
- Will the site exploit the dynamics of one-to-one marketing?
- Can the site be used to develop a dialogue with the audience?
- Can the organisation cope with dialogue – non-response will insult the audience?

Strategic links

- How will it be promoted?
- Will it be integrated across all communications?
- What links, alliances and hot spots should we develop (particularly with related but non-competing products) to increase the number of entry points?

Strategic communications

- Will the site have personality, set a good tone and build content areas around useful metaphors?
- Is the user invited back again?
- Is the user given a reward/reason to come back?

Resourcing

- How much resources will it require to: (a) set up; (b) maintain?
- Who will pay for it – which budget: advertising, PR, database, customer service?
- Who will service the site, answer e-mail questions, update content, etc?

So the online strategy might be to provide a new channel for customer services by developing an online availability with multiple entry points and internal routes to nurture and convert an enquiry through to a sale. Alternatively, the online strategy might be to develop an online presence with a view to developing a database for future one-to-one marketing campaigns. Ideally the strategy should encompass answers to the previous 26 questions.

Planning how visitors will find you (online signposts)

Register with search engines
There is a service which does it all for you available at URL:http://www. submit-it.com. This service will then post your announcement to the following companies: Yahoo, Webcrawler, Lycos, Starting Point, Infoseek, Opentext, Galaxy, WWW Worm, Harvest, Whole Internet Catalogue, Apollo, Pronet, Jump Station, Netcenter, Nerd World Media, Nikos (*New Media Age*, 30 November 1995, p 6).

Leave trails
Cyberspace is a vast frontier of isolated sites. Travellers tend to dart around unseen on a web of electronic back roads. There is a need to help the traveller to find your site by erecting signposts on those back roads. This includes getting listed in specific directories, eg for shopping listings and business-to-business directories. Do not hide your Web site. 'In the cluttered world of Web, a familiar brand has powerful appeal. Surprisingly some rivals have buried their brands online, eg Sports Illustrated was crammed into Time Warner's pathfinder. "That's a huge mistake. They haven't carried their brand onto the Web"' (*Fortune*, March 1996, p 98).

Unseen travellers zip through cyberspace:

'Despite the rush to colonise cyber-space, this vast frontier has many isolated sites. Travellers zip around unseen on a web of electronic back roads. Marketers need to erect signposts along the back roads of cyber-space to help guide the fast moving customer to their trading post or home page. Once there, travellers don't wait without reward. Items of interest have to pull the customer further into electronic rooms. Amidst a sea of multi-mediocrity, the sophisticated traveller moves on – never to return if disappointed by the first visit.'

(Source: Smith, 1996)

Develop links

Find where your target market travels. Identify which are the heavily used sites, then forge links, hot spots, etc. Location is one of the most important things. This may mean buying space and erecting your own electronic advertising billboard on someone else's site. 'It is important to post messages and run promotions in the most well trafficked areas of the net to generate interest' (*New Media Age*, 12 October 1996).

Promote the Web site both online and offline

Promote your Web site on all communications tools from bottles to product packs and sales literature to advertisements and mail shots, etc. Put your Web address on to business cards, letterheads, fax cover sheets, postcards, invoices, etc. Use online and offline activities to ensure the world knows your Web site is up and running. Send out news releases every time something new is on the Web site.

Don't forget to test, test, test

Do an online dress rehearsal before releasing.

Home page design

The home page is the first screen which a visitor sees when he or she keys in your URL (Web address) or when he or she clicks on a link (hot spot) on another site. Your homepage is your handshake – it can be wet, limp, strong, welcoming, enthusiastic. Designing the right emotional tone can mean the difference between success and failure.

The main page or the home page is a general index. Make it snappy yet informative. There is a trade-off between dull pages stuffed with text and glitzy pages packed with elaborate images – the former downloads quickly on to the visitor's PC, while the latter downloads so slowly that many visitors simply switch off after waiting for more than a minute. Keep pages to 20 kilobytes of data at most, but certainly no more than 30 kilobytes. Give a brief outline of any links so that the visitors know what to expect if they choose to click.

The click of a mouse = success or failure:

The industry… could turn out to be as important for society and business as the telephone; yet for any contender, the margin between success and failure will come down to nothing more substantial than the click of a consumer's mouse.'

(Source: *Fortune*, 1 May 1997)

But aesthetics is only one aspect of a good Web site. Whether the site is designed to generate sales or just to build a database, there has to be effective calls to action. The most beautiful looking Web pages in the world will never generate any sales if the Web site does not have some good calls to action to persuade the visitor to take the next step. It is surprising to see so many Web sites with ineffective or, worse still, missing calls to action. Visitors must also be rewarded: their trip must be a worthwhile experience otherwise they will never return. This means that both the actual content, the structure/routes within the Web site and the level of interactivity must be suitably good. This, in turn, means that the graphical interface must be pleasing and easy to follow, the content must be interesting, useful and constantly updated, and the minimum level of interactivity must be satisfied by speedy responses to the visitor's requests/communications.

To build a brand without the constraints of time and space would be a creative's dream. Web sites are arguably a marketer's dream – the opportunity to engage in 'two-way brand building'.

Appendix 10.2 provides some additional tips on the design of the home page.

Content

Keep asking the questions: 'What does the customer want?' 'What problems do they have which I can solve economically?' Ragu's Spaghetti Sauce Web site offers recipes, Italian phrases and sweepstakes. The site must make the visitor want to come back for more. The content must be updated so that the site remains interesting for repeat visits. Miller beer offers e-mail with the brewer, regional news stories, items on sports that Miller sponsors (striving for a similar audience), colourful graphics and athlete interviews. Mastercard provides information on what to do after losing a credit card; a 'Masterclass' to learn how to surf the net; a 'Master tour' of other interesting places on the Web; 'Visionarium' showcases of new credit card technology; and stories which demonstrate Mastercard's global reach by presenting folklore from around the world (*Adweek*, 27 March 1995). Maybe the Web site can provide product demonstrations and price lists, but ask what else could it deliver which customers would like? Some organisations get celebrities to talk to people through, for example, an online conference or simply post the celebrity's thoughts each week/month.

Out of date content costs money

'Virgin Atlantic Airways overlooked updating its prices on its www and was fined $14,000 for violation of advertising regulations.'

(Source: *Wall Street Journal*, March 1996, pp 30-33)

Sponsorship, product placement, advertorials and competitions are all part of the cross media marketing mix which can appear on a Web site. Brand building activities can include campaigns that hype logos, mascots and images. Mission statements, exhibition dates and venues, distributor addresses, customer survey forms and order forms are all commonly found on Web sites around the world.

Why bother accessing your site?

'TV has 80 channels now. There's video on demand, live entertainment, movies, amusement parks and more. But with all these expanding options the consumer still has the same two to three hours of free time. There must be a compelling need for consumers to access you.'

(Source: Fred Rosen, President, Ticketmaster, 1998)

Size, routes and flow

Will the site have flow? Does the site carry calls to action in the right places. Is the main menu available from every screen? Is there an easy exit route? Is the visitor tempted to see more and more? Is the visitor routed around the site in a sensible manner. If generating sales is the main objective, is the visitor carefully carried through the various stages of the buying process so that an enquiry is comfortably converted to a sale? If the main objective is to build a database, is the visitor rewarded for exchanging data? Is there an inbuilt satisfaction of completing a finite experience (ie is the site the right size in so far as visitors do not get lost or become frustrated by not being able to see everything)?

Watch other sites

See what is excellent and consider why they are excellent.

Interaction

Ideally the interaction should not be so complicated that large software applications have to be downloaded before the visitor can interact with the site. Keep interactions relatively simple so that most PCs can engage in a similar level of interaction. Alternatively build in a menu of interaction to accommodate different levels of visitor hardware.

Images

Images, pictures, graphics and photographs should be clearly labelled so that users know what software and hardware is required to successfully download material on to another PC. This reduces frustration when users try to download when they have not got the right hardware to download quickly. The images should be labelled so that the user has an idea of how big the file is before trying to download. If it takes three minutes to download it can really be a source of irritation and therefore do more harm than good.

Graphics should be saved as gif. or compressed jpeg. files. (preferably JPEG); 256 colours are standard. If using a custom Palette keep to the 16 colours that Windows uses. Lower the resolution on scanned graphics to less than 96 dpi. Crop unwanted/useless peripheral imagery. Allow for lowest spec access to site. Flag up estimated downloading times for video etc. You would be advised against repackaging existing media such as existing advertisements – they have got to be redefined to fit a PC screen.

APPENDIX 10.1: COSTS

In the UK, Web site costs vary enormously, with an average of over £20,000. This covers development and registration plus any annual fees, maintenance/ updating but not servicing (customers' or visitors' enquiries etc). The 1:3:5 rule of thumb suggests that the Web development budget should be multiplied by three for servicing and maintenance and multiplied by five for promotions (promoting the Web site and generating traffic). In some cases, companies seem to reverse this to 5:3:1.

In the USA, a decent site on which people might linger for five minutes or longer and return over and over can be built for less than $150,000 compared to approximately $500,000 for a single 30-second spot on *Seinfeld* (34 million viewers). Perhaps smart companies will be allocating between 5 and 10 per cent of their marketing budgets to interactive online activities.

Electronic billboard costs

Prodigy, the US service, charges $4,000 pw for a space on its home page. America On-Line asks advertisers to pay $240,000 pa for it to develop and maintain an interactive marketing area.

Microsoft Network online service starts at $7,500 for a 12-month commitment and provides a billboard-like icon on a directory screen which will signpost users to the advertiser's Web site.

> Until the consumer networks begin to offer advertising on a 'pay per response' basis more akin to the direct marketing model, as opposed to the traditional TV audience measurement model, advertising on these media is unlikely to achieve real success.
>
> (*Admap*, February 1996)

APPENDIX 10.2: TIPS FROM COMPUSERVE HOMEPAGE WIZARD

Don't

- *Don't:* Use italics (hard to read).
- *Don't:* Use different font sizes and types.
- *Don't:* Use textured backgrounds.

Do

- *Do:* Ensure there is a link to the home page on every page/screen.
- *Do:* Ensure the opening graphic displays fully on 640 × 480 pixels.
- *Do:* Reuse graphics such as title banners (once downloaded they can be called up from cache).
- *Do:* Always ALT! give surfers something to look at while your pictures trickle down the pipe.
- *Do:* Use Centre-ing liberally.
- *Do:* Replace the standard grey background – white is safe.
- *Do:* Show file sizes.
- *Do:* If changing the colours of visited and unvisited links – make them fit with the colours on the page.

APPENDIX 10.3: THE INTERNET – USEFUL OR USELESS?

Useless things on the Internet

- *Discover how many cans of Coke are left in a Coke machine.* Students at Carnegie Mellon University wired photo-sensors to indicator lights on a Coke machine and programmed a computer to count the cans as they were dispensed (finger coke@cs.cmu.edu).
- *Watch live coffee being brewed in a coffee pot.* University of Cambridge students aimed a camera at the computer lab's coffee pot and transmitted on demand digital snapshots of the state of the brew.
- *View laboratories all over the world.* There are live cameras accessible through the Web, pointed at busy labs all over the world.
- *See the time and date of someone's most recent phone call.* Brian Gottlieb from St Louis, Missouri wired his telephone to display to Internet users this vital information.
- *Check the temperature of refrigerator and hot tub separately.* Paul Haas from Ypsilanti, Michigan, hooked up his computer to achieve this feat.
- *Talk to a cat.* Michael Witbrock uses a voice synthesiser to let online visitors 'talk' to the cat that likes to sleep in the warmth of his modem. You can also listen to Bill Clinton's cat.

'You think they're weird? Well what's really weird is that people visit these sights not in hundreds but in thousands.'

(Source: *Time*, 16 January 1995)

'Smart networks to electronic agents or programmable filters, means consumers will be able to bypass adverts more easily. However they will also choose to seek out advertisements as and when they require information.'

(Source: *CIP* executive briefing, 1995)

'Classic information, toxic-data syndrome with more and more messages to read and less and less time to read them. "A solipsistic time sink that makes television watching seem like a social event... the modern world is not dying for want of more information."'

(Source: *Time*, 17 April 1995)

Download music:

It takes 90 minutes to download three minutes of music.

Useful things on the Internet

- *Watch Rolling Stones live concerts.*
- *Go back to the future.* A virtual tour of Universal Studios (http://www.mca.com) costs $35.
- *Tour a country.* Available as Le Tourist Cyber, Le Web Louvre and Central Culturel Virtuel (http://gertrude.art.uiuc.edu/mcornh/french/ccv.html).
- *Save a life with a global ambulance call.* A 13-year-old Chinese girl, Yang Xiaoxia, lost an arm to a mysterious disease. The mystified medical researcher sent out a desperate message on the Internet detailing the girl's condition and requesting help. Within days, 200 replies poured in from around the world and the cause of the disease was identified as a flesh-eating bacteria that had killed 11 people in Britain in 1994. Yang's treatment was altered accordingly and she is now recovering in hospital (*Time*, 10 April 1995).

- *Save a city – instant letter to the White House.* Reebok had preset letters written to the White House about inner-city hunger.
- *Save a continent.* Hold Hands across America, started on the Internet.
- *Save our planet.* Data can be pulled together on insurance industry losses due to typhoon activity to demonstrate how these climate effects relate to increases in global greenhouse gas emissions. The Web democratises information exchange. The chemical release inventory page (http://foe.co.uk/cri) allows you to enter a postcode and get a local map of sites of registered chemical releases. This information is freely available from the DOE but only in a table format requiring a chemical degree (*New Media Age*, 14 December 1995, p 6).
- *Lobby government officers.* Opinion makers and pressure groups are using the net as a means of communications. For example, multiple sclerosis groups shared information on the supply and cost of a new drug (Beta Seron) in the US and Europe. Now patient groups can compare progress on drug trials globally (*PR Week*, 9 June 1995).
- *Real time discussions.* Relay Chat (called IRC among 'net heads') is like CB radio except that messages are typed in via the keyboard.

DISCUSSION TOPICS FOR CHAPTER 10

1) How can the Internet assist a marketing manager?
2) How can the Internet hinder a marketing manager?
3) Is the Internet simply overhyped?

REFERENCES

Arden, Z (1995) Open road, *PR Week*, 17 March

Clarke, A C (1997) Interview in *The Daily Mail*, 11 March

Coulson-Thomas, C (1996) Will the Web take over?, *New Media Age*, 25 July

Dibbell, J (1996) Smart magic, *Time Digital*, 1 July

Dwyer, P (1996) The enabling agent will not dumbdown humans, *New Media Age*, 25 July

Dwyer, P (1997) Forecasting the future of the media, *New Media Age*, 30 January

Elms, M (1996) *Marketing Business*, March

Graham, A (1997) Exclusion zone – how can new media reach millions of people worldwide while bypassing the public?, *New Media Age*, 30 January, p 9

Haigh, D (1997) Accountability, *Marketing Business*, March

Handy, C (1995) *Visions of Heaven & Hell*, Channel 4 broadcast

Hubbard, S (1996) *Skills for an Information Society: A review of research*, reported in System overload, *Time Magazine*, 9 December

Hutton, W (1995) *Visions of Heaven & Hell*, Channel 4 broadcast

Jobs, S (1996) Interview in *Wired*, February

Kanter, R M (1996) *Integrated Marketing Communications* (CD ROM), Multimedia Marketing Consortium, London

Kavanagh, J (1996) Time wasters in the office caught on the Web, *The Times*, 2 October

Libbenga, J (1996) Pull on your shoes and boot up, Network, *The Independent*, Section 2, 9 September

Marshall, B (1996) IT focus, confidence booster, Guardian Education, *The Guardian*, 24 September

Negroponte, N (1995) Interview in *The Sunday Post*, 2 July

Port80.com (1998) Flawed Web site survey, http://www.port80.com

PR Week, 17 March 1995

Quittner, J (1996) The Netly News, *Time Magazine*, 11 November

Schrage, M (1995) The prisoners of CPM, *Adweek*, 27 March, p 25

Sheldon, N (1996) How will advertisers meet the challenge of an interactive age?, *New Media Age*, 4 April

Smith, P R (1996) *Integrated Marketing Communications* (CD ROM), Multimedia Marketing Consortium, London

Standage, T (1996) A hundred years of surfing, Connected, *The Daily Telegraph*, 27 September, p 9

Stipp, D (1996) The birth of digital commerce, *Fortune*, 9 December, p 99

Toor, M (1996) Artificial life – how genetic engineers will revolutionise gaming, the Internet and everything, *CD ROM Magazine*, August

Watts, R (1995) Media: travelling the international superhighway in Focus, *PR Week*, 2 June

World Futurist Society, The futurist, summarised in *Crystal Globe: The haves and have nots of the new world order*, St Martin's Press, New York

Wurman, R S (1996) *Information Anxiety*, reported in System overload, *Time Magazine*, 9 December

Strategic issues: branding

LEARNING OBJECTIVES

- Understand how brands are built as combinations of rational and emotional benefits for the customer.
- Distinguish different types of brand, and the situations appropriate to their use.
- Understand the forms of language and social meaning which enable brands to be effective.
- Appreciate the brand playground and its rules.
- Understand the concept of brand personality.
- Be able to distinguish the relative strengths of own-label and manufacturer brands.
- Understand basic strategic approaches to branding, and the current debate about the valuation of brands.

TOPICS COVERED BY THIS CHAPTER

WHAT IS A BRAND?

Despite the importance of brands in marketing, there is no generally agreed definition of what a brand is. However, if you locked three marketers in a room and asked them to describe the characteristics of a brand, they would probably emerge with an agreed press release. Most marketers would not disagree with Peter Doyle's definition of a brand as a 'specific name, symbol, design or, more usually, some combination of these, which is used to dist-inguish a particular seller's product' (Doyle, 1994). This is very similar, for example, to the American Marketing Association's definition adopted by Philip Kotler (1994). Doyle qualifies his definition by describing *successful brands* as having both a product that satisfies the functional needs of customers, and also added values which make the customer feel confident that *the brand is of higher quality or more desirable than similar brands from competitors*. Kotler goes somewhat further than this, and focuses on the relationship of trust between a seller and a buyer, describing a successful brand as 'essentially a seller's promise to consistently deliver a specific set of features, benefits, and services to the buyers.' Other authors, such as Lambin (1993), prefer to approach brands in terms of the level of awareness of customers and their ability to recognise or recall a brand.

Default branding (the unintended brand)

Many products and services in both consumer and industrial markets carry symbols, names, unique designs and colours, but without the image-nurturing and constant investment in marketing communications which generally support a brand. Potterton Boilers, for example, have a well-known name and reputation in domestic and industrial heating. Rolls-Royce is synonymous with the highest technical quality of aero-engines. Over a period of time, as these products and services are experienced in a market, their name becomes associated with a specific price–quality level, and will become one of the variables of customer choice. The public activities of a manufacturer will also affect the cognitive (knowledge-based) perception of the manufacturer's name. There is evidence that the credibility of marketing messages will be affected by a well-known name (Smith, 1993) or a name which has established associations of quality and reliability (eg ICI in agricultural fertilisers and industrial paints). This has more to do with the mechanism of source credibility (see Chapter 2) than with branding, and although a proportion of customers will not buy from an unknown company, there is no evidence that attaching a particular name to a product or service will by itself constitute a factor in a buying decision.

However, businesses have extensive and often highly publicised relations with their customers, employees, shareholders, creditors and market environments. Even without any deliberate planning of its corporate identity, or the perceived image of its products and services, a business will have, to a greater or lesser extent, a public reputation. Values of environmental care, community involvement, and professional and technical leadership will inevitably attach to that reputation (eg BP's public announcement of a new corporate ethics system announced in early 1997). Attitudes of customers and non-customers will become more positive towards a business which is seen to be involved in or sponsoring public non-profit-making events (eg NatWest Bank's sponsorship of lunchtime concerts in the City of London). Even without the intentional development of branding, some of the characteristics of brands will attach to all that business's products and services. This is the default or unintended brand, which is *the expectation held by a customer of how reliable and trustworthy a business is, independent of any planned marketing communications* (see Figure 11.1).

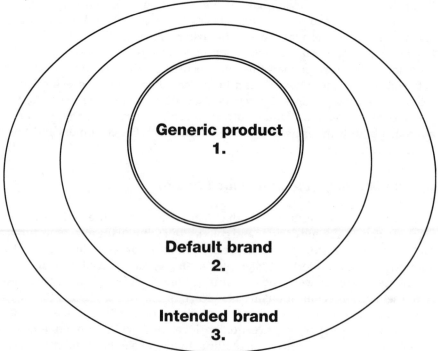

1. Generic or basic product
2. Default brand (unintended and unplanned communications)
3. Brand (intended and planned communications)

Figure 11.1 How the customer sees a product

A considerable part of a business's communications with its markets can therefore be unplanned, *ad hoc* and inconsistent with the image it would prefer to convey and which its brand marketers need it to convey. A dirty delivery truck will carry negative messages about the business, and even more so if the driver is not considerate and polite to other road users. A percentage of an advertising budget or the cost of a sales campaign can be wasted if the delivery trucks are not routinely washed. This example shows that failure to spend small amounts of money in one part of the business (eg washing the delivery trucks daily and routine driver courtesy training) can negate, and possibly destroy, the impact of the marketing communications budget for a substantial number of customers (Hill and Hillier, 1977). The default brand is unavoidable, ever-present, and waiting to explode like a land-mine with negative communications to the world at large, which includes the customers.

The importance of the default or unintended brand in brand communications is that if customers have difficulty in assessing the intrinsic qualities of a product (experience qualities such as taste, colour, smell), they will shift their attention to the extrinsic qualities of the brand (name, manufacturer, image, advertising) in order to evaluate the product (Zeithaml, 1988). To prevent the default brand having a negative effect on customer attitudes towards a brand, and to ensure the maximum impact of the marketing communications budget, businesses should have an overall policy on how to integrate all aspects of their public identity. Levitt (1962) has argued that this default brand can be managed through the implementing of *centripetal marketing* (see Chapter 1), a concept which is central to integrated marketing communications. Practical integration can be achieved by:

- a rolling public relations programme, focused towards target markets and committed to ensure that customers and other people within the customer environment perceive in the business a consistent set of values which are similar to the underlying values of the company's main brands;
- a design policy which covers all visual aspects of the business, from van livery and cleanliness to headed notepaper and letter style, so that a consistent visual identity is maintained.

Industrial brands

Most of this chapter is concerned with brands in consumer markets. In *industrial* (or business-to-business) marketing, brands are seldom used as a marketing communications tool. There are several reasons for this:

- Studies of buying preference in industrial markets generally rank price, quality, technical service and delivery as the main criteria in deciding a supplier. Responses to marketing communications by industrial buyers tend to be high involvement and focused on the current technical needs of their business (see the discussion of the professional customer in Chapter 3 and Figure 3.6). Ideas of fun, leisure and social meaning, which are inherent in consumer brands, are largely restricted to the business lunch after the deal is made.

- Industrial businesses do invest in corporate identity to communicate quality and other attributes (eg ICI, BOC, Dupont), but despite this, the reputation of a supplier is generally ranked low as a buying criterion in studies of industrial buying preference.
- The relationship between industrial businesses is normally complex, involving a number of specialists in the selling business (eg sales rep, technical manager, transport manager) contacting and dealing with their opposite numbers (eg buyer, production manager, warehouse manager) in the buying business. This complex relationship is called *organisational mating*, and it is in these personal relationships that the qualities of trust and reliability (the key characteristics of consumer brands) are built.
- Although industrial marketers do use advertising, sales promotions and public relations, their main communications tool is personal selling. Industrial sales reps and managers build direct relationships of trust and dependability with their customers, and there is generally no need for this to be replaced by the surrogate personality of the brand.
- Industrial businesses tend to segment their markets by size of business, Standard Industrial Classification, end-use of product and geographical location (Wind and Cardozo, 1974). They have no marketing planning basis on which to target the psychological attributes and social meaning of brands.

There are three aspects of industrial marketing which do, however, have some characteristics of branding. Firstly, large industrial businesses invest sometimes quite substantial budgets in developing corporate identity, and this can have an effect on the credibility of their sales reps in communicating with buyers. Corporate identity can be particularly important in the process of public sector tendering, which accounts for a substantial proportion of all purchasing in most countries (eg 15 per cent of GDP in the EU in 1996), as public image and reputation can be an influential factor in winning a tender bid at above the lowest tender price submitted. Secondly, some businesses (eg telecommunications companies) serve both consumer and industrial markets. They need to maintain at least the design quality of their consumer brand image on brochures, letterheads, exhibition stands, vans, uniforms and public notices in order to keep the image consistent. Thirdly, many process and fabrication consumables (non-durable products which are consumed as part of a production process, eg sanding discs, saw blades, flooring, cylinder oxygen and acetylene, welding rods, car components, fertiliser) are frequently purchased *ad hoc* by small and medium-sized businesses rather than under a negotiated supply contract. These consumables are purchased through industrial retail channels sometimes serving both industrial and consumer customers (eg builders' merchants), and many products stocked by these *industrial retailers* will carry either retailer or manufacturer names and logos which appear to play some role in customer preference. This is far short of the deliberate personality and social traits built into consumer brands, but it does raise the question of whether or not products and services can be identified with a latent or default brand.

COMPONENTS OF A BRAND

What is generally agreed by marketers is that a successful brand:

- is a visual signature or *brand mark* (symbol, name, design, colours or combination of these) which is attached to products and services;
- fosters a relationship of trust, reliability and exclusivity between a business and its customers;
- adds value to the basic product or service;
- provides some kind of psychological pay-off to the customer;
- simplifies the problem of differentiation;
- possesses personality traits which will allow customers to form a relationship with the brand.

Table 11.1 Tangible and intangible components of a brand

Tangible brand components	Intangible brand components
● Product itself	● Trust, reliability
● Brand name	● Psychological pay-off
● Brand mark	● Added value
● Description of benefits	● Quality of differentiation

A brand therefore consists of both tangible and intangible components (see Table 11.1). The tangible components (eg the quality of the product and product features) and the external markings (eg brand name, brand mark and description of benefits) are the outcomes of a complex planning process. This process also researches and identifies the special intangible qualities of the brand which the customer can gain by buying the brand (eg trust, reliability, added value, quality of differentiation and other forms of psychological pay-off). These tangible and intangible components enable brands to sell at higher prices than unbranded (or what are called *generic*) products because the brand adds value to a generic product (see Figure 11.2). The difference between the price customers are prepared to pay for a generic product and the price they are prepared to pay for a brand is called the *brand premium*, and so brands are referred to as being *premium priced*. There is normally a disproportionate relationship between the cost of adding value through branding and its impact, so relatively modest additional investment in branding can achieve significant brand impact and sustain a price premium over other unbranded products.

For practical planning purposes, a brand is a relationship which has a number of measurable variables, including the perceived quality of the branded product, the experience of consuming the brand, the psychological

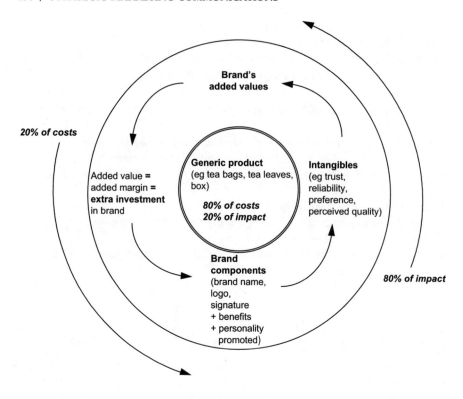

Figure 11.2 The concept of added value will add only a relatively small amount of cost but it will make an enormous difference to the impact on the customer

and social pay-offs from using the brand, and the value added to the product by the brand. For any brand, each of these variables consists of a set of attributes which can be researched and measured by the marketer in building and maintaining a brand and for positioning the brand against other brands in the market.

In the concept of IMC (see Chapter 3) the brand is the focal point of the relationship made in consumer markets between the marketer and the customer, as is illustrated in Figure 11.3.

It not only enables a business to focus its efforts around all the needs of the customer (functional, psychological and social), but it also provides the language which articulates that relationship. It is the definable social area in

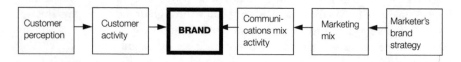

Figure 11.3 The brand is the point of interaction between the marketer and the customer

which customer activity melds with the communications and marketing mixes developed by the marketer. A brand is therefore 'a statement of a psychosocial relationship and dependency between a customer and a marketer'.

As a statement, it is conveyed in unique language, visual and verbal (the communications mix will include branding symbols, names, marks, colours and graphics). It provides social meaning, and will be adapted by the marketer to the social needs of the customer as those needs become apparent. It is psychological, in that it is a subjective cognitive experience for a customer. The marketer is as dependent on the acceptance and adoption of the brand by the customer as is the customer dependent on the marketer's competence to modify the brand when the customer's needs change. It is a relationship built on both information and experience, on an amalgam of meanings and styles. Above all, it is a relationship of reliability and trust.

CORE CHARACTERISTICS OF A BRAND

At the heart of a brand is a core of rational and emotional benefits. A well developed brand is capable of adding value and differentiation to almost any kind of product or service, but as brands contain a strong experiential element (eg the experience of consuming and enjoying the brand), they tend to grow in relation to specific classes of products or functions. Coca Cola, for example, has been built on an association with soft drinks, colas in particular, and has many line extensions in that product class. As some of its core benefits are *entertainment, youthfulness* and *happy leisure*, it can transfer its capacity to add value to products such as T-shirts and leisure bags. Trustworthy and reliable as it is, Coca Cola would not easily transfer to technical products such as motor cars or sound systems because of the historical limits of association between the brand and the functional attributes of soft drinks. On the other hand, a brand such as Virgin has grown quickly away from its early associations with record distribution and has transferred effectively into games, soft drinks, air travel and financial services. These are *brand extensions* of Virgin, based on the observable core benefits of youthful vitality and personal success, often expressed in the PR exposure of its founder, Richard Branson.

This relationship can be expressed at a number of levels of intensity. Levitt (1980) has proposed four levels:

1) generic product, where the function of the product and its support services are basic to the relationship. The customer evaluates the product through *recognised quality*;
2) expected brand, which satisfies the customer's minimal requirements. The customer evaluates the product through *recognised quality* plus *a recognised name*;
3) augmented brand, which includes a brand personality. Evaluation is through *recognised quality* plus *a recognised name* plus *recognised personality traits attached to that name*;

4) potential brand, which encourages the customer to pay a premium price to gain added value through benefits, usage and value chain activities. These means to added value define the activities which are included, in this chapter within the concept of the *brand playground*.

In each of these levels, the customer is making a defined relationship with the brand based partly on their perception of certain attributes and partly on what the marketer has done to add attributes to the product or service. The customer's idea of what he or she is buying will change, and in the process of building a brand, the brand may be shifted from one level of intensity to another.

The potential of brands to carry their ability to add value from product to product, and service to service, raises questions about what lies at the core of a brand. Generally, marketers agree that at the core of any market offering, product or service, lies the *core or generic benefit*. For a medium family car, the core benefit might be the facility of safe family transport. For a cosmetic, it might be the availability of style or self-confidence. When a business does not recognise the core benefit of a product, it can miss market opportunities. Bojana Fazarinc, Hewlett-Packard's marketing communications manager expressed this jokingly: 'In the past, if we were trying to sell sushi, we would market it as cold, dead fish.' If a brand conveys reliability, then that value will also attach to the core benefits, which will be perceived by the customer as having the reliability of the brand. Further, the experience of buying and consuming the brand will attach qualities of play and personality to those core benefits. There is therefore a dual core at the heart of a brand, consisting of both product or service benefits and brand benefits (see Figure 11.4). The core product or service benefits tend to be perceived rationally, and are about the functions and tangible benefits of the brand (eg a watch needs to tell the time accurately, possibly with the date and day of the week, and perhaps in 20 metres of water). The brand benefits are emotional and are based on the core psychological and social values of the brand.

Around this dual core will be added the actual product or service (eg functions and features), together with the physical attributes of the brand (such as symbols, colours and graphics) and the communications designed by the marketer. The brand can only become complete when the customer has experienced consumption of the brand physically, psychologically, socially and emotionally.

There is thus a dichotomy in brands between:

- *physical product benefits* – the physical attributes of quality, such as flavour, taste, colour, handiness of packaging; and
- *non-physical brand benefits* – the social and emotional values of the brand to the customer, such as status, dream realisation, and the symbols, colours, brand marks and graphics which the brand uses as visual shorthand for these.

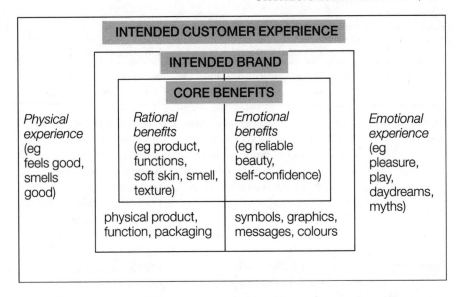

Figure 11.4 The dual core benefits of a cosmetic brand are delivered to the customer through its physical, informational and experiential attributes

These two sets of benefits will be assessed and relied on in different ways by customers (see Table 11.2).

BRANDS ARE ADDED VALUE

Branding, the marketing process of creating brands, is the great achievement of twentieth century marketing. For the marketer, branding is the basic method for differentiating one market offering from another, and without it, modern marketing as we know it would not exist. As Philip Kotler (1996) has said:

> Brands are extremely important. In fact the art of marketing is partly the act of branding because without brands you are in a commodity market and price is essentially the key determinant.

In a commodity market the customer will perceive all products as generic, having roughly equal quality and features (eg one packet of salt has the same value as any other). When a brand is added, the customer will perceive differences of image and associated attributes between one product and another (see Figure 11.5), and these differences will become part of the customer's search and choice process. The addition of certain product variations and features (eg salt anti-caking agents, sea salt, table salt, dietary salt) will increase the value and potential price of even a fairly generic product.

So, for the customer, branding has transformed the chore of shopping into social theatre and brightened the household shelf with trusted and familiar

Table 11.2 The rational/emotional dichotomy in action

	Physical product	**Emotional brand**
Benefits	Physical attributes, eg flavour, colour, texture.	Social and emotional benefits, eg status, dreams.
Assessment of quality	Quality can be sensed by touch, feel, colour, etc. If customer does not have time to evaluate, or finds it difficult to evaluate, he or she will move their attention to extrinsic benefits, eg branding.	Customer depends on extrinsic characteristics to assess quality, eg branding. If extrinsic characteristics have high predictive value (eg 100% fruit juice = no additives) customer will infer quality.
Positioning	Add features which confirm the unique attributes of the brand personality, eg a carrying handle on a washing powder pack confirms helpfulness.	Create or maintain a unique personality through visual association (eg Esso Tiger) and brand activity games which foster the values of the brand (eg Esso Tiger and a wildlife save-the-tiger campaign).
Adjustment of brand to changing customer needs	Cannot be modified without altering the nature of the product.	Can be retuned as customer perceptions and needs change.

friends. Brands such as Kellogg's, Heinz, Zanussi, Bosch and Electrolux have brought routine and reliable quality into kitchen foods and household appliances. Tourists can travel confidently with Kodak film, American Express and Thomas Cook traveller's cheques, global payment cards such as Mastercard and Diner's Club, and BP, Shell, Total or Esso fuel. In a world of more and more products and services, bringing increasingly complex choice processes, the customer has learned to trust and invest in the familiar brand as a guarantee of known quality. Even the high costs and risks of buying a family motor car are softened by the assured quality features of Ford, Honda, Mercedes-Benz and Volvo. Whatever the price–quality relationship desired by the customer, there is a brand ready to supply it. Brands are the denominators of price–quality. Even if a customer does not purchase a major brand, his or her choice will be guided by the standard qualities set by the leading brands in the market. In the consumer landscape, brands are the signposts of social meaning and the arbiters of price–quality.

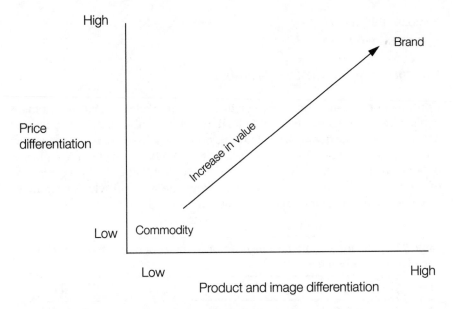

Figure 11.5 Commodities are developed into brands through adding value

WAYS OF LOOKING AT BRANDS

For the marketer, in a sense all products and services are brands. However generic a product or service, marketing will add some of the attributes of branding. With a generic product such as coffee, for example, customers may identify significant differences in quality through the description on the pack, such as whether it is Colombian or Arabica, high caffeine or low caffeine. UK supermarkets now distinguish on-pack and on-shelf a wide variety of coffee attributes, often supplementing a 1–5 grade caffeine content classification with taste ambience descriptions, such as *French, Breakfast* or *Mediterranean*. Virtually every product and service in consumer markets to some extent possesses qualities of branding, which means that there is an enormous variety of brands.

There is no generally accepted classification of brand types used by marketers. This is understandable, as brands are built in relation to the specific market situation of a business and its individual analysis of, and approach to, that situation. Just as no two competing businesses will segment their market in precisely the same way, every marketer will describe their brand in terms of its strategic value to their marketing objectives. Nevertheless, there are several ways of looking at brands which can show when and how to use different types of brand. These are:

- consumer and industrial brands;
- quality attributes of brands;
- level of reliance on brands;

- monolithic brands;
- strategic usefulness of brands.

Consumer and industrial brands

Consumer brands are icons of twentieth-century marketing culture. Customers live in a world of brands (see Table 11.3), which are universally recognised as markers of specific quality and status. Straplines such as 'There are rivets and there are Levi's rivets' and 'Coca Cola is it') are more than creative fantasies of advertising copywriters. They express the cultural and social significance of the brands they promote. They also articulate ways in which customers can give meaning to, and take meaning from, these brands.

Table 11.3 The top ten brands ranked in order of recognisability and preference for major world markets

Ranking	Europe	USA	Japan	Russia
1	Coca Cola	Coca Cola	Sony	Sony
2	Sony	Campbell's	National	Adidas
3	Mercedes	Disney	Mercedes	Ford
4	BMW	Pepsi-Cola	Toyota	Toyota
5	Philips	Kodak	Takashimaya	Mercedes
6	Volkswagen	NBC	Rolls-Royce	Fanta
7	Adidas	Black & Decker	Seiko	Pepsi-Cola
8	Kodak	Kellogg's	Matsushita	Volvo
9	Nivea	McDonald's	Hitachi	Fiat
10	Porsche	Hershey's	Suntory	Panasonic

(Source: Lander Associates in de Mooije (1994).)

There is also an element of playfulness about consumer brands, a quality which is about pleasure rather than drudgery, leisure rather than work, games rather than tasks, beauty rather than functionality. The importance of brands for the individual customer is far more than just a reliable product with a recognisable design signature. Brands are a way in which marketers make relationships with customers, and those relationships have an important dimension of social meaning which enable customers to express their images of themselves in a painless and socially acceptable way. They are not simply safe and reliable product choices, but rather they are statements by individual people of social meaning. What enables brands to be so successful at doing this is the fact that they are generally attached to products, and so they become a normal and acceptable part of the 'empire of things' (Douglas and Isherwood, 1980) with which people express themselves and their social values. Coca Cola, for example, has been described by its own management as a 'catalyst of social pleasure' (Bradt, 1996) because offering to buy someone a Coca Cola, wherever they might be in the world, can be construed only as a sociable act.

Industrial products and services, on the other hand, are not generally given brand identities with social or personal meaning, and the reasons for this have been discussed earlier in this chapter.

Quality attributes

Brands can be classified in relation to the ability of the customer to identify attributes of quality in a product or service. Kotler (1994: 445) distinguishes deep brands and shallow brands. A deep brand possesses six characteristics which can be visually perceived by the customer: attributes, benefits, values, culture, personality and suggested user. A shallow brand has only some of these characteristics. Where there is high on-pack exposure of quality attributes, brands can be shallow, often using simple name association or brand marks (see Figure 11.6). Where quality is more difficult for the customer to assess, brands need to be deep, with well developed personalities.

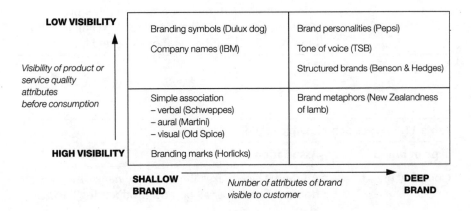

Figure 11.6 Relationship of visible quality and depth of brand

Level of reliance on brands

Brands can be classified according to how the customer relies on the brand in making a buying decision (see Table 11.4).

Monolithic brands

A company name can be added to a product or service where that name is generally recognised by customers as being associated with qualities of reliability, trust, pleasure or excitement. This may be called a company brand, a monolithic brand or a corporate endorsed brand. There are several types as listed in Table 11.5.

Table 11.4 Brand classification via reliance of customer on brand

Type of brand	Reliance of customer on brand
Ideal brand*	A brand which a customer uses to compare other brands. If the brand is not in stock, customers will choose the brand which is closest to their ideal brand.
Referent brand	An ideal brand which acts as a reference influence on the customer's perception of another brand, and which provides most of the emotional core of that other brand, eg perception of own-label brands will be influenced by the emotional core benefits of the leading brands in that product category.
Conjunctive brand*	A brand which is selected after the customer has set a minimum standard on all performance criteria.
Disjunctive brand*	A brand which is selected after the customer has set a minimum standard on only a small number of performance criteria. The customer will eliminate those brands which do not meet those selected criteria.

* See Green and Wind (1973).

Table 11.5 Types of monolithic brand

Type of brand	Association
Company brand	A brand which makes the company name the dominant brand for all or most products (eg Shell, BP, Esso).
Manufacturer brand	A brand owned and developed by a manufacturer around a specific group of products or product lines (eg Heinz).
Retailer brand	A specific design of packaging and labelling used to identify products as carrying the quality and reliability intended by the retailer on all its products. Some retailers break this identification into sub-classes of *value, premium* or *top of the range* products, and change elements of the design accordingly (eg Sainsbury's).
Multiple brand	A product or service which carries two brand signatures: (a) the brand of a family of products or services; and (b) the manufacturing company's name, or the brand attached to a particular set of generic benefits within that family, eg Cadbury's Milk Tray.

Strategic usefulness of brands

Brands can also be classified in terms of their strategic usefulness in positioning against other brands in the market, as shown in Table 11.6.

Table 11.6 Brands classified by strategic usefulness

Type of brand	Strategic usefulness
Leading brand	A brand which has a dominant share of a market by volume or value, and which is the preferred choice of the customers who purchase it.
Fighting brand	A brand which is developed to attack a specific competing brand.
Niche brand	Niching is a technique used mainly by small businesses to gain and keep position in a market against one or several leading brands. A small part of the market is selected for special levels of service and quality. This *specialness* is sometimes identified as a brand (eg The Royal Leamington Spa Water Toffee Company, also known as RLS Promotional Confectionery).
Global brand (see Chapter 12)	A global brand is a mostly standardised product or family of products which have a common brand identity wherever they are marketed. They are promoted with unified global communications, often supported by localised sales promotions. The personality and lifestyle values of the brand are common to all global cultures (eg the friendliness of Coca Cola).

Marketing and advertising agencies often have their own in-house terminology for and classification of brands, which are part of their own style of marketing strategy. BMP DDB Needham, for example, use a classification of *young, green* or *exciting*.

Branding is a shared language

Branding is also a common language which is used and understood by both customers and marketers. It has structure and meaning, so its effects can be measured and quantified, and as customers (without realising it) have learned this language, they expect it to be used.

Structure and meaning

The presence of brands in a market provides a structure of reference points which enable customers both to fix standards of product quality and to understand the meaning of what are often quite complex visual and verbal communications. Many of those reference points are represented by visual signs, symbols and metaphors associated with certain product qualities and creative strategies established over many campaigns and long periods of time, often to the extent that the brands and their associated meanings become a part of the culture of society. This is the process of linguistic evolution which turns brand communications messages into *semiotics*. This is a form of language in which specific symbols or words are innately and uniquely associated with certain meanings and values for the customer (Dyer, 1988). Barthes (1993) argued that repeated associations of values and symbols over time create a special semiotic language which will continue its meaning over several generations and be absorbed into the culture in which it is used.

Where Father Christmas got his clothes

Coca Cola, for example, has promoted the association of social happiness with a unique and consistent visual identity since the early 1900s. Pictures of happy, often youngish people were as much a feature of 1920s and 1930s Coca Cola advertising as they are in today's television commercials. The symbolic curved stripe, embodying the profile of the hobble-skirt bottle, has been reworked periodically as a design, but retains its essential form on square profile cans to preserve the semiotic curve. In early 1997, Coca Cola market tested a hobble-skirt can in the US. Coca Cola has been responsible for an even more significant semiotic, as the traditional red and white outfit of Father Christmas in the US and Western Europe can be traced back to an early seasonal advertising campaign by Coca Cola.

POSITIONING

As customers evaluate brands on both tangible physical benefits and intangible emotional benefits, the brand marketer needs to measure both these as perceptions by customers in the market. The emotional perceptions can then be related to the physical perceptions, and the position of each brand plotted on a *perceptual map* of the market (see Figure 11.7).

For a major brand, this process of measuring and mapping positions in a market is often a complex procedure requiring the measurement and analysis of a wide range of customers' emotional perceptions. Position mapping can also be based not on specific attributes of brands, but on the degree of similarity or difference between brands, to give an overall impression of how customers see the distance between brands in a market.

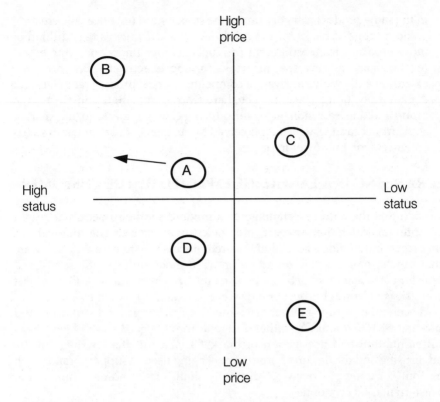

Figure 11.7 Perceptual map of brand positions in a market

When the positions of all brands in a market have been established and mapped, the brand marketer has to make a number of key strategic decisions and judgments, including:

- What adjustments need to be made to the marketing and communications mixes to keep the brand in its current position? This may involve developing the mixes in order to defend the brand against its nearest competitors (eg by adding value to improve price–quality perception). In Figure 11.7, if brand B's marketer feels that the brand may be attacked by brand A, should the status enhancement attributes of Brand B be increased, or should the physical product be improved to increase perceived price–quality? This is a typical branding problem in car markets.
- Should the brand be moved to a new position in the market? Brand A could be improved in status enhancement qualities through marketing communications and packaging improvements to move it closer to brand B and take some of B's market share. This would be typical in the major brand-dominated UK washing powder market.
- Can the brand be extended through brand or line extension to take more of a competitor's market share? A *line extension* is the addition of more products

in the same product category under the same brand (eg Lucozade creating a wider range of packs for the drink). A *brand extension* is the addition of more products from a different product category under the same brand (eg Lucozade adding special drinks for sports activists). Brand or line extension will involve analysis of competing brands' product ranges. Brand A is in a position to take market share from Brands B, C and D through brand and line extension (eg by introducing economy packs to take market share from brand D, which is perceived by customers to be similar in status enhancement, but lower in price).

BRANDING IS A LANGUAGE EXPECTED BY THE CUSTOMER

Branding is the cultural language of a modern market-based society (see Chapter 2). Customers expect and look for marketing communications messages and brands as part of the search process. Customers are also aware that purchase of a certain brand will reward them with specific status, and look for particular types of brand personality. Even in the pre-1990 Communist countries of Central Europe, brands were used and promoted by the central-ised economic planning system as a method of optimising distribution and production. Their aim was rather different from the marketer's objectives of differentiation and acquisition of market share, but the language of the advertising and the design of product packaging used to support brands such as Tomi washing powder were distinctly similar to branding promotion in Western market economies.

In three of the four typical customer profiles described in Chapter 3, brands play an important role in enabling the customer to avoid a long process of product comparison and information gathering. For some, such as the routine customer, brands are a usual choice. As discussed in Chapter 3, the routine customer will shift between brands, but will be unlikely to move to products which have very little branding unless there is a major price incentive, and will certainly return to major brands after that.

BRANDS ARE A PLAYGROUND OF SOCIAL MEANING

Meanings derived from communication of any kind are social. They have to be interpreted in the context of the individual receiver's lifestyle, values, social commitments, family and working relationships, and these contexts have to be clearly understood by marketers if communications, no matter how attention-grabbing, are to be interpreted and translated into social action. This common area of interpretation and understanding between the customer and the marketer is defined by the overlap in their respective *fields of perception* (discussed in relation to understanding messages in Chapter 2). With brands, however, the fields of perception are specialised (see Figure 11.8).

The *perception* by the customer is of the brand image, derived from both marketing communications and experience of consuming the brand. The brand experience is therefore important in the formation of customer attitudes towards the brand, because many of the emotional values will only become apparent to the customer during or after consumption. Associations might develop, for example, between the taste of a breakfast cereal, its convenient packaging, the images, graphics and colours on its packaging, and a wish for a calmer atmosphere during the family breakfast. Customer responses to brand communications are therefore best seen in terms of a whole brand experience, and not simply in terms of decoding a message and buying a product. This brand experience is to an extent self-reinforcing, as the consumption experience will intensify every time the customer consumes the brand.

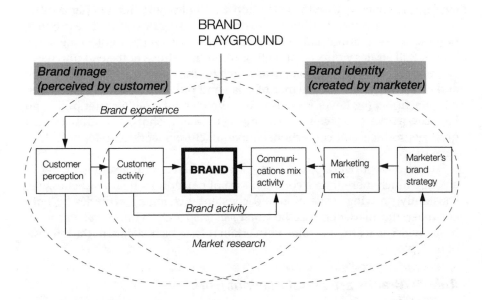

Figure 11.8 The flow of activity in and out of the brand playground

The brand is both a message and an experience. The brand communications mix, and many elements of the marketing mix, need to include messages and features which enhance the experience of consuming the brand. This brand experience is an essential part of the customer's attitude towards the brand, and will cause further activity aimed at repeating the brand experience.

Perception by the marketer is of the brand identity which has been created. The area of overlap, as with conventional communications, is an area of common understanding, but that understanding is progressive. Often, the marketer will express the brand in a personality, new traits of which are constantly being revealed to the customer as the marketer continues creatively to manage the brand. As the customer builds up both information and emotions about the brand from marketing communications and from experience in consuming the brand, this will be fed back to the marketer:

- by conventional market research (eg measuring perception); and
- by observable customer activity which expresses consumption of the brand (eg responses to on-pack competitions, special offers, attendance at sponsored events, use and consumption by non-buyers).

This common area of understanding is built on a number of relationships which the marketer can make with the customer both directly and through distribution. These are included in the larger model of the integrated marketing communications process shown in Chapter 3 (see Figure 3.9), and are principally the push and pull elements of marketing communications strategy. Push strategy is concerned with promotion to wholesalers, retailers and other intermediaries in the distribution channel, providing discounts, free product, point-of-sale promotion and other incentives to encourage the stocking of the brand. Pull strategy directs marketing communications to the end purchaser and user, to encourage customers to search for the brand on the retailer's shelf and create demand. The balance of push and pull strategies varies between manufacturers (eg Lever Bros use push, Procter & Gamble prefer pull), and between markets (eg where lead-time to market is short, as with packaged grocery products and confectionery, manufacturers tend to prefer pull strategies).

So this area of overlap, unlike a conventional communications model, is actually much more than a common area of perception. It is a wide range of constantly growing perception and constantly changing activities by both customer and marketer. It is the *brand playground*. As with any playground, the activities in it are constrained by certain rules which safeguard the interests of both players.

Rule 1: Brands are about play not work

The concept of play is fundamentally important in the brand playground, as this gives consumer brands their special quality of social meaning. A dull and unentertaining brand which implies hard work or household drudgery will not last long in a market as it will imply the creation of more problems than it solves. Brands are therefore designed to be bright, entertaining magic wands which wish away household and other chores.

For social anthropologists, the difference between work and play is quite distinctive, and brands fall on the play side of the work–play dichotomy. This dichotomy was characterised by Loizos (1980) as follows:

Work	Play
obligatory	voluntary
tiring	refreshing
disciplined	spontaneous
serious	not serious
done for others	done for oneself

Loizos qualifies this dichotomy in two ways. Firstly, in advanced industrial societies many tasks lack any intrinsic reward and do not seem directly and immediately related to meeting immediate needs. Secondly, a great deal of what goes on at work, such as joking, making friends and going to lunch together, is not work. This dichotomy has similar features to the apparent differences between left and right activity in the human brain, where the right cerebral lobe is concerned with aesthetics, creativity, pleasure and play, and the left lobe with analysis and task performance (see Blakeslee, 1980).

There is a relationship between this work–play dichotomy and the ways in which customers respond to brands. Brands emphasise play rather than work in a variety of ways. Household cleaning and washing products, such as washing powders, emphasise the simplification or elimination of work, as in a campaign for one washing powder which promised that it would 'Wash your cares away'. Motor car promotions frequently emphasise the effortlessness of driving, just as train companies emphasise the comparative effortlessness of train travel.

The traditional approach to consumer behaviour and attitudes towards brands is focused on the ways in which customers receive and process information. Two sets of functions are generally considered in the information processing approach:

1) attitudes formed by customers towards functional qualities of products and services, and the preferences which arise from these;
2) attitudes formed by customers from their analysis of the semantics (word meanings) of communications.

This is mainly about left-side (analytical) brain activity. Customer perceptions discovered in small-scale qualitative research are frequently converted into large-sample research based on the meaning of words (semantic differentials). Brand personality and attributes, and the marketing communications expressing them, are therefore generally created on the basis of the semantics of liking and disliking.

It has been pointed out by Holbrook and Hirschman (1982) that this information processing approach ignores or gives insufficient emphasis to playful leisure activities, sensory pleasures, daydreams, aesthetic enjoyment and emotional responses. They argue that consumption is a primarily subjective state of consciousness with a variety of symbolic meanings, and that fun, enjoyment and pleasure are outputs of purchase and consumption. The hedonic (pleasure seeking/enjoying) response of customers is much more than simply liking or disliking. This approach suggests that function and pleasure are parallel but different parts of the brand relationship between customer and marketer. In brand marketing communications, there are thus two parallel processes taking place:

1) information processing, in which customers learn the meanings and associations of messages, symbols, names and designs; and
2) consumption experience, in which customers become aware of pleasures, myths, aesthetics, daydreams and emotions in relation to the brand.

The consumption experience is about play rather than work, and is developed by marketers in order to produce the high levels of interest which have been observed in relation to leisure, entertainment and art (Holbrook and Hirschman, 1982). The methods used by marketers are games, whether obvious and overt such as on-pack competitions, or implicit and covert as in the case of enigmatic (puzzle-based) advertising.

Rule 2: The customer must not play with other brands

Differentiation is an innate strength of brands, and at both strategic and tactical levels can justify their relatively high cost. Lambin (1993) identifies six conditions for successful differentiation:

1) it must provide customers with value;
2) that value can be either higher satisfaction or reduced cost;
3) customers must be prepared to pay a price premium for that value;
4) rival brands must not be able to copy the differentiation;
5) the additional sales revenue generated must more than cover the cost of differentiation;
6) the differentiation must be communicated clearly to the customer.

Branding is a particular kind of differentiation, which involves creating an exclusive relationship between customer and marketer in which the brand most interesting to a customer becomes the standard by which all competing brands are assessed by that customer. The highest form of this relationship is *brand loyalty*, where the customer buys only the brand to the exclusion of all others. There are other, less intense relationships where customers may ultimately prefer a brand, but may not necessarily buy it. A *routine customer*, for example, (see Chapter 3) will be aware of many brands, but will not want to spend time analysing their differences. He or she may be persuaded by shelf-presence, point-of-sale promotions or price-off coupons to switch to an alternative brand, even if that alternative is marginally below the quality level of the brand they generally prefer. The communications task of the brand marketer is therefore twofold:

1) to establish the brand as significantly different from competing brands in ways that will appeal to the target customer;
2) to constantly remind the target customer of the availability and significance of the brand.

This emphasises the importance of reminder advertising and promotion in maintaining differentiation from competition, and ensuring not only customer preference for the brand, but also purchase. Reminder advertising, however, is more than just regular and routine communication. It is part of the process of making the relationship with the brand a continuous one, in which selecting the same brand becomes an autonomous action by the customer. That continuous relationship can be strengthened and sustained in many other lower cost ways, such as on-pack coupons and games, price-off coupons mailed direct to the target customer and social meaning promotions such as the computers-for-schools coupons given by UK supermarket multiples. Even more exotic games are created for the consumer through loyalty systems, such as retailer loyalty cards and air-miles. The design and colours of the brands can be updated as customer style preferences change (eg the eight changes of Shell – see Smith, 1993). The brand playground should be a rich and pleasurable assortment of games, continuously played to keep out other brands.

Rule 3: The games must reflect the social life of the customer

In addition to common perceptions of language and culture, branding requires a joint perception by customer and marketer of the social significance and situation of use of the brand. When customers opt to pay a premium price for a pair of designer jeans, they are developing their self-image in a particular way under the influence of a relevant reference group. Marketers therefore put the label on the outside of the jeans as well as the inside. With fashion clothing and accessories this process is easily observable, but does the same apply to branded grocery products? In the 1950s Mary Baker Cake Mix was successfully promoted with images that confirmed the mother-housewife as a provider of good food for the family, despite the simplicity and lower cost with which the same target customer could have mixed self-raising flour and margarine herself. The Katie advertising for Oxo carried the same message about family status. Contrast the Kellogg's sunshine breakfast approach to that most difficult of family meals with the 1980s Midland Bank advert in which the symbolic griffin climbed through the kitchen window and ate the family breakfast while giving advice on how to run their bank account and borrow money for a holiday. The extent of social meaning derived by the customer from the brand will depend on the *brand personality*, its traits and lifestyle (see the discussion of brand personality later in the chapter).

Rule 4: The playground must last for ever

The marketing objective in creating and sustaining brands is to gain long-term competitive advantage in a market. Marketing communications are the key factor in achieving this through making brands into continuous rather than occasional experiences, and by giving brands a myth-like quality.

With regard to time, customers are sometimes rational and therefore construct their social universe partly in an organised, demarcated time dimension. The passing of the year is marked by seasons, festivals, birthdays and other periodic events, and the passage of time can be laden with meaning (Douglas and Isherwood, 1978). The continuous experience of the brand is therefore a series of time-marked events. Customers do not eat the same standard meal three times a day, every day of the year. Some master-marketing businesses have used this time dimension to segment and target customers. McDonald's, for example, segment in the UK by time of day, with different offerings through the day backed by different marketing communications targeted at specific groups of customers. This is reflected in their advertising strapline, 'At McDonald's there's a time for you.'

The dimension of time is also used in branding to establish brand strength through the creation of interlocking myths and dreams. Social anthropologists work in what they call the ethnographic present, which concentrates past, present and future into a continuous present. Douglas and Isherwood (1978: 23) explain it in the following terms:

> Whatever is important about the past is assumed to be making itself known and felt here and now. Current ideas about the future likewise draw present judgements down certain paths and block off others... The individual treats his past selectively as a source of validating myths and the future as the locus of dreams.

This sense of the ethnographic present is therefore used by marketers to select and put together certain myths (past) and certain dreams (future) so that the customer can decide what to buy. This process is not about analysing brand or product attributes, which are often too functional to provide the materials of myths and dreams. Rather it is about using facts to create myths that correspond and work in parallel with the myth beliefs of the customer. Hovis bread, for example, is routinely given the nostalgic treatment of a nineteenth-century child relishing the delights of home-baked bread and fresh butter, expressed in browns and sepias like an old and trusted photograph of some long departed but dearly loved aunt. Hovis is, of course, produced by a late nineteenth-century patented process of bread-making, but modern brands, such as Mr Kipling cakes, also succeed on the basis of creating myths parallel with the myth world of the customer. In any brand, the potential of myth can be unlocked by the marketer, and is often implicit in the customer's consumption experience, as exemplified by Guinness and many malt and bourbon whiskies, where the presentation of facts and images stimulates the recognition of an implicit and unstated myth embodied in the brand.

This use of the ethnographic present should not be seen as a form of manipulation, as the creation of myth will considerably enrich the customer's experience of consuming the brand. It must also involve providing a high quality of functional value in the product itself, or there will be inconsistency between the brand promise and the product or service to which it is attached. Many of the brands which rely on the interlocking of myths and dreams are attached to products of substantial functional quality, and it may be that this is also an interlocking quality of their brand strength. The brand playground can last for ever.

Rule 5: Everybody wins a prize

Brands provide intrinsic reward for their purchase and use. This is generally achieved by messages which increase the self-esteem of the purchaser and user. This is particularly prevalent among brands of beer. By the 1990s most developed markets had voluntary or legally binding rules preventing advertising and other communications tools from suggesting that consumption of alcohol increases social performance. Creative strategies are therefore focused on the notion that a discerning drinker will select the brand. For Guinness, in the 1970s this was achieved through the creative strategy of the Guinness Supporters Club; in the 1980s Guinness emphasised individuality, and in the 1990s mature individuality. Sometimes, the reward offered is the consumption of the brand, as in the strap-line 'Have a break, have a KitKat.'

Reward can be more social, as in countline biscuits which keep children occupied and happy at critical times of the family day, as when they return home from school. Reward can also be financial, as in price-off coupons redeemable at the supermarket, though the relatively low rates of redemption for many coupons and coupon media may indicate that over-couponing can cheapen the brand and actually reduce its value. In 1995 only 5 per cent of door-to-door coupons and only 15 per cent of on-pack coupons were redeemed (according to NCH Promotional Services – see also AA/NTC, 1997).

The brand playground has no spatial or temporal limits. It can be anywhere at any time. Whiskas catfood is there whenever your cat purrs around your ankles. Kellogg's Cornflakes can be the sunshine breakfast, lunch and afternoon snack when the children come home from school. It is this all-pervasiveness of brands, and their ability to provide social meaning at any time which makes the brand playground so effective for marketing communications.

BRAND PERSONALITY

These deeper levels of branding which carry social meaning and ideas of playfulness are usually expressed through the *brand personality*. This is a set of psychological and social traits which express the main attitudes, values and lifestyle of the target markets. In many brand communications this personality is visualised by using a well-known actor, musician or sports star to endorse the brand. This enables the brand to *travel* easily across different segments in a market and across different national and regional cultures, because film, television, music and sport are increasingly part of a global (rather than national or local) culture (eg Pepsi campaigns have sponsored and coordinated local promotions with Tina Turner concert tours). Some brands suggest certain dominant personality traits by using animals (eg the

Esso tiger), or by anthropomorphising (giving human characteristics to) animals which have special photogenic qualities (eg PG Tips use of chimpanzees). Other brands suggest personality through storylines which project the lifestyles and daydreams of TV soap operas (eg Maxwell House and Nescafé compete head-to-head in the UK with alternative romantic storylines). Even when inanimate physical products are used, they are given human characteristics (eg milk bottles bobbing up to a front door, Polo mints queuing up excitedly to have the hole inserted, low quality and implicitly anti-social peas being excluded from the Birds Eye frozen pea bag). Whatever kind of brand personality is developed, it will always convey suggestions about the pleasure, fun or excitement of consuming the brand.

The brand personality, together with the functional and emotional attributes required at the time the marketing communications are planned (eg the planning of an advertising campaign), forms the basic formula for all creative strategies for the brand. This formula is called the *brand platform*, though what is included in it will vary from marketer to marketer and agency to agency. The brand platform will generally consist of the symbol, name, designs, colours, lifestyles and brand personality which will be built into the brand, but as lifestyle is a more useful variable for market segmentation, personality and lifestyle are usually both treated as aspects of brand personality for planning purposes. The kind of relationship which the brand makes with customers in the market will depend substantially on how the brand personality is developed. There are two basic purposes for the development of the personality and lifestyle traits of a brand:

1) They must be uniquely different from the personality traits and lifestyle attributes of other brands in the market. This will enable the brand to be positioned strongly against competition.
2) They must reflect the most salient (strongest and most obvious) personality and social traits of the customers in the target market. This will enable the customers to identify themselves with the brand, or to accept the brand into an imaginary social relationship with themselves.

Both these purposes imply that brand personality must be a key variable for segmenting markets. There are three basic approaches to understanding personality: the psychoanalytic approach, the psychosocial approach and the personality trait approach (Engel, Blackwell and Kollat, 1978).

The psychoanalytic approach

Influenced by the work of Freud, this approach describes personality in terms of three elements:

- *the id* consists of biological and instinctual drives;
- *the ego* is the hedonistic (pleasure-seeking) activities resulting from the drives of the id, and the personal morals which may constrain them;

- *the superego* is the interaction of the id and the ego in the unconscious mind, which results in human behaviour.

This psychoanalytic approach was the basis of the customer motivation research carried out in the 1950s. Behavioural psychologists such as Dichter used indirect assessment of customer motivation to identify the relationships between the drives of the id and purchase preference. For example, Dichter (1964) construed:

- a man buying a convertible car as seeking a mistress;
- baking a cake as giving birth;
- the smell of cigar smoke as masculine aroma.

The psychosocial approach

This approach assumes that personality is based on social variables, not biological instincts. It therefore explains the formation of personality as a process of self-image and attitude development which is a reflection of the environment in which a person grows and lives. Motivation to behave in a particular way operates at an unconscious level. As a process of social adjustment, personality will derive from the individual giving meaning to and taking meaning from objects, and will be influenced by reference groups (eg family, schoolfriends, colleagues at work). The psychosocial approach is used in this chapter for brands in general.

The personality trait approach

This is a useful quantitative method of assessing personality through analysing traits. A trait is a predisposition of a person to behave in the same way in similar situations. This approach assumes that the same traits may be common to many individuals, that they will remain stable in all situations, and that they can be inferred from the measurement of human behaviour. This approach is used in this chapter for brand personality.

While all these approaches are used in developing brands, the problem for marketers is that there is no evidence for a direct correlation between personality and product choice (Engel, Blackwell and Kollat, 1978). Even if there was, it would constitute only one of many variables in the customer's search for and purchase of products and services. There are also practical problems for marketers in using personality as a main or independent variable in customer choice:

- there is no significant correlation between demographics (age, sex, location, etc) and personality, so segmentation based on personality is likely to create segments of customers so small and scattered that they will be impossible to access;

- similar personalities can have different product choices, and different personalities can have similar product choices.

So personality only becomes useful as a sub-segmentation variable after initial segmentation, eg as a way of analysing brand choice within the same product type. For this reason, personality is subsumed within the lifestyle character-istics of a market, and this is the typical way in which personality is used in the creation of brands. Brand personality is normally incorporated into a lifestyle.

BRAND CONFLICT: OWN-LABEL VS MANUFACTURER BRANDS

Within distribution channels there is a constant battle between manufacturers and channel intermediaries (wholesalers and retailers) to acquire the largest share of margin (the difference between manufacturers' ex-works price and the price paid by the end customer). During the 1970s and 1980s in the UK, this battle was won largely by the multiple retailers (see Figure 11.9).

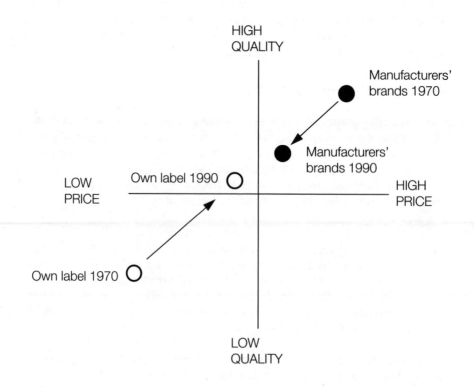

Figure 11.9 The changing nature of retailer and manufacturer brands

The two main reasons for this change in power within UK distribution channels were:

1) When OPEC doubled the price of oil in 1974 and again in 1979–80, manufacturers slashed advertising and sales promotion budgets, and the retailers filled the communications vacuum with their own advertising. As a consequence, customers began to rely much more on the choice of a particular retailer as a criterion of assured quality.
2) In some product areas, such as packaged grocery products, supermarket multiples had developed enormous buying power. Sainsbury, for example, controlled 12 per cent of the grocery market by the early 1980s.

This trend towards a concentration of channel power into the hands of the multiple retailers has continued into the 1990s, affecting not only grocery products, but also brown goods (radios, TVs, sound systems, etc), and white goods (cookers, refrigerators, dishwashers, etc) (see Figure 11.10). Retailers have also in this period developed their *own-label brands* (or *retailer brands*) to undercut the price–quality levels of manufacturer brands. This has continued the process of weakening manufacturer brands (see Figure 11.11). Despite this, retailers still stock strong manufacturer brands, because they act as benchmarks of price–quality for their customers, and enable retailers to offer several distinct choices of product in distinct bands of price–quality.

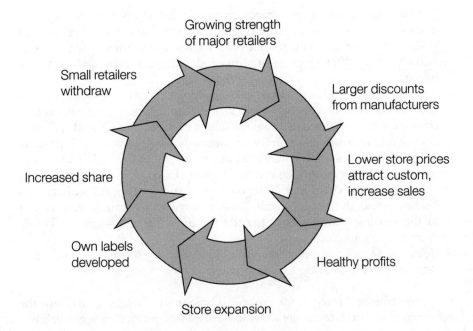

Figure 11.10 Retailers' increase in power

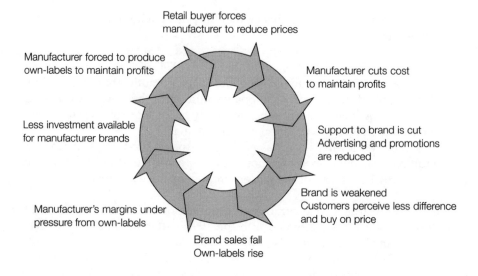

Figure 11.11 Manufacturers' loss of power

Many retailers make their highest margins on their own-label brands, yet they still continue to give substantial shelf space to strong and growing manufacturer brands. There are several reasons for this:

- For the retailer, strong manufacturer brands define the top price–quality available, and own-label products can then be positioned at lower levels of price–quality for sale to the routine price-conscious customer. Often a retailer will offer two different price–quality product ranges to compete with the brand.
- The strong manufacturer brands also provide many of the emotional attributes in the core of the own-label brand through their own marketing communications. The emotional attributes of the leading brand will thus act as a reference influence on the customer, who will perceive at least some of the added value of the own-label as a reflection of the added value and personality of the leading brand (see Figure 11.12).
- To achieve the level of marketing communications support required for a leading brand, the retailer would have to increase price much closer to that of the leading manufacturer brands to cover the necessary marketing communications costs.
- Retailers do not generally have the brand management experience that manufacturers can bring to their brands.

Communications strategies for own-label brands should therefore define the retail promise. This is the general standard of quality, product range, reliability, service and comfort provided across all products by the retailer. This also constitutes an important element of the emotional core benefit of an own-label brand (see Figure 11.13).

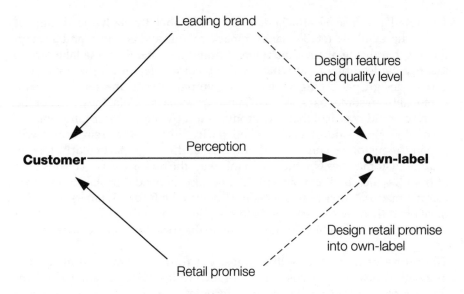

Figure 11.12 The leading (referent) brand and the retail promise of the retailer provide the focus for own-label brand development

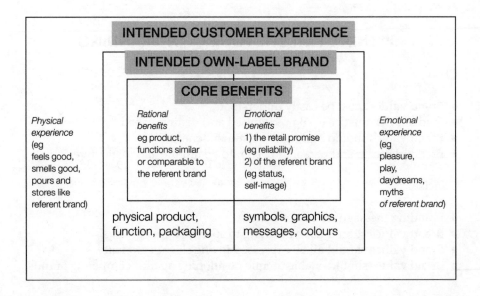

Figure 11.13 Core rational and emotional benefits of own-label brands

The retail promise is attached to the own-label through the design of packaging, symbols, retailer name or mark, colours and graphics, and through the merchandising against the referent brand in-store. Retailers take care to identify the leading brand which will act as the referent for the own-label, and to design packaging which is in sympathy with the referent brand personality. In some cases, as with Sainsbury's Classic Cola, the owner of the referent brand may feel that this produces a copy brand. Merchandising the own-label alongside of and in shelf parity with the referent brand will maximise customer comparison, impulse and choice, particularly for the routine customer (see Chapter 3). In this way, the own-label is a curious type of brand, which both competes with and also depends for its success on a leading manufacturer brand. At some point in the future, retailers will have developed their own-label brands to the point where they can exist without the referent brands which for now provide the social meaning of a product.

The future of marketing will be mostly a future of brands, but not the monolithic, heavily advertised mass brands of the 1990s. Channels of communication will continue to fragment technically to provide a narrower and more targeted focus on specific, and often quite small, groups of customers through new electronic media and the refined positioning allowed by database marketing. Customers will want more customised products and services, and more personally customised brands to give them social meaning. Retailer own-labels will be the only mass brands, and current global brands will niche at national level into a thousand different bespoke marketing relationships. The day of the personalised brand, customised at the individual level as much as a tailor-made suit or a home-cooked meal, is only a few technological paces away.

APPENDIX 11.1: THE FOUR Cs OF BRANDING

Clear

- Brand values must be easily understood.
- Trademarks must be easily recognised and distinguished.
- Brand values should highlight consumer benefits.
- Brand platform and personality should be unique and distinctive.

Concise

- Branding message should be simple.
- Brand values should have meaning to specific target groups.
- Brand values should all be expressed in one clear personality.
- Brand values should enable unique positioning against competing brands.

Consistent

- The emotional benefits of the brand must be consistent with the rational benefits.
- Communications strategies across the business should be coordinated.
- Reminder advertising and other communications should be consistent over time.
- Perception of the brand should be constantly reinforced.

Competitive

- The brand should be distinctly positioned.
- Brand values must be unique.
- Brand values should be developed to make imitation difficult.
- Brand designs should be legally protected in all present and potential markets.

APPENDIX 11.2: MEASURING BRANDS

Branding can be measured

Apart from the financial measurement of brands (see Appendix 11.5), branding is a special form of marketing language in which the degree of customer understanding can be factorised and measured by marketers. This enables campaigns to be aimed at achieving specified changes in market understanding of a brand. To assess understanding, marketers measure recall and perception.

Measuring recall

There are various techniques for measuring the percentage of customers in a market who can remember an advertisement or message during or after a communications campaign. It may be important to know if a new brand name has been remembered by customers, and this would be researched by *recognition testing*. This is normally carried out by asking respondents to identify words or pictures. Alternatively, it may be necessary to know if both the brand and the message from a particular piece of communication (eg a cinema commercial) have been noticed and remembered by customers. To measure this, respondents will normally be asked if they recall an advertisement for a specific brand (*aided recall*) or for a product or service without any mention of the brand (*unaided recall*). This will measure the extent to which the message as well as the brand is being seen and recognised, so is a useful test of whether or not the communication is being given *attention* by the target customers. Recall testing does not measure the effect of communication on customer attitudes or behaviour.

Measuring perception

Attention precedes perception. The human senses constantly take in vast amounts of information (sight, sound, taste, smell, vibration, texture), but only a very small amount of this is used by the human brain. The largest intake of sensory information is by the eye. (There are 10 billion nerve cells in the human brain. Information comes into the central nervous system from 260 million visual cells, 48,000 auditory cells and 78,000 receptor cells.) There are mechanisms both in the sensory organs and in the brain which select only certain information for processing. The cones on the retina of the eye, for example, have inbuilt recognition of certain patterns such as discs and rings. What the brain selects for processing is probably a result of learning.

This process of taking in information, organising it and making sense of it is called *perception*, and the selection of only certain information for processing is called *selective perception*. This can be measured in a variety of ways, including:

- measuring the perception of the attributes built into a brand (such as personality and lifestyle) to test whether the brand is being understood in the way the marketer intended;
- measuring customer perception of the similarities of brands to assess how customers see other brands in the market;
- measuring the importance to customers of a wide range of brand attributes, so that a perceptual map of the market can be produced showing the position of competing brands relative to customers' preferred attributes.

APPENDIX 11.3: BASIC DECISIONS IN BRANDING

Decision	Focus of decision	Options
Need for a new brand or not?	Branding decision	Brand Non-brand Default brand
Who should own and control the brand?	Brand sponsor decision	Manufacturer brand Retailer own-label brand
Should each product be individually branded?	Brand family decision	Individual name Family name Multiple brand (both)
Should other products be included under the brand?	Brand extension decision	Brand extension Line extension No extension
Should two or more brands be developed in the same product category?	Multi-brand decision	One brand Several brands
Should the brand be repositioned?	Repositioning decision	Change mixes to gain new position No repositioning
Does the brand need defending?	Brand defence decision	Retune to changes in customer perception Strengthen attributes to prevent loss of market share to competitors Brand is already well defended

APPENDIX 11.4: BUILDING AND MAINTAINING STRATEGIES

'Stop + Sit'	Analysis	Building tasks	Maintenance tasks
Segmentation	Demographics Lifestyles Personalities Price-quality Social values	Match brand personality to lifestyles	Add personality attributes
Targeting	Market objectives, functions and emotions of brand	Define market share required, sales and margin	Market share: – recover share – gain new share – protect share
Objectives	See above	See above	See above
Positioning	Competitor brands Default brand Perceptual map Price–quality map	Build personality Find unique position Brand name or mark	Protect, extend, rejuvenate by brand extension, line extension
Sequence	Market change next 12 months and in 2, 3, 4 years	Market objectives Brand audit Strategy Criteria for name Test personality Screen and select	Retune designs Modify mix New games New investment
Integration	Default brand PR effectiveness Check that the communications tools below integrate	Assess impact Develop programmes Use PR to adjust image of whole business	Update information system Relate games to whole business and its image
Tools	Sales force Advertising Sales promotions Direct marketing Public relations Sponsorship Exhibitions Corporate identity Packaging Point of sale promotions and merchandising Word of mouth Internet and new media	Image advertising Sales promotions Databasing Pricing to channel	Reminder advertising Games as promotions PR profiling

APPENDIX 11.5: VALUATION OF BRANDS

Brands are now regarded as key assets of a business. They are protected by copyright, design registration and trademark registration, and this enables them to be bought and sold by businesses. Their value is generally referred to as *brand equity*, although this term is also often applied to the extent to which a brand has gained recognisability and trust in a market. In a sense, the two meanings are similar, as they both represent the practical worth of the brand as a means of securing sales revenue and margin. The value of a brand will depend mainly on the strength and extent of awareness of the brand in the market (Kotler, 1994: 445). There are five levels of brand awareness which will affect the calculation of brand value:

1) *Brand loyalty* is where customers buy only that brand and will not switch even if the brand is out of stock. This is the most valuable level of brand awareness.
2) *Brand preference* is where customers prefer the brand, but may purchase another brand in certain circumstances (eg if the brand is out of stock).
3) *Brand acceptance* is where customers feel sufficiently well disposed towards a brand that they will accept as credible the messages in brand com- munications, and the brand will become one of a number of brands which they may choose.
4) *Brand awareness* is where the customers in the target market can recognise and recall the brand, but have formed no special preference for the brand.
5) *Brand non-awareness* is where few customers know about the brand.

The calculation of brand equity is a difficult area for both accountants and marketers because brands exist at these different levels of awareness. In order to put a money value on a brand, it is necessary to quantify its potential in terms of sales revenue and profit. There are many different methods used for this, and the following are examples:

- *Added value of the brand*. This is the price premium times the additional volume sales gained by the brand over the average brand in the market. This will enable a calculation of the annual added value sales volume deriving from the brand which can be converted into a purchase price for that brand (eg a common multiple would be two and a half times annual added value sales revenue), or it can be discounted back to net present value.
- *Brand asset valuator (Young & Rubican)*. This measures what Young & Rubican call *brand strength* (differentiation and relevance to customers) and *brand stature* (esteem and knowledge of the brand) for some 450 global and 8000 local brands in over 20 countries. From this Young & Rubican produce an analysis of dynamic brands, niche brands and tired brands.

- *Brand vision (AGB Taylor Nelson).* This measures customers' attitudes to brands and identifies customers less committed and more committed to a brand in order to identify customers who may switch brands.
- *Equitrend (Total Research).* This measures brand salience (customers who have a stated opinion of the brand) and correlates this with the average rating of quality given to that brand by customers and non-customers. This is used to assess potential price elasticity of a brand.

There are several problems with all these approaches to measuring brand equity:

- Many of the variables, such as attitude and opinion, are difficult to measure, and two different research instruments may produce quite different attitude profiles in the same market. Even if the added value approach is used, there remains the problem of how to define the average brand in the market.
- Some of the value of brand equity lies in the potential of the brand, which may be managed to a different level of profitability by another business. Two different businesses may therefore assess quite different values for the equity of a brand.
- A brand may also have an impact on different parts of the marketing mix, and may be leveraged across the mix in quite different ways (eg an established brand will gain distribution easier and at lower cost; demand will be relatively inelastic to price; new products and line extensions can be launched at lower cost). These potential effects of a brand are again difficult to estimate.
- If a brand is to be valued for inclusion in the balance sheet as an asset of a business, where are the professional valuers who can apply strict and consistent criteria? Ignoring the problems which accountants have experienced with valuing other assets of a business such as its property portfolio, this is the main argument used by the UK accounting profession for not including brand equity in the balance sheet, although this has been the practice in Australia for some years.

These problems have all been addressed by marketers, particularly in the pioneering work of marketing consultants Interbrand which has developed techniques of brand valuation that comply with accounting standards in the UK and elsewhere. Measurements of brand equity are an important indication of the effectiveness of brand management, and can also be used in mapping the positions of brands in a market. As accounting practices change in Europe and the US, as they have already in Australia, and brands are placed as assets in the balance sheets of businesses, brand marketing will move to the centre of the relations between businesses and customers, and this will start to redefine the nature of marketing practice and its role within business.

DISCUSSION TOPICS FOR CHAPTER 11

1) How can the default brand of a business be managed by a marketer?
2) Describe three promotions which could become games in the brand play-ground for a leading washing powder brand.
3) Discuss the role of merchandising in brand communications.
4) What are the differences between retailer own-label brands and manu-facturer brands?
5) What types of brand are used by the customer to evaluate quality?
6) Select useful variables and draw a perceptual map of the household furniture market. Suggest positions for IKEA, Habitat, MFI and other furniture retailers with which you are familiar.
7) Outline the main arguments for and against capitalising brands in a comp-any's balance sheet.
8) Identify the different ways in which rational and emotional benefits are used by the customer to evaluate a brand before purchase.
9) Discuss the importance of the consumption experience in brand com-munications. How would you communicate ideas about the consumption experience for a chocolate bar?
10) How do customers derive social meaning from brands?

REFERENCES

AA/NTC (1997) *The Marketing Pocket Book*, Advertising Association/NTC Publications, London, p 125

Barthes, R (1993) *Mythologies*, Vintage, London

Blakelees, T R (1980) *The Right Brain: A new understanding of our unconscious mind and its creative power*, Doubleday, New York

Bradt, G (1996) Multimedia Marketing Consortium, London

Dichter, E (1964) *Handbook of Consumer Motivations: The psychology of the world of objects*, McGraw-Hill, New York

Douglas, M and Isherwood, B (1980) *The World of Goods: Towards an anthropology of consumption*, Penguin, Harmondsworth

Doyle, P (1994) *Marketing Management and Strategy*, Prentice Hall, Englewood Cliffs, NJ

Dyer, G (1988) *Advertising as Communication*, Routledge, London, ch 6

Engel, J F, Blackwell, R D and Kollat, D T (1978) *Consumer Behaviour*, 3rd edn, Dryden Press, Hinsdale, IL

Green, P E and Wind, Y (1973) *Multiattribute Decisions in Marketing: A measurement approach*, Dryden Press, Hinsdale, IL

Hill, R W and Hillier, T J (1977) *Organisational Buying Behaviour*, Macmillan, London

Holbrook, M B and Hirschman, E C (1982) The experiential aspects of consumption: consumer fantasies, feelings, and fun, *Harvard Business Review*, September

Kotler, P (1994) *Marketing Management and Analysis, Planning Implementation and Control*, Prentice Hall International, Englewood Cliffs, NJ

Kotler, P (1996) *Buyer Behaviour* (CD ROM), Multimedia Marketing Consortium, London

Lambin, J-J (1993) *Strategic Marketing: A European approach*, McGraw-Hill, New York

Levitt, T (1962) Centripetal marketing, in *Innovation in Marketing*, Pan, London

Levitt, T (1980) Marketing success through differentiation – of anything, *Harvard Business Review*, January–February, p 83

Loizos, P (1980) Images of man, in *Not Work Alone: A cross cultural view of activities superfluous to survival*, ed, J Cherfas and R Lewin, Temple Smith, London

de Mooij, M (1994) *Advertising Worldwide*, Prentice Hall, Englewood Cliffs, NJ

Smith, P R (1998) *Marketing Communications – An integrated approach*, 2nd edn, Kogan Page, London

Wind, Y and Cardozo, R (1974) Industrial market segmentation, *Industrial Marketing Management*, **3**

Zeithaml, V A (1988) Consumer perceptions of price, quality, and value: a means–end model and synthesis of evidence, *Harvard Business Review*, **52**, July 1988, pp 2–22

T W E L V E

Strategic issues: global implications for communications

LEARNING OBJECTIVES

- Understand the globalisation process and its opportunities for growth.
- Consider the problem of barriers and the challenges of international markets.
- Be aware of global growth restrictions imposed by non-global brand names.
- List global communications strategic options.
- Appreciate the strengths, weaknesses and implementation issues of a centralised/standardised approach to global communications.

TOPICS COVERED BY THIS CHAPTER

GLOBALISATION OF MARKETS

This chapter examines the opportunities, the challenges, the problems and the strategies facing organisations operating in the international marketing communications arena.

The global opportunity – is it really happening?

Today, yoghurt, pizza, spaghetti, rice, kebabs, Indian cuisine, Chinese meals, Mexican food and American burgers are both popular and easily available in many countries around the world. The Rolling Stones and Shakespeare also have a universal appeal. There are more people learning English in China than speak it in the USA. Back in 1985 approximately one billion people from different time zones across the world watched the Live Aid charity concert simultaneously. In 1994 two billion people watched football's Brazil versus Italy World Cup final. Perhaps the global village is still growing. Or are clichés like 'the world is getting smaller' nothing more than oversimplified general-isations cast upon a culturally complex world? Some say that human beings have more things that bind them together than separate them. Others say that market differences are greater than market similarities. There are, in fact, what the Young & Rubican advertising agency call cross cultural consumer characteristics. These identify the common ground. The man or woman living in a smart apartment block in London's Knightsbridge has probably got more in common with his or her counterpart living in a smart apartment block off New York's Central Park than he or she has with someone living in some drab south London suburb. There are indeed some common denominators and some common sets of needs and aspirations which can be identified, particularly in similarities of lifestyle. Suffice it to say that the young and the rich have very similar tastes throughout the world.

Touching a global nerve

It follows that if a manufacturer or service supplier targets roughly the same socio-demographic groups in different countries and touches a common nerve within these target markets, then the same product or service can be packaged and promoted in a uniform manner. The pricing and distribution may vary but the branding, packaging and even the advertising can be the same. The manufacturers of world brands can therefore position their products in a similar manner in the minds of millions across many different cultures. This is the result of careful analysis and planning by expert marketing professionals rather than a trial and error approach to market extension. The next challenge lies in moving the rest of the communications mix in a uniform manner so that not just advertising and packaging but sales promotions, direct mail, sponsorship, etc reap the benefits of a global approach.

Forces driving globalisation

Globalisation is not just a product-orientated corporate push for growth but more of a market-orientated reaction to the emergence of common global lifestyles and needs. These are emerging as cheap travel combined with higher disposable incomes allow travellers to leap across borders, visit other cultures and return home with a little bit of that culture's soul in their own. Television itself has brought into the sitting rooms of British homes pictures and images of America's *Miami Vice*, Australia's *Neighbours*, Africa's famines and Tiananmen Square's students. It has also brought stunning scenes from the depths of the oceans to the balmy beaches of the Caribbean, the rugged beauty of the bush and the once rich and fertile Amazon forest. This global awareness is exploited by the corporate push for growth, which has forced many suppliers from saturated local markets to venture into overseas markets. Improved production, distribution and marketing techniques have accelerated the movement of products and services from all around the world into local markets. Political barriers are falling in China and the Eastern bloc and, of course, Europe's own internal political barriers are being dismantled also. The doors of the world's markets are opening. The key, it seems, is to identify core benefits which are common to different cultures along with any relevant cultural idiosyncrasies.

The elite global players

The significant benefits derived from a global brand and a global communications strategy are reserved currently for a relatively small number of players. This elite band recognise the right conditions and apply thorough research and planning to exploit the brand's assets on a global scale. Although Rein Rijkens (1992) has identified a 'trend towards greater internationalisation and centralisation' it should be remembered that a single communications strategy (incorporating everything from branding through to the complete range of communications tools) rarely works for all the players operating in international markets. The desire to harness the global opportunity is natural because international markets offer huge rewards. They also present intricate problems. Careful cultural homework needs to be included in the detailed research and planning that goes on below the surface.

Look for below-the-surface similarities

Similar buying behaviour and buying patterns do not necessarily mean a uniform market with uniform needs, uniform communication channels, uniform decision-making processes, uniform decision-making units or even uniform reasons for buying. Take the case of buying premium priced water. In a Khartoum slum an impoverished family pays twenty times the price paid by families with water main connections, while half a world away a middle-class family buys bottles of mineral water. This demonstrates 'unreal similarities'. The buyers appear to behave similarly by purchasing expensive water. They are, however, very different – in fact they are from totally dissimilar groups with different aspirations, motivations, lifestyles and attitudes, not to mention disposable income. On the surface there is a market for private water in both countries, but the distribution channels, communication channels, advertising messages and levels of disposable income are poles apart.

An analysis that goes below the surface (or below the sales results) will reveal a range of different motives, aspirations, lifestyles and attitudes to the same product. Surface information can create a false sense of simplicity. International markets can also suggest surface solutions that ignore the cultural complexities and intricacies of distant markets. As Sir John Harvey-Jones (1988) once warned:

> Operating in this milieu requires much greater sensitivity to national differences than we are accustomed to having. The mere fact that one stays in the same sort of hotel almost anywhere in the world, that one arrives in the same sort of car, that it is now possible to call by telephone or telex directly from almost anywhere in the world, all gives a superficial feeling of sameness which is desperately misleading and must never be taken for granted.

Globalisation, intertwined with cultural idiosyncrasies, appears to be emerging in many markets around the world. The marketing maxim 'think global, act local' remains valid. The challenge goes beyond communicating with new international customers and into working with international partners whose idiosyncrasies and languages pose many problems. Take nomenclature for a moment. The French normally refer to advertising as 'publicité' which can cause some confusion, while the Yugoslavian word for advertising is 'propaganda'. Other cultures have difficulty translating 'marketing', 'marketing communications' or 'advertising' as they have not yet created such words.

Despite all of this globalisation is occurring and offering huge rewards.

GLOBAL CHALLENGES

International markets are riddled with hidden cultural differences that make global advertising an intriguing challenge even for the most capable international marketing expert. Some of the intricacies which contribute towards the difficulty of global marketing are described in a little detail in the sections which follow.

Language
Language obviously requires translating, although there are exceptions to the rule (where the language reflects beneficial cultural aspects of the product, eg Audi's 'Vorsprung durch technik' strapline). Some expressions simply do not translate (see discussion of the wrong strapline below).

Literacy

In many developing countries literacy is low (Dudley, 1989). This limits the amount of explanation possible in advertising. Even with high literacy, the reading of translated Western-style advertisements still causes problems, eg before and after toothpaste advertisements which are not adjusted for Arab populations, who read from right to left.

Language, literacy and logic

Combine these three in the international arena and a new challenge emerges – writing clear instructions is a skill in one language, but a complex skill in several. Try this set of instructions for assembling a 'Knapsack':

'Directions for assembling:

1) Lead the hind leg in an opened position.
2) Lead the frame of the sacksupport up.
3) Insert the blushing for blocking in the proper split, push it deeply and wheel in an anti time sense till it stops.'

Colour

Colour has a direct access to our emotions. Watch how red is commonly used in advertising in the West. Colour, however, does not have uniform meaning across the world, eg blue in Iran means immorality, white in Japan signifies death (hence McDonald's white faced Ronald McDonald has problems), purple in Latin America also means death, brown/grey in Nicaragua is disapproved, and so on (Winick, 1961).

Gestures

Humour is rarely globally appreciated, and even basic body gestures are not global. In some parts of India shaking the head from left to right means 'yes'. Touching the lower eyelid may be just an itch, but it also suggests to a South American señorita that you are making a pass and to a Saudi that he is stupid. Scratching an earlobe has five different meanings in five Mediterranean countries: 'You're a sponger' (Spaniard), ' 'You'd better watch it' (Greek), 'You're a sneaky little...' (Maltese), 'Get lost you pansy' (Italian), while a Portuguese will feel really pleased. Even thumbs up is deemed to be a devastatingly obscene gesture to a Sardinian woman. Thrusting your palms towards someone's face may be meant to be endearing but to a Greek there is no greater insult since this gesture, called a 'moutza', comes from the Byzantine custom of smearing filth from the gutter in the face of condemned criminals. The 'A-OK' gesture (thumb and index finger in a circle with the rest of the fingers open) means money to a Japanese, zero in France, 'OK' in America and 'I'll kill you' in Tunisia (Morris, 1988).

Culture

Culture creates a quagmire of marketing problems: religion, sex, eating, greeting, habits, lifestyles, the role of women – the list is endless. Ferraro (1990) points out nine critical dimensions that contrast the US with the rest of the world's cultures. She says that US culture places a high value on (a) individualism, (b) a precise reckoning of time, (c) a future orientation, (d) work and achievement, (e) control over the natural environment, (f) youthfulness, (g) informality, (h) competition and (i) relative equality of the sexes.

Original national identity

National identity can be an asset or a liability. For example, Dudley (1989) reports that Marathon Oil makes a point of stressing its US association in Italy where American high technology is beneficial, but in Germany Marathon avoids the issue of its American parentage because of the German concern over US control in the German energy industry.

Media availability

Television is sometimes unavailable since (a) developing countries do not have a high penetration of televisions in domestic households, (b) some countries do not have commercial TV stations, and (c) others do but they restrict the amount of advertising time. Unilever and BAT make their own medium available in East Africa by running their own mobile cinemas.

TV helps:

The further away from a TV screen, however, the more difficult many experts say it becomes to create and to deliver a pan European message (Mead, 1993).

Media overlap

Television and radio from one market can spill over into other markets, eg half the Canadian population has access to American television. Kahler and Kramer (1977) report that 'Belgium, with no commercial TV, can be reached through two Dutch, three French, three German, two English, and one Luxembourg channel.'

Lack of media data

Great Britain and Ireland have well-structured and categorised media analysis data (audited data). Without reliable media data, the optimum cost and effectiveness of the overall campaign is unlikely to be achieved. Properly structured media markets are easier to work in.

Lack of media credibility

In some countries unregulated or poorly regulated media may flaunt the principles of legality, decency, honesty and truth, which in turn may make these media untrustworthy or create audience scepticism about the particular source of information.

Varying media characteristics

Coverage, cost and reproduction qualities can and do vary from country to country.

Different media usage

Kahler and Kramer (1977) suggest that the British tend to see TV as a visual medium while TV to the Americans is a visual accompaniment to words.

Different media standards

A lack of uniformity of standards means different types of both film and artwork may be required for different markets, eg different page sizes may require different artwork, which increases cost.

Different price structures

Different countries have different forms of negotiation and bartering. The Americans and the Japanese are poles apart. In less developed countries, cash may not be available but barter, or counter trading, can offer an acceptable alternative.

Legal restrictions

Whether in the form of voluntary codes or actual legislation, there is as yet no harmonised set of laws or regulations. This presents the advertiser with different problems in different countries. As Majaro (1982) says, 'In Germany, superlatives are forbidden by law. In Sweden, misdemeanours by advertisers may be charged under the criminal law with severe penalties.

Competition

Different markets have different key players using different strengths. For example, Ford's position of 'safety engineering' worked in many countries but not in Sweden, where, of course, Volvo occupied the position. Competition may react in different ways in different markets.

Non-global names

Some brand names simply restrict themselves from seizing the global opportunity. The section on global misses below includes a list of many unfortunate examples.

Central agency, local creative:

'The trend towards using the same creative work across Europe is developing more slowly than the tendency to use the same advertising agency network.'

(Source: Rachel Kaplan, 'Ad agencies take on the world', *International Management*, April 1994.)

GLOBAL MISSES

Some marketers carefully choose names that work for their local domestic market. This insular perspective is more than likely to restrict any future growth opportunities into international markets and almost certainly restricts development into a global brand.

Wrong name

Here are a few examples of how to get the name wrong:

Sic (French soft drink)
Pschitt (French soft drink)
Lillet (French soft drink)
Creap (Japanese coffee creamer)
Irish Mist (in Germany 'Mist' means manure)
Bum (Spanish potato crisp)
Bonka (Spanish coffee)
Trim Pecker Trouser (Japanese germ bread)
Gorilla Balls (American protein supplement)
My Dung (restaurant)
Cul toothpaste (pronounced 'cue' in France, which means 'anus')
Scratch (German non-abrasive bath cleaner)
Super-Piss (Finnish car lock antifreeze)
Spunk (jelly baby sweet from Iceland)

Even sophisticated marketers can get it wrong. General Motors discovered that Nova meant 'it won't go' (*no va*) in South America. Ford launched the Pinto in Brazil and soon realised that it was slang for 'tiny male genitals'. Coca Cola's phonetic translation in China meant 'Bite the wax tadpole'. After launching into English-speaking markets, Japan's second largest tourist agency was surprised to receive a steady influx of enquiries for sex tours. The Kinki Nippon Tourist Company soon changed its name.

These translation problems are not insurmountable. For example, Curtis shampoo changed its name from 'Everynight' to 'Everyday' for the Swedish market since the Swedes wash their hair in the mornings. Mars changed their well-known 'Marathon Bar' to 'Snickers' to fit in with the world-wide brand name communications strategy.

Wrong strapline

The New York Tourist Board found 'I love New York' difficult to translate into Norwegian since there are only two Norwegian verbs that come close: one translation is 'I enjoy New York', which lacks something, and the other is 'I have a sexual relationship with New York'. Kentucky Fried Chicken's 'finger lickin' good' came out in China as 'eat your fingers off'. Frank Perdu's slogan 'It takes a tough man to make a tender chicken' was misunderstood when translated as: 'It takes a sexually excited man to make a chick sensual'. Other expressions which have sometimes been imprecisely translated include: US cigarettes with low asphalt (tar), computer underwear (softwear) and wet sheep (hydraulic rams).

Wrong product

In the attempt to get the packaging, advertising and branding right, global marketers can sometimes forget the fundamental product and whether it is suitable for the market in the first place. Here are some examples of international product failures arising from the basic product itself. Many campaigns fail because the product or package is simply not suitable for the market in the first place. Examples include Christmas puddings in Saudi Arabia (where the word 'Christmas' is illegal and 50,000 of the Anglo-Saxon population go on holiday during Christmas anyway) or toothpaste to combat beatlenut stains (where stained teeth imply wealth in some cultures, as does being overweight in others). Other examples include Kellogg's 'Pop Tarts' in the UK since (unlike the US, too small a percentage of British homes have toasters). General Foods' packaged cake mixes found the Japanese market too small for them (only 3 per cent of homes have ovens). Coca Cola had to withdraw their two-litre bottle from Spain because few Spaniards owned refrigerators with large enough compartments. Tennent's Caledonian, a successful Scottish lager, flopped initially in the UK because it came in 24-packs rather than six-packs. Phillips had to change the size of its coffee-makers to fit into the smaller Japanese kitchens and its shavers to fit smaller Japanese hands.

GLOBAL COMMUNICATIONS – STRATEGIC OPTIONS

More and more businesses have to compete in the global arena. For many companies there is nowhere left to hide. Those that do not move into the global market will probably find that the global market will come to them as new international competitors target the once safe local market. There is a need to be proactive rather than reactive. Those that ignore this small part of the globalisation process may not be around in 50 years.

A defensive strategy (eg consolidate existing customer base, stay native and block competition from entering with, for example, a series of flexible distributor promotions) may safeguard the company, at least in the short term. Offensive strategies are required if a company is seeking entry into new markets, eg increasing promotional spend in key national markets, supported by a flexible operations system. Strategic alliances and joint ventures offer a lower-cost, lower-risk (and possibly lower-margin) method of entry into these new, large and increasingly competitive markets. Global competition has even prompted global cooperation in the marketing communications industries. Independent advertising and PR networks are popping up alongside the global agencies who have expanded to meet their clients' global requirements.

Warren Keegan (1984) identified five product/communication strategies for multinational marketing. These were determined by the state of the various international markets, analysed by (a) whether the need (or product function) was the same as other markets; (b) whether the conditions of product use were the same as other markets; and (c) whether the customer had the ability to buy the product. The strategies are:

1) *Same product/same communications*. This applies to markets where the need and use is similar to the home market, eg Coca Cola with its centrally produced advertisements which incorporate local differences in language.
2) *Same product/different communications*. This applies to markets where the need or function is different but the conditions of product use the same, eg bicycles in Europe and bicycles in Africa (recreation and transport respectively).
3) *Different product/same communications*. This applies to markets with the same product function or need but with different conditions of product use, eg different petrol formulae but same advertising image in Esso's tiger.
4) *Different product/different communications*. This applies to markets with different needs and different product use, eg greeting cards and clothes are held to be 'culture bound' but it should be noted that some clothing companies like Levi's use the same, centrally produced, wordless advertise-ments – internationally.
5) *New product (invention)/new communications*. This applies, for example, in the case of a hand-powered washing machine.

Whether the complete communications mix can be standardised by centralised control and production of everything from advertising to sales promotions to point of sale to PR to direct mail, etc is highly unlikely because of, firstly, the differences in regulations and laws which vary from country to country, and secondly the array of differences highlighted in the earlier section on global challenges. There are, of course, exceptions to the rule. IBM's Aptiva ran a 'Win tickets to the 1996 Olympics' across 12 European countries, while a new point-of-sale campaign rolled out to 15 European countries. Mars also developed a pack specifically for the Euro 96 football championships featuring a green colour base with white netting effect which appeared in shops in the UK, France and Germany.

Not totally pan-European approach

'All promotional ideas for Snickers' sponsorship of Euro 96 were shared with each European office and the individual brand managers then assessed the viability for their market place. Language barriers will often dictate the feasibility of an individual promotion. For example the 'Snickers – tackles your hunger in a BIG way' strapline was not utilised in any country other than the UK due to language interpretation difficulties.'

(Source: Gordon Storey, Mars External Relations Manager, *Marketing Business*, September 1996.)

The question of whether at least the advertising can be standardised (same communication) is a source of great discussion. Kahler and Kramer (1977) suggest that successful standardisation:

> is dependent on the similarity of the motivations for purchase and the similarity of use conditions. For culture-free products such as industrial goods and some consumer durables the purchase motivations are similar enough to permit high degrees of standardisation. Culture-bound products, in contrast, require adaptation. Customs, habits and tastes vary for these products and customer reaction depends on receiving inform-ation consonant with these factors.

James Killough (1978) felt that 'buying proposals' (the benefits proposed in the advertisement) had a good chance of being accepted across large geo-graphic areas, whereas the 'creative presentation' (creative treatment) did not. Essentially, if the international market had a similar set of needs and interests (to the established market), then a successful adaptation of the advertising message was more likely (as in the case of pattern advertisements. Simon Majaro (1982) observed that:

> ...the gap between the time a product reaches its decline stage in the most advanced market and the introduction stage in the slowest market is narrowing. If this trend continues the point will be reached where the pattern of the lifecycle in a domestic market will become identical with the pattern in the foreign markets. This will of course have tremendous impact on the communications strategy of firms operating internation-ally. It would mean that in time it would become possible for the communications objectives of such firms to become more and more homogeneous, thus allowing for a larger measure of standardisation. In other words if the trend continues it should become possible for the same campaign, subject to the manipulation necessitated by linguistic and cultural variations, to be undertaken in all markets. This is indeed the kind of standardisation that Coca Cola has achieved in world markets.

This strategy stems in the main from the fact that the product lifecycle profile of Coca Cola is pretty homogeneous throughout the world.

Rein Rijkens (1992) confirmed the trend towards 'greater internationalisation and centralisation' where basic creative ideas are centrally produced for international use. Kahler and Kramer (1977) felt that transferability of advertising was dependent on the possibility of a more homogeneous consumer who might, for example, evolve out of the ever-integrating European Community.

If the European consumer showed a willingness to accept the products of countries within the Community and if that consumer was motivated similarly to those in other countries, a common promotional approach would be practical, but if national identities prevailed, separate campaigns would be more likely to succeed.

GLOBAL COMMUNICATION STRATEGIES

The four basic strategies available for global marketing communications are:

- central strategy and production;
- decentralised strategy and production;
- central strategy and local production (pattern advertisements);
- central strategy with both central and local production.

Central strategy and production

Advertisements are controlled and produced by the head office (or its agency). This includes message modifications like translations and tailor-made editions for various markets. Examples of centrally controlled and centrally produced advertisements include Coca Cola's emotion-packed 'General Assembly' advertisement showing the world's children singing happily and harmoniously together. Similar to their 1971 'I'd like to teach the world to sing' (McCann's) ad, it was packed with emotion and carried a universal theme. The 21 language editions of this advertisement opened with 'I am the future of the world, the future of my nation' and ended with the tag line 'A message of hope from the people who make Coca Cola'. Each country then edited in their own end shot of the appropriate child's face. (Incidentally, the German edition was dubbed slightly out of synchronisation since the Germans associate quality films with dubbed (ie slightly out of sync) American and British films.) Scottie's nappies save production costs by omitting any dialogue and just using a different voice-over for each country. Levi's do not bother with voice-overs, dubbings or translations as there is no dialogue, just music. Their unified logo and brand image does away with the need for different pack shots (close-ups of the pack/label) for each country, so their commercials produced by the London agency BBH are used throughout Europe.

Decentralised strategy and production

Advertisements are controlled and produced by each local subsidiary and its agency specifically for the local market. This approach generates lots of different advertisements by the same company. Each division or subsidiary works with its own local agency to produce tailor-made advertisements for the local market. As well as being an expensive approach, it can destroy uniformity and a consistent global presence but it does allow more creativity to suit the specific needs of the local market.

Central strategy and local production (pattern advertisements)

The pattern provides uniformity in direction but not in detail, which allows the advertisements to be locally produced but within the central strategic guidelines.

These advertisements work to a formula or pattern (eg buy product and family is happy and healthy). In the Blueband Margarine advertisements, whether in Scandinavia or Africa, the appropriate happy mother can be seen spreading margarine on bread with her happy family sitting around eating it. Impulse fragrance uses a 'boy chases girl' formula across Europe but still allows for cultural idiosyncrasies like eye contact, sex appeal and law abiding citizens to be tailored into each country's different production. Renault's pan-European strategy was to 'endow the car with its own personality'. In France the car was shown with eyes. In Germany the car talked back. In the UK the end line was 'What's yours called?'

Central strategy with both central and local production

Centrally produced non-verbal commercials are used to build a unified identity, while local productions supplement this platform. This is demonstrated by the Levi's example below. Although 'standardised' generally refers to production it can also include centrally controlled media strategies, planning and buying. The centralised/standardised global campaign problems are discussed later in this chapter. As Rein Rijkens (1992) says:

> As far as advertising is concerned, the company will continue its policy of central production of non-verbal commercials and cinema films, to be shown throughout Europe and intended to establish a uniform identity for Levi Strauss as a business and for its products. Advertising produced locally by the Levi Strauss subsidiaries will respond to local circumstances and to the local competitive scene. This formula, also applied by other companies marketing a uniform product and using one advertising strategy on an international scale, has proved successful and may well be further developed once the single market comes about.

CENTRAL STRATEGY AND CENTRAL PRODUCTION

The advantages

- *Presents consistent image.* A consistent image (and positioning) is presented around the world, allowing consumer awareness and familiarity to prosper.
- *Consolidates global position.* Leaves the brand in a stronger position to protect itself from any attack.
- *Exploits transnational opportunities.* Reduces message confusion arising when (a) advertising in one country spills over to another (eg boundary-crossing satellite TV), or (b) when migrants and tourists physically travel to another geographic area (geographic segment).
- *Saves costs.* Economies are enjoyed by not having several different creative teams (and production teams if using central production) working on the brand around the world (ie saves reinventing the wheel). Possibility of centrally produced (or at least centrally designed) point-of-sale material also. Levi's have found that they save £1.5 m by shooting a single TV ad to span six European countries (at £300,000 per each one-minute TV ad) (Mead, 1993).
- *Releases management time.* And/or reduces the size of the marketing department, which might otherwise be tied up briefing creative teams, approving creative concepts, supervising productions, etc. It may even save time invested with packaging designers, sales promotion agencies, etc if pack designs and promotions are run from central office.
- *Facilitates transfer of skills.* Within the company and around the world since, in theory, it is the same job anywhere around the world. It also stimulates cross-fertilisation of company ideas if staff are moving around internationally.
- *Eases management.* Centralised management is easier since there are, in total, a smaller number of decisions and projects to consider. One creative decision facilitates the harmonisation of creative treatments, particularly in areas of media overlap. Media policies to manage the media overlap between countries can be put in place to maximise effectiveness and recommend the preferred media choice in specific territories. Local budgets may be determined for each product in each market so that the method of allocating resources is balanced, while activity programmes and a specific reporting system may be agreed to facilitate easier management.

The disadvantages

- *Stifles creativity.* Stops local creative contributions from both company staff and local advertising agency (whether part of an international group or independent agency). The account may be considered by the local agency staff to be dull and boring with the supposedly 'best brains' (from the creative department) avoiding being involved with it.

- *Frustrates local management.* Although the local office may be accountable for its performance, it does not have control over its own destiny since advertisements are centrally produced or directed. This may lead to a sense of frustration.
- *Minimises effort from local agency (if using an international agency with its network of overseas branches).* The high global advertising spend may put the brand high on the agency's head office list, but the local agencies may find it is uneconomic to spend too much time and top brains on it.
- *Loses opportunities.* The opportunity to react quickly to changes in the local market is lost.
- *Does not adapt to different product lifecycles.* Different markets may be at different stages of their lifecycles, which may make the standardised approach unsuitable. It may, however, still be possible to standardise each stage of the brand's development, eg Boot's launch of Eurofen in the UK and Northern Europe.
- *Provides the wrong idea.* Some central advertising concepts may simply not work as well as another locally created original idea. Sales therefore perform below their potential.
- *Proves difficult to translate.* Some ideas just do not lend themselves to translation, eg Pepsi's 'Come Alive' was translated in some countries as 'come from the dead' or 'come out of the grave'.
- *Provides false savings.* Local language adaptation/modification costs may negate the cost savings generated by the centrally controlled creative work.
- *Does not take into consideration market complexities.* The many other local market differences (eg variations in consumer protection regulations and media availability, etc) may make a standardised message extremely difficult.
- *Lacks experienced staff.* A lack of suitably qualified expert staff who can manage the coordination of transnational standardised campaigns may make the whole centrally controlled advertising concept too risky.

The key to successful centralised communications

'If Shakespeare and the Rolling Stones can do it, so can advertising.'

Maurice Saatchi.

Rather than engaging in high-risk new product development many corporations prefer to consider the lower-risk new market development approach. Harmonisation of brand strategy across different markets has been on the agenda for years. Making it actually happen is another thing altogether. Take advertising – although more and more advertising is used in more than one country only some of it works successfully.

Understanding the disadvantages in addition to the advantages is the first step towards implementing centralised communications. Identifying the barriers reveals the levels of resistance among distant marketing managers. It follows that internal marketing skills are also required. Before international communications are standardised (centralised) 'management thinking must first be harmonised internationally' (Kashani, 1989). Reducing local autonomy without reducing local responsibility requires skilful management handling. Indeed, maintaining management motivation requires all the more people skills, particularly when their responsibilities for advertising budgets are being slashed.

Many local managers will perceive the central advertising campaign to be lacking in inspiration and disappointing because it is based on the lowest common global denominator – those cross-cultural characteristics which somehow find commonality across borders resulting in dull ideas.

Inspiring managers to continue to excel under a blanket of apparently bland advertising is a challenging job. It becomes more challenging if internal communications are delayed. Excellent external communications strategies are not enough. Excellent internal communications (internal marketing) is also required to bring the most vital element in communications on board – the team.

If it does not work internally, it is unlikely to work externally. Internal communications, ideally, should create a certain sense of ownership understanding and pride in all external marketing communications. Then the strategy has a better chance of success.

APPENDIX 12.1: EUROPE

Europe's single market

The single market has the potential to expand beyond the initial European Community and into Northern, Central and Eastern Europe. The EU's single market means freedom of goods, services, people and capital. The new single market is just what it says – one big new market with many more customers, more competitors, more suppliers, more choice and lower costs. This brings with it a web of cultural idiosyncrasies, language barriers and a reported sense of xenophobia that sometimes translates into a pattern of what the Henley Centre for Forecasting call, 'patriotic purchasing impulses' (though this does not stand in the way of getting good value for money, which proves that behaviour does not always follow attitudes and aspirations). Net result? Opportunities (and threats) galore.

Is it really single? In practice, the single market is splintered by different levels of economic development (north and south), culture, attitudes and lifestyles, languages, retail trends, direct mail trends, sources of information, time taken to make a decision and so on. John Mole (1990) says that 'southern Europeans work to live and northern Europeans live to work.' The agency Ogilvy & Mather say that 'The national cultural, social and psychological differences will remain for so many years to come that the reality of a truly common market may never exist.' Some of the EU idiosyncrasies reported by Philip Kotler (1988) are that the average Frenchman uses twice as many cosmetics and beauty aids as his wife does. The Germans and the French eat more packaged branded spaghetti than the Italians while Italian children like to eat a bar of chocolate between two slices of bread as a snack.

Some of the differences in lifestyles across Europe are reflected by the different trends in retailing and direct mail shown in Table 12.1.

Table 12.1 Main trends in retail and mail order

Main trends in retail and mail order	Belgium	Denmark	France	Germany	Greece	Ireland	Italy	Netherlands	Portugal	Spain	UK
Source: O&MD Survey											
Retail											
Concentration to large stores	*	*	*	*			*	*			*
Shopping moving out of town			*	*	*				*	*	*
Proliferation of credit cards	*	*	*			*		*			*
Retailers offering financial services		*	*								*
Shopping becomes leisure activity											*
Development of specialist shops											*
Customer revolution underway					*	*			*	*	
Mail order											
More working women: consumers need convenience	*	*									*
Becoming fashionable/ more acceptable			*	*		*	*	*		*	*
Rapid growth				*			*		*	*	*
Mail order companies offering financial services				*							limited
Retailers entering market				*							*
Developing specialogues for niche needs				*					*		test*
Electronic media in use/ experiments			*	test*			test*			test*	test*

Different mixes for different EU countries

Different marketing mixes and communication mixes are required for different European countries. Oral B toothbrushes found different distribution and promotional routes in different countries. In Holland, dentists derive 40 per cent of their turnover from the sale of products like toothbrushes. In Germany, supermarkets are expected to sell only cheap, utilitarian brushes while the pharmacies handle the premium brands. In Italy, a premium brush has to carry a fashionable, exclusive label. This makes any above-the-line campaigns difficult. The communications mix was built around direct mail to dentists supported by point-of-sale and product literature, packaging design and sales presenters.

In the business to business sector different communication mixes are used in different countries. Table 12.2, again from Ogilvy & Mather Direct, shows how buyers from just three countries (France, Germany and the UK) have wide variations in their choice of information sources (communications mixes) when buying Rank Xerox machines. In Germany, magazines dominate while word of mouth or networking (meaning buyers talking to other buyers) is uncommon. In the UK trade fairs are unimportant whereas France and Germany rate them highly.

Table 12.2 Preferred information sources

Rank	France		Germany		UK	
1	Magazines/Journals	44%	Magazines/Journals	65%	Magazines/Journals	43%
2	Trade fairs/exhibitions	35%	Trade fairs/exhibitions	32%	Word-of-mouth	39%
3	Sales visit	25%	Direct mail	29%	Catalogues	17%
4	Catalogues	17%	Sales visit	26%	Direct mail	16%

Different purchasing decision processes

Table 12.3 shows the varying amount of time taken to make a final decision, again for the purchase of a Rank Xerox machine.

Table 12.3 How long does it take to make a final decision to purchase?

	France % Co's	Germany % Co's	UK % Co's
One week or less	61	12	36
Up to one month	29	19	9
1–3 months	19	20	19
3+ months	4	10	9
Average no. of weeks	**4.9**	**5.1**	**6.8**

EU effect on client/agency relationships

Advertising agencies may see a concentration of clients with bigger (and fewer) marketing communications budgets. It will be interesting to see if client head offices and advertising agency head offices will concentrate geographically. Arguably, this will lead to the big agencies getting bigger. Perhaps there will still be room for the small local agency, while the medium-sized agencies may be caught in no man's land and become extinct. This may lead to many more mergers and acquisitions, even stock market listings to raise more funds. Whether this will improve the quality of client service is debatable. Agency management may have to devote resources to their stockholders and focus on half-yearly profit figures rather than client service. In the short term these priorities can be mutually exclusive, with one being chosen at the expense of the other. Clients obviously do not like being treated as second class citizens. The larger, less personal, listed corporation may lose the charm of having direct and immediate access to the agency's chairman. The inevitable staff changes may cause key teams to leave. Sometimes the clients go with them. At other times the client fires the new agency because it is now part of a group that holds competing accounts, or the agency resigns the account because the new corporation has acquired some competing accounts which create a conflict of interest.

Culture

The complexities of working within EU cultures

To some overcoming local customers' idiosyncrasies may seem relatively easy compared to overcoming local partners' working practices. Whether they are suppliers, distributors, sales agents, advertising agents, strategic partners or just prospect contacts, understanding and overcoming each other's approach to business is essential. Below is an excerpt from John Mole's excellent book on other cultures, *Mind Your Manners* (1990), which considers how various Europeans see each other.

The Europeans

Somewhere in the world there are people who think the Germans are messy and unpunctual. (The chances are they are in Switzerland.) There are countries where Greece is regarded as a model of efficiency. There are countries in which French bosses would seem absurdly egalitarian and others where Italian company life would seem oppressively regulated. 'They are so inefficient. It is hard to get them to do things. At home I ask for something to be done, politely of course, and it gets done on time without any fuss. Here there are always reasons why it can't be done the way I want it. If it gets done at all. Sometimes they just ignore me. You have to follow up much more here. Set deadlines. They always want me to discuss things instead of doing them. Punctuality? Meetings never start on time. And they always drag on. You invite a customer to lunch at 1 o'clock and he arrives three-quarters of an hour late and thinks nothing of it. It is very frustrating. I get very irritated and I don't know how to handle it.' Was this said by a Danish manager about working with British employees or by a British manager working with Italians? The answer is yes to both parts of the question.

(Mole, 1990)

APPENDIX 12.2: AGENCIES

Types of agency

There are several different types of agency from which an international advertiser can choose:

- international agencies (multinationals);
- independent networks/associations/confederations of agencies;
- local independent agencies;
- house agencies.

In addition to deciding whether to centralise control over advertising (and effectively standardise it), another dilemma facing the international marketing manager is whether to put all international advertising in the hands of one international agency or hand it out to local independent agencies.

Many local independent agencies have grouped themselves into networks or associations, which means that they have a ready network of contacts with the other network member agencies in the various international regions. A fourth and less common option is for the client to set up its own house agency specifically to handle its own world-wide advertising. The two extreme options will now be considered, ie whether to choose a single international agency or choose several independent local agencies.

Choosing an international agency or independent local agency

This question is linked to whether the communications should be controlled centrally or left to run autonomously. Should the marketing team at headquarters work with just one large multinational advertising agency or should they allow a range of independent agencies to use their unique skills on a local basis? A coordinated message can be developed in either situation. For example, centrally produced advertisements (with local modifications/translations, etc) and pattern advertisements (formula advertising) can work under either system.

Although a centrally produced advertisement is more likely to be handled by a large international agency, there are exceptions where local independent agencies with local media buying and production skills (if pattern advertisements are required) may be preferred. It is possible to choose to work with a range of independent local agencies while adhering to centralised policies.

These policies can help the client to manage the whole advertising process by giving specific guidance on creative directions, media strategies, budgets and activity programmes.

As Majaro (1982) says: 'Obviously where the product profile justifies communications standardisation, it may be advisable to use the services of an international agency with offices in all markets.' Majaro continues: 'Hoping to attain the same results by using a host of local agencies with no international expertise is a formula for waste in world-wide marketing.'

Advantages of using an international agency

Compared to local agencies, the international advertising agency claims the following advantages:

- *Full service* – because of the international agency's size, it can offer a full range of services, including research, planning and translation under one roof.
- *Quality* – some clients feel reassured by the quality feeling of a large international agency (as opposed to taking a chance with a smaller local agency). Quality and standards should, in theory, be universal.
- *Broad base of experience* – training and transferring personnel is common among the international agencies.
- *Presence* – in major advertising centres, the agency branches are located at the centre of most major cities/marketing territories.
- *Cost saving* – less duplication in areas of communication, creative and production departments.
- *Easier to manage* – a single central contact point combined with the points listed in the section on the advantages of centralisation.

Disadvantages of using an international agency

It is arguably easier for a single international agency to standardise the message. The disadvantages of standardisation therefore apply where central control moves in. In addition, the overseas agency subsidiary may lack enthusiasm if the account was won elsewhere. It is as if, by necessity, various branches of the international agency are brought in. The lack of excitement may be compounded, particularly where all the creative work has been handled by head office. In a sense, the branch's job is relegated to media scheduling and planning.

DISCUSSION TOPICS FOR CHAPTER 12

1) Does global marketing affect all markets? Why?/Why not?
2) How can cultural idiosyncracies be accomodated in global communications plans?
3) Explore some typical problems which occur in international marketing communications programmes.

REFERENCES

Dudley, J (1989) *1992: Strategies for the single market*, Kogan Page, London
Ferraro, G P (1990) *The Cultural Dimension of International Business*, Prentice Hall, Englewood Cliffs, NJ
Harvey-Jones, Sir J (1988) *Making It Happen*, Collins, London
Kahler, R and Kramer, R (1977) *International Marketing*, Southwestern Publishing, Cincinatti, OH
Kashani, K (1989) Pathways and pitfalls of global marketing, *Marketing Business*, June
Keegan, W (1984) *Multinational Marketing Management*, 3rd edn, Prentice Hall, Englewood Cliffs, NJ
Killough, J (1978) Improved pay-offs from transnational advertising, *Harvard Business Review*, July–August, pp 102–10
Majaro, S (1982) *International Marketing*, Allen & Unwin, London
Mead, G (1993) A universal message, *The Financial Times*, 2 May
Mole, J (1990) *Mind Your Manners*, The Industrial Society, London
Morris, D (1988) Watch your body language, *The Observer*, 23 October
Rijkens, R (1992) *European Advertising Strategies*, Cassell, London
Smith, P R (1998) *Marketing Communications – An integrated approach*, 2nd edn, Kogan Page, London
Winick, C (1961) Anthropology's contribution to marketing, *Journal of Marketing*, **25**

Index

VISIT KOGAN PAGE
ON-LINE

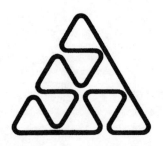

http://www.kogan-page.co.uk

**For comprehensive information
on Kogan Page titles, visit our website.**

Features include

- **complete catalogue listings, including
  book reviews and descriptions**

- **special monthly promotions**

- **information on NEW titles and
  BESTSELLING titles**

- **a secure shopping basket facility for
  on-line ordering**

**PLUS everything you need to know about
KOGAN PAGE**

THE MULTIMEDIA MARKETING CONSORTIUM PRESENTS
THE MARKETING CD ROMS
a series of ten world class CD ROMs
covering a complete course on marketing

Enter the world of multimedia. Improve your organization's marketing skills and save money simultaneously. Watch world gurus and top marketing managers reveal their secrets of success. Enjoy a whole new experience.

Why use The Marketing CD ROMs?

- Improve your organization's marketing skills
- Create a new awareness of marketing throughout the organization
- Reduce mistakes by copying how the experts do it first time
- Reduce training costs by saving time and money tied up in travel and accommodation
- Reduce costs even further by sharing the CD ROMs around
- Broaden the access to marketing training – let everyone come on board
- Reward staff with state of the art training materials
- Learn the right marketing jargon

How does it work?

Choose an area of interest. Listen to the expert and enjoy the slide show. Explore additional examples in the hyperlinks. Assess yourself with Questions and Answers. Visit the Hall Of Fame where Theodore Levitt, Rosabeth Moss Kanter, Kenichi Ohmae, Philip Kotler and Peter Doyle reveal the secrets of marketing success. Watch them, convert them to text, add your own notes. Mix your thoughts and theirs. Use the video browsers to see marketing managers, from Coca Cola to Concorde and Microsoft to Manchester United, explain how they market their products and services successfully. Use in a group, in a department meeting or on your own, at work, at home or while travelling.

THE TEN MARKETING CD ROMS

1. History, Definition and Concept of Marketing
2. Segmentation, Positioning and the Marketing Mix
3. Marketing Planning
4. Buyer Behaviour
5. Marketing Research
6. Product Decisions
7. Service Decisions
8. Pricing Decisions
9. Distribution Decisions
10. Integrated Marketing Communications

EACH MARKETING CD ROM CONTAINS:

- Tutorials – up to 12 tutorials combining video with graphics
- Self Assessment – 100 + Questions & Answers
- Hall Of Fame – World Wide Gurus reveal the secrets of success
- Picture Browser – Over 100 images
- Video Browser – Additional video clips of top marketers in action
- Glossary – Over 200 pieces of jargon defined
- Text-tools – convert video into text
- Notepad – mix your own electronic notes with the gurus text
- Summary – progress check & key point summary
- Hyperlinks – related examples and linked materials
- Save – your progress, scores, notes taken and hyperlinks explore

'...**exciting new material**...' The Chartered Institute of Marketing
'...**instantaneous access to the best marketing minds in the world**...' The Marketing Council
'...**a valuable resource to industry**...' The Institute of Practitioners in Advertising

For more information visit the web site below or contact Paul Smith directly at:
The Multimedia Marketing Consortium, London Guildhall University, 84 Moorgate, London EC2M 6SQ
Telephone: (0171) 320 1454 Fax: (0171) 320 1465 Email: psmith@lgu.ac.uk Web: www.lgu.ac.uk/lgu/mmm

Also by Paul Smith with Chris Berry and Alan Pulford

Marketing Communications (Second edition)
An Integrated Approach

'I welcome the second edition of this best-selling book... I commend the integrated approach to marketing communications to the reader, whether they be a student coming to grips with the subject or a practitioner aiming to obtain maximum effectiveness from a limited promotional budget.'

Alan Pulford, Visiting Fellow, Manchester Metropolitan University and
Manchester Business School

First published in 1993, *Marketing Communications* is firmly established as an international bestseller: Paul Smith's contribution to the acceptance and understanding of an integrated approach to marketing communications is now universally recognised. Both marketing professionals and students alike have benefited from his pragmatic and original approach. Indeed, it is the recommended reading text for the Chartered Institute of Marketing's Promotional Practice module and included on the Marketing Society's prestigious list of marketing classics.

This latest edition has been thoroughly updated and revised: new short cases, up-to-date statistics, fresh illustrations and photographs, along with a more pan-European flavour, all combine to bring it right up-to-date with the current international business scene. Several chapters have been completely rewritten, and the larger format and redesigned text layout will make it easier for reading and studying.

Three major features of this new second edition are:

- golden rules of IMC (Integrated Marketing Communications) – a new section which covers the benefits, the barriers and the golden rules;
- SOSTAC Planning System – a unique system, tested on hundreds of marketing managers, which provides a simple and structured approach to planning.
- the Internet – a major new chapter giving an in-depth look at the benefits and barriers and how to integrate the Internet into an overall marketing communications strategy.

The prime aim of *Marketing Communications* is to provide readers with a comprehensive framework to better understand the individual elements of the marketing communications mix and their collective effectiveness.

Continuing in the same lively style as before, the new edition is packed with visuals, practical tips and useful insights. The cases and examples are drawn from a diverse range of organisations and show successful solutions in action.

Paul Smith lectures in marketing at London Guildhall University and is the director of the Multimedia Marketing Consortium. He has worked extensively as a marketing consultant and speaker in the European and US markets.